Motherness

More praise for *Motherness*

"How do you find your way as a parent when the standard rules of parenting don't seem to apply? This is a book that grapples with that question while also having important things to say about motherhood, autism, and self-compassion."

—Ann Douglas, author of *Parenting Through the Storm*

"Motherness is that rarest of books—a memoir that looks inward but also out, shining a light on the personal in a way that refracts out to dazzle us all. In her unflinching and yet wholly tender focus on *seeing*—seeing and celebrating her child and then also, ultimately, seeing and celebrating herself—Julie Green has charted a path for all of us, parent and non-parent alike, to follow into a brilliant, better world."

—Amanda Leduc, author of *Disfigured: On Fairy Tales, Disability, and Making Space*

"Raw, honest, and thought-provoking, *Motherness* will resonate with any neurodivergent parent who recognizes parts of themselves in their child and wants to embrace these common threads to foster deeper connection and acceptance."

—Debbie Reber, founder of Tilt Parenting and author of *Differently Wired: Raising an Exceptional Child in a Conventional World*

"Julie Green's debut memoir *Motherness* is informative, offering interesting insights into a multi-faceted history of autism spectrum disorder, and it is also a deeply felt, personal account of what it is like to raise a neurodivergent child as a neurodivergent mother. But much greater than the sum of those parts, Green's gorgeous writing carries this deeply human story, which is filled with curiosity, honesty, humour, and above all, love."

—Harriet Alida Lye, author of *Natural Killer* and *Let It Destroy You*

"*Motherness* is a beautifully told, deeply validating account of late-discovered autism and the intersecting experience of being both an autistic woman and the mother of an autistic child. This is more than a memoir, it's a mirror for those who have long felt unseen, bringing visibility, validation, and hope to a new generation navigating late discovery, motherhood, and identity."

—Catherine Asta, author of *Rediscovered* and host of *The Late Discovered Club* podcast

"*Motherness* is powerful, thought-provoking, and frankly, impossible to put down. It left me questioning my own assumptions and considering how we can create a world where autistic individuals are truly understood, supported, and celebrated."

—Ingrid Smith, parent educator and coach

"As more women are recognizing their own neurodivergence, Julie has gifted us with a beautifully written and incredibly relatable memoir. Readers will come away feeling seen, understood, and never again alone."

—Emily W. King, PhD, child psychologist and author of the *Learn with Dr. Emily* Substack

Motherness

*A Memoir of Generational
Autism, Parenthood and
Radical Acceptance*

Julie M. Green

Published by ECW Press
665 Gerrard Street East
Toronto, Ontario, Canada M4M 1Y2
416-694-3348 / info@ecwpress.com

Editor for the Press: Jen Sookfong Lee
Copy editor: Crissy Boylan
Cover design: Jo Walker

LIBRARY AND ARCHIVES CANADA CATALOGUING IN PUBLICATION

Title: Motherness : a memoir of generational autism, parenthood, and radical acceptance / Julie M. Green.

Names: Green, Julie M., author.

Description: Includes bibliographical references.

Identifiers: Canadiana (print) 2025021783X | Canadiana (ebook) 20250217864

ISBN 978-1-77041-802-8 (softcover)
ISBN 978-1-77852-486-8 (ePub)
ISBN 978-1-77852-487-5 (PDF)

Subjects: LCSH: Green, Julie M.—Mental health. | LCSH: Green, Julie M.—Family. | LCSH: Autistic women—Canada—Biography. | LCSH: Mothers of autistic children—Canada—Biography. | LCSH: Motherhood. | LCGFT: Autobiographies.

Classification: LCC RC553.A88 G74 2025 | DDC 616.85/8820092—dc23

This book is funded in part by the Government of Canada. *Ce livre est financé en partie par le gouvernement du Canada.* We acknowledge the support of the Canada Council for the Arts. *Nous remercions le Conseil des arts du Canada de son soutien.* We would like to acknowledge the funding support of the Ontario Arts Council (OAC) and the Government of Ontario for their support. We also acknowledge the support of the Government of Ontario through the Ontario Book Publishing Tax Credit, and through Ontario Creates.

Canada

Canada Council Conseil des arts
for the Arts du Canada

ONTARIO ARTS COUNCIL
CONSEIL DES ARTS DE L'ONTARIO
an Ontario government agency
un organisme du gouvernement de l'Ontario

Ontario

ONTARIO CREATES

PRINTED AND BOUND IN CANADA   PRINTING: FRIESENS   5 4 3 2 1

*This book was written on the traditional territory
of the Anishinaabe, the Haudenosaunee, and the
Huron-Wendat. I gratefully acknowledge my privilege
to be able to live, learn, and play on these lands.*

For my Irish Londoner,
through whom all things are possible.

Contents

Like son, like mother:
A prologue

Forty-four years. That's how long you wait to hear the words that will change your life.

"How do you feel?" A voice reaches through the computer screen. The man seems flimsy in 2-D, unreal. A hologram. A virtual man. Because the world is in the grip of a pandemic, your appointment is via video call, which suits you fine. Better than fine. In fact, you prefer it.

You run a hand through your prematurely greying hair, once, twice—a nervous habit you've had for as long as you can remember.

"I don't know," you tell him. It's the truth. You don't know what you feel at that moment. You rarely do. That's the problem, or at least part of it.

The man, who is a doctor of some sort (more PhD than MD), asks if you found the assessment stressful, and you find yourself nodding vigorously. Three hours of direct observation and standardized testing followed by a thorough personal and medical history. Afterwards, you had crawled into bed, utterly spent even though it was only mid-morning.

It was almost comical, the degree of exhaustion you had felt. After all, you had not performed a triathlon. You had not pieced together strings of code or analyzed data on spreadsheets. All you had done was sit at a desk and talk to a panel of doctors. All you had done was list the steps involved in brushing your teeth and describe what was happening in a picture book without words. In other words: child's play.

When they asked you to make up a story using random household objects, you stared at the pen and plastic cup in front of you, your mind hollow as a tree. Seconds stretched into minutes. You swivelled in the office chair and wrung your hands together under the desk. You wondered why, if it was located in the cavity of your chest, you could feel your heart booming inside your head.

It was all you could do to stay in the room.

You are autistic, the doctor says now.

Impossible. I can't be on the spectrum is your first thought. *I am not Rain Man, Sheldon Cooper, or even Temple Grandin.* You have no visible quirks—well, none that you know of. You couldn't care less about planes, trains, or automobiles. You've never sat through a single Marvel movie, and you'd rather have a root canal than attend Comic-Con. No offence to those who are into those things. Autism is a spectrum, not a stereotype, after all. And if anyone should know that it's you, having spent the past 12 years raising a child on the spectrum.

The doctor ends the call, and for a long time you sit staring at the blank computer screen. Random scenes flash before you in your mind's eye:

A brown-haired child in a strange bed, tossing and whimpering in the dark.

A young girl with her nose in a book, absorbing every word on the page while the world around her slips away.

A teenager picking at the skin around her cuticles until pearls of blood appear.

And, older now, in an ivory gown with ornate roses stitched to the bodice, smiling at the tall man with pale blue eyes standing beside her.

Cut to another scene—

Her naked in a Jacuzzi-sized pool, reaching into the claret water and fishing out a baby, pressing his small, writhing body to her chest.

And later still: curled on the closet floor, her hair greyed at the temples, rocking and dog-panting in the dim light.

It's hard to believe these girls and women are the same person. That they are all iterations of people you have been. Like a cat, you've had nine lives, or at least nine personas.

Maybe, it occurs to you, this is what autism is.

⌒

Ever since Austrian-American psychiatrist and physician Leo Kanner first described "early infantile autism" in 1943,[1] the face of autism has been white, cis, and male.[2] It's not that autistic girls and women did not exist. We have always been here, hidden in plain sight. Unless we exhibit obvious developmental delays, our autism tends to go undetected. Given our presentation of autism can appear more "subtle," we sometimes fly under the radar. Compared to males, the female autist tends to exhibit fewer stereotypical or repetitive behaviours.[3] We may appear to be socially motivated and may even have friends. Those of us who are able to, often camouflage or "mask" our differences, copying others and adopting interests that seem socially appropriate for our gender. In other words: We do what we can to fit in.

Research has shown that prolonged masking comes at a cost to mental health and can lead to low self-esteem, stress, exhaustion, anxiety, depression, even suicidality.[4] Instead of autism, we are frequently diagnosed with depression, anxiety, or mood disorders, such as borderline personality disorder and obsessive-compulsive disorder.[5]

Since diagnostic testing has historically focused on a single (male) phenotype, females did not fit these criteria and have therefore been undercounted for generations. The gender bias runs deep, with boys around four times more likely to be diagnosed with autism than girls.[6] Fortunately, as understanding of the unique female phenotype continues to develop—with new research identifying underlying differences in brain connectivity between the sexes—this bias is shifting.[7]

⌒

When I eventually tell my son about the assessment, he shakes his head. "You can't have autism," Carson says. I don't have his kind of autism, he means. And he's right. My kind of autism is another garden variety altogether. Apples and oranges may both be classified as fruit, but that's where the similarities end. There is no comparing a 12-year-old boy with a 44-year-old woman. And yet I feel certain that if plotted on a Venn diagram, our respective autisms would intersect. For one, we share the same hypersensitivity to smell, sound, and touch. We agree that jeans are made of sandpaper; clothing tags are razors. We are both highly anxious. Whereas Carson tends toward dramatic explosions, I can usually feign composure, only to implode later in the privacy of my home—or else I hold it in for so long that I get sick.

Faking it. I realize that's what I have been doing my entire life. Armed with this new twist, my script begs to be rewritten. Entire plot lines and characters that previously didn't make sense now shine with clarity. I'm not alone. In recent years, countless adults have experienced a similar epiphany on the back of their child's autism diagnosis. The apple doesn't fall far, etc. It's something that professor and autism researcher Simon Baron-Cohen describes as "a phenomenon."[8] Contrary to popular belief, it's not that there are suddenly more autists in the world; there are simply more of us being diagnosed, particularly those who were previously overlooked: girls, adults, and racialized people.[9] Forty years ago, only those with significant or intensive support needs were likely to be identified as autistic. Today's net has been cast much wider. Awareness has spread. Diagnostic criteria have improved and expanded (and need to expand more).

So, how do I feel? Relieved. Angry. Sad. Afraid. Overwhelmed. I feel like Dorothy waking up from a dream I could have sworn was real.

Three words, and suddenly everything—absolutely everything—makes sense.

You are autistic.

Dark side of the mom

This story starts the way every fairy tale does, with us driving through the narrow, winding lanes of English countryside, past hedgerows and pubs and cottage-like houses that are every bit as quaint and charming as they look on TV.

The prince's name is Aidan. He is tall, dark-haired, and predictably handsome, with Irish freckles and twinkling blue eyes. He parks our Fiat. We hold hands as we stroll along the high street, acting the part of newlyweds even though we've been married for eight years. It's a Sunday morning, not long after we moved out of the pressure cooker of London. I like it here. I like buying a pint of milk from the co-op and walking our bull terrier through fields of bluebells. I find that I can breathe here in a way that I never could in the city.

We step inside the café we always go to—our café. The prince orders croissants and tea (of course) while I order a latte. My favourite part is the first frothy sip. Aidan spreads out *The Times* on the round table between us. The paper is thicker on the weekend on account of the glossy supplement. We read different sections, and then we swap. This is our ritual. It's an indulgence, this time we spend lingering over the paper and pastries. We don't know that yet.

Something about today feels different, though. Someone we know—a colleague of Aidan's, maybe—is having a baby, and we start bouncing around the idea of starting a family of our own.

Should we?

Shouldn't we?

What do you think?

What do *you* think?

"My biggest fear," I say as I lick my index finger and dab a flake of croissant, "is that we'll live to regret it if we don't."

My biggest fear, in fact, is being attacked by a bear. Grizzlies, black, brown, polar . . . bears of all stripes; I don't discriminate. But my second, more realistic, fear is of missing out. I want a life that is technicolour, not one that is greyscale. Even though I am an only child, I'm not the least bit concerned about continuing the family line. And I believe that being child-free is a valid choice. The trouble is, so far being child-free hasn't felt like a conscious decision so much as a diversion, a pleasant bout of amnesia. Eight long amnesiac years. I have always suffered the worst kind of indecision and inertia. I never know my own mind. When faced with a decision, even a seemingly inconsequential one like what dish to order, I get so anxious that I end up unable to decide at all. Other times I assume I want one thing only to panic and switch at the last second, thinking maybe I should go for the other thing, after all—regardless of what that other thing happens to be. I am a notorious waverer. An incurable waffler. Aidan sometimes jokes that restaurants should offer me a menu with only one item on it.

Starting a family isn't a decision that comes lightly. It's not a choice, say, between ordering the cheesecake or the tiramisu. Not all women plan to have children, mind you. My mother certainly didn't; I came into this world after a whirlwind romance when she was only 18. And since my father had no intention of settling down, she was left holding the baby, literally. When it comes to starting a family of my own, I want to be sure. I want to want it beyond a shadow of a doubt. My situation is not my mom's situation. Aidan and I have a good life, better than good. We are in love, *still*. We own a house and a dog and a car and a king-sized bed. The full fairy tale. But what if, years from now, we look up from the Sunday papers at each other and think, *What's the point of all this?*

⌒

Motherhood was never my dream. I was not one of those little girls who fantasize about becoming a mommy, who rhyme off the names of all the babies they will have. Little girls who dress, burp, and cuddle their dolls. Girls who *rehearse* motherhood while they themselves are still babies. It's not that I actively disliked babies or children. I mean, I played with dolls. I even had a realistic-looking baby named Molly, with wispy white-blonde hair and watery blue eyes that flicked open creepily when you sat her upright and closed when you lay her flat. Despite being crazy about Molly, who was far superior to the Cabbage Patch Kids that dominated the '80s, I had no grand aspirations of motherhood. When I grew up, I wanted to be either an astronaut or a *Solid Gold* dancer, strutting around stage in shimmering leotards and stilettoes. I also briefly entertained the thought of becoming a nun (before Sister Marie-Hélène ruined that dream for me). I imagined myself being married. But a baby? Never even crossed my mind.

By the time I met Aidan in 1999, those shimmering leotards and stilettoes were a distant memory, as was the dream to make it to space. I was 21 on a gap year in London. The plan was to work as a temp and travel around Europe while I figured out what to do with *the rest of my life*. Falling in love hadn't been the plan, but it sure was romantic. Aidan's parents were glad that he had at last found a good Catholic girl. But gladness soon turned to dismay when they learned I wasn't such a good Catholic girl, after all.

By the time we travelled to Ireland for his cousin's wedding, Aidan and I had been living together ("in sin," as it were) for several months. While my prince stayed in his grandfather's house, I was expected to stay at his aunt's place down the road. I had never met any of his extended family before. That first night, Aidan said goodnight and left me with strangers in a strange home whose walls were hung with an assortment of dead animals—each one personally hunted, stuffed, and mounted by Aidan's uncle. Foxes and deer stared at me, glossy-eyed and accusing, as though I were somehow responsible for their fate. Matters only got worse when Aidan's aunt showed me to my room. On the wall leading upstairs was a black bear, spread-eagle, its fangs exposed. The only way to get to my room was to pass the dead bear. Panting, I gripped the handrail and took two steps at a time. As soon as I reached the landing, I locked myself in my room until morning.

Soon after my bear encounter, Aidan and I exchanged vows— never again would I be forced to sleep in a house populated with dead animals. Catholics are funny creatures. Before marriage, everyone is obsessed with chastity and abstinence. But the second you tie the knot, everyone is on you to get making babies already.

Much to the dismay of our respective families, Aidan and I took our sweet time. We travelled and worked, then travelled some more. A year or two passed, then a few more. Gradually our families lost faith in our reproductive powers, and the hints stopped. So much for babies.

In the time it takes to get to the milky sediment at the bottom of my latte, it's settled. We are officially "trying." Turns out, I am one of those annoying women who falls pregnant almost immediately. And, aside from some mild nausea that requires me to bake and consume entire batches of ginger cookies, I have an easy time of it. I gain lots of weight because I give in to every single craving I have for McDonald's and the large sausage rolls from our local bakery.

When I study the ultrasound photo of what appears to be a giant prawn, I have a rough idea of what being a mom will entail. I imagine playground-swinging, sandcastle-building, cookie-baking, lots of handholding and snuggles. Like most first-time mothers, though, I haven't got the faintest clue.

Carson is two weeks late arriving. After being induced at a local hospital, I suck nitrous oxide from a canister and listen to whale sounds playing on a CD I brought from home. A few hours later, my giant prawn is born into a giant pool. The lights in the room are dimmed—not so much to create ambiance but to conceal the staggering amount of blood in the water.

After I am stitched up and whisked off to the ward, I can't sleep. *How can anyone sleep after what I've just done*, I wonder. I hold Carson in my arms and stare at him for what feels like hours. He doesn't look real. He looks like Molly, I decide, but without the creepy eyes. He is, in every way, perfect.

In the middle of the night, the adrenaline starts to wear off, and I am suddenly aware of a searing pain between my legs. I waddle over to the nurses' station. Around 3 a.m., the midwife on duty gives me paracetamol and makes me a cup of hot cocoa. I waddle back to bed, but I don't sleep. Instead, I stare at Carson sleeping in the bassinet beside me. Sometimes he wakes screaming, and I hold him to my chest for a while before placing him back in the bassinet. The next day I tell the prince I have to get out of there. He meets me at the hospital. We bundle our little prawn into the Fiat, and head home.

For the first hour or so we sit in the living room staring at Carson who is sound asleep in his Moses basket. We watch his chest rise and fall with each breath and study his fluttering eyelids in complete awe. *We did this. We made this.* Then awe swiftly turns to panic when our prawn wakes and starts wailing. Only then does it dawn on me just how far out of our depth we are. Our depth is not even another postal code; it's another continent. *We did this. What the hell have we done?*

The first 72 hours are a blur. A bender without the booze. I nurse Carson around the clock, struggling to remember everything my midwife taught me. Breastfeeding is all about the latch. The latch must be just right or else the baby won't nurse. Carson is a powerful sucker, yet no matter how secure his latch, he's never satisfied. He just cries and cries and cries. The expression on his angelic face says it all. He's pissed, downright enraged at the world. At me, it seems. Of course he is. One minute he's safe in the womb. Next there is an assault of light and sound, hunger and cold. And so, he responds the only way he knows how. He clenches his tiny fists and screams his high-pitched screams.

And I respond the only way I know how. By clenching my jaw and crying quiet tears. We are trapped in a vicious circle, each feeding off the other's overwrought nervous system. My baby cannot calm himself until I am calm. But I cannot begin to calm myself with him screaming all through the day and night.

When my father-in-law visits for the first time, he declares me a superwoman. To him, giving birth without modern interventions like anaesthetics or epidurals makes me a marvel. But as I sit gingerly on a donut ring, my stitches raw, my breeze-block pad heavy with postpartum blood, I feel anything but heroic; I feel like the walking wounded. I have returned home a changed woman. A shell of my former self. Shell-shocked. Childbirth is not a war, yet so far motherhood feels like an ambush for which I was unprepared.

The visiting nurse is concerned: Carson is not producing enough wet diapers. And there are crystals in his urine, a troubling sign. He's not getting enough nourishment, she says, meaning milk or that other stuff, colostrum. Nectar of baby gods. She tells me I need to switch to formula right away.

I shake my head. "I just need to get the latch right," I say, remembering my midwife's mantra. I can do it; I know I can. I just need more time. I don't reveal to the nurse the carnage of my post-birth body. I don't let on that underneath my stained T-shirt, my areolas are cracked and bleeding despite the copious layers of Sudocrem I apply every hour.

Once she leaves, I sit on the couch and sob. Then I go into the kitchen and start mixing up formula. My baby is a week old, and I have failed him already. I have failed us both.

Although Carson takes to the bottle easily, greedily, he still cries around the clock. How much does the average baby cry *on average*, I should ask the nurse. How long is a piece of string? It's a question so arbitrary yet one to which I feel I should intuitively know the answer. I don't. I am an only child who knows nothing about babies. What the hell was I thinking?

Another day, another hour, indistinguishable from the last. Carson spends them much the same way: crying and sometimes screaming while you stand frozen in the doorway to his nursery. It doesn't matter what you do—whether you hold him, change him, feed him, rock him—the outcome is the same. He keeps crying. Keeps screaming.

So, you take long too-hot baths that sting where your stitches are, and you stare ahead at the white tiles until the water turns lukewarm. The voice inside your head says, *This is not normal. This cannot be normal.*

Your parents fly over for a week, then they fly out again. And after a brief paternity leave, the prince returns to work as you know he must. But you hate that he is gone. When he arrives home in the evenings, he barely gets through the front door before you thrust the baby into his arms. That's what you call him at such times. Not Carson, not our son, but *the baby*.

"Here, you take him." You try not to sound quite as brittle as you feel. You wonder whether you might have actual hearing damage from all the screaming.

Every night you stand at the stove preparing food you have no desire to eat. As you fry, sauté, julienne, and sear, tears cascade down your cheeks, seasoning the food. This would be handy if you were a chef. While you cook and cry, Carson sits in a vibrating chair, momentarily lulled by its rhythmic movement. The second you finish eating, the crying resumes. You and Aidan take turns pacing between the kitchen and living room while Carson howls in your arms. At one point, you stuff foam plugs into your ears just to take the edge off. The soundtrack of his screaming plays around the clock. It plays on repeat every evening and during the few hours that you manage to sleep. In your dreams, you run from room to room in a billowing white nightgown you don't own in real life. In your dreams, you keep running toward the source of the crying—toward where you think your baby is—but you never find him. You never can find him. Then you wake up.

During the day, you push the pram around your quaint village, past the bakery and the co-op, past the curry house and the estate agents, in a fugue state. No matter how grey the English skies, you wear oversized sunglasses. You hope the glasses make you look sophisticated and untouchable, like Anna Wintour or Jackie O, instead of how you really feel, which is washed out and sad. You defy anyone who walks past you in the street to peer into the pram and coo at your sleeping baby. Of course, Carson is asleep. He always falls asleep the second you leave the house. On bad days, you imagine it's a conspiracy. You imagine he does it on purpose, that he falls asleep outside to get back at you.

At dinner one evening, Aidan looks at you and says, "We should talk to the doctor." You nod and blink. You stare blankly at this man, who is your husband, across the expanse of the dining table. He looks so far away, as though you're looking at him in a rearview mirror. You cannot remember the last time you had anything close to enough sleep.

⁓

The pediatrician looks young, ridiculously young, and square with his neat side part. I answer his questions (no, the baby isn't vomiting, there's no fever, no diarrhea, no blood, no mucus in his stool) with a few questions of my own.

"Are there any tests you can run?" What if Carson is in pain? You figure he must be in some kind of pain. It doesn't make sense for a baby to scream and cry like that for no good reason.

"It's probably just colic," the pediatrician says with what looks like a smirk. *Is he smirking?* I want to reach across the desk and punch him or, at the very least, mess up his immaculate hair.

At home, I read everything I can get my hands on. Colic sounds like a medieval disease. The definition is decidedly less romantic: intense or prolonged crying "for no apparent reason."[10] It usually affects babies in the first three months, for at least three consecutive hours, at least three times a week for at least three weeks. So many threes. Despite my research, I am no closer to understanding what colic is or why it is happening to my baby.

In fact, a whole decade will pass before I read about a possible link between colic and a neurodevelopmental condition known as autism spectrum disorder.[11] When Carson is born in 2008, the few existing studies on the subject offer mixed findings. The only consensus on colic is that it usually goes away on its own after three to four months. Usually.

So, with giddy anticipation, I count down the days and weeks. Three months pass, and then six. The crying continues. We try swings and various baby slings. A friend loans me a long strip of brown fabric, which I wind around my torso, looking like Obi-Wan Kenobi. When I wear Carson in this contraption, my back aches but eventually he screams himself into exhaustion.

Such times I stare down at my baby, sound asleep against my chest. It's been awhile since I had a chance to get a good look at him. His features are so peaceful, his porcelain skin so perfect. Carefully, urgently, I reach for the camera so as not to rouse him. I need to document this moment, so I can remember it.

This, I think, *is how babies are supposed to look.*

⌒

That Christmas we visit my family in Canada. My grandmother meets Carson for the first time. By then Nan's hair is a shock of white, and there's a film over her eyes. She's almost completely blind. She loves babies. And she is instantly smitten with Carson, as I knew she would be. I only wish she could see him clearly. She breathes in his skin as though it's freshly baked bread. She breathes him in like she wants to eat him. I know the feeling. My baby is especially delicious.

When I tell her about the crying and the colic, my grandmother is dubious. I expect some wisdom, maybe some homemade remedy. After all, Nan grew up in a family of 12 kids and raised six babies of her own. Surely she knows a thing or two about this ancient affliction that is colic. But instead, she turns to me and says, "If you can't look after him, then maybe you should consider giving him up for adoption."

Her words are a slap. I don't know what I was expecting. My mother's mother is a proponent of tough love. A woman of her generation. I know she means to shake me out of my wallowing. Her words are the emotional equivalent of smelling salts. And yet—this is the worst thing anyone has said to me in the history of worst things, and it came from one of the people that I love most in the world. I am stunned into silence. But worse, beneath the hurt and the indignation is a niggling fear that she's right.

We try white noise. The vacuum cleaner. Lullabies. Television. The ubiquitous car rides. Nothing helps. I read some more. We try gripe water, cooled fennel tea, every single brand of colic drops on the market. Walks in the stroller in the pouring rain. Long drives at night.

Several weeks pass, but I no longer notice or care. One day bleeds into the next. The more Carson cries, the more I feel myself slip away. I jab a pacifier in his mouth and close the nursery door behind me. Nap time.

During the day, I sit on the couch and watch TV. Or rather I stare at the moving shapes and colours onscreen. I watch them swirl and shift and pull, unable to make sense of what is happening. Over time, a fantasy begins to form in my mind, vivid as any of my dreams: There I am heading downstairs, grabbing the keys from the hook by the front door, and stepping outside. I get behind the wheel of the Fiat and now I am reversing out of the driveway, alone . . .

At dinner, when Aidan suggests I return to the doctor's office, I detonate.

"But we've already done that. It's just colic, remember? *Totally normal.*" I don't realize I am shouting until Aidan reaches across the table and brushes my arm. His touch is feather-light, yet I flinch and pull back.

"No," he whispers. "Not for Carson."

Oh. *Oh*, I think, and for some reason I think of that iconic Pink Floyd cover. That's what this is like. That's how it has been since Carson was born. An eclipse. A dark orb blotting out the light.

Postpartum depression is the chicken, and colic is the egg; I am not sure which entered our home first, but both threaten to destroy it. I would not hurt myself—at least I don't think I would. And I know I would never hurt Carson. I love him because he is part of me, he is *of* me. And yet I keep fantasizing about disappearing, convinced that he and Aidan would be better off without me. Every day I tell myself, *If you were stronger, you'd be able to cope. If you were a good mother, you'd know how to do this. You'd be able to look after your baby.*

Feelings of stress, frustration, exhaustion, guilt, thoughts of harming the baby, irregular sleep, and attachment issues are common in mothers of colicky babies.[12] More than half of autistic mothers report having experienced postpartum depression.[13] Specific stressors related to pregnancy and motherhood are amplified for autistic mothers, it seems. Sensory sensitivities and executive function skills involved in childcare—in some cases difficulty breastfeeding, social interactions with other moms, communication barriers when dealing with health-care providers, adapting to new routines, facing judgment, stigma, and isolation as a new parent—all these things may contribute to postpartum anxiety and depression. Autistic women can and do make great mothers, yet we clearly need more help than we ever get or are prepared to ask for.

Did Carson's colic make me depressed, or did being autistic make me depressed? It's a moot point. Before long, I make an appointment to see the doctor and return with a prescription for antidepressants. A little white pill under my tongue every morning. It's that simple—except it's not. Over time Carson cries less, yet he still cries an awful lot. Most days the moon shifts just enough to let the light pass, for us to see a way forward.

⌒

One afternoon I lay next to my baby on my king-sized bed. For once, I have showered and dressed in clothes that are not pyjamas. In his blue onesie, Carson grips his toes and gurgles at the ceiling. I can't stop looking at him. There is a novelty to his face. It is as though I am seeing it for the first time. It makes no sense, of course; I am with him all day long. My own face hurts from smiling. At one point he looks over at me, and I swear he smiles back. Then again, it could just be trapped wind.

On Sundays, we drive to our café. The prince heads to the counter to order croissants while I hold Carson. Since my hands are busy, Aidan reads to me from the newspaper spread out on the table. From the outside, we look like any other family sitting in a café together. I look like any other new mom cradling her sleeping baby. But I know the truth. The ordinariness of this day feels extraordinary, and I want to savour every bit of it.

With my free hand, I lick my fingertips and dab at the pastry crumbs on the plate. The croissants taste so good—the perfect marriage of flaky and greasy. I had almost forgotten how good they could taste.

The Griner

It's all my fault. When Carson is six months old, we pack all our worldly belongings and move back to Canada. Far from being a fly-by-night decision, it takes the better part of a decade to convince my Ireland-born, London-raised husband to immigrate to my homeland—land of igloos and polar bears. To convince him that the latter won't be camping out in our backyard. I needn't have worried; Toronto confounds his expectations in the best possible way: skyscrapers scrape the sky in this multicultural mecca that is his new home.

"See," I reassure him, "*civilization*." His relief is palpable.

By the time we arrive in Canada, Carson's colic has mostly subsided, yet I'm still convinced that he cries more than any baby in the history of babies. Over time his cry evolves into a distinctive sound that is part whine, part groan—a *grine*. It's a sound redolent of Stevie Nicks's vocals in "Edge of Seventeen." Carson hereafter becomes known as the Griner. Whenever he is grining, well-meaning friends, even strangers at the playground, attempt to prevent him from making this deeply annoying sound by pulling funny faces and tickling him. Usually to no avail.

For all his notable faults, my stepdad has a hidden gift. When Carson won't nap, and I have nothing left in the reserve tank, Mitch quietly steps in. He paces and jiggles Carson in his arms or else rubs his back. My stepdad stays in the nursery for as long as it takes, and it often takes a long time to settle Carson. Not normally a patient man, when it comes to his grandson Mitch exudes a calm and steadfastness that is incredible to witness. I am left gobsmacked by his baby-whispering magic. Such times I can't help but wonder, who is this marvel of a man and where did he come from. He's certainly not the Mitch I know.

Mitch came into my life when I was around nine. Having just gone through an ugly separation from his first wife, he was fighting to retain custody and some vestige of a relationship with his own two children when he and my mom got together. So it's perhaps not surprising that he wasn't too stoked about acquiring a young stepdaughter. And in fairness, I wasn't exactly stoked about acquiring a stepdad, either—particularly one who expressed zero interest in getting to know me.

With Carson, though, everything is different. Time has softened Mitch's rough edges. He shows up for my baby in a way that he never showed up for me. While I don't pretend to understand the reason for this sudden, radical transformation, I know better than to question it. Given my close relationship with Nan, I appreciate how important grandparents can be. Many kids don't get the chance to really know their parents' parents. I've never met my biological father or any member of his family. Since my mom was raising me on her own, my grandmother stepped in and became a kind of second mother to me. I want that kind of bond for Carson, too.

When my boy turns three, we enroll him in daycare a few mornings a week. Everyone tells me this is a necessary step in preparing him for kindergarten next year. Next year he will be four, going on five. That seems young, much too young to start school. Is he ready? Am I ready, for that matter? Dropping him off at daycare for the first time is hard yet secretly exhilarating. Carson, to my surprise, handles our inaugural separation well. A bit too well, in fact. Unlike some of the kids, who wail and cleave to their moms and dads at drop-off, there are no heart-wrenching scenes for us. Carson remains dry-eyed. Just as well. Had my baby been that committed to missing me, I don't think I could have gone through with it. At the same time, a few parting tears might have been nice for my ego. Will he miss me at all? Will he even notice I'm gone?

Unlike the other children, Carson doesn't bring a special blanket or stuffed animal with him to preschool. In fact, he expresses zero interest in any of the plush toys gifted to him by various friends and family. The stuffed animals—a sad, neglected zoo—sit collecting dust in a pristine row on his shelf. At bedtime, instead of reaching for one of them, Carson cuddles an old remote control.

At daycare, he immediately heads for a bin that contains items for playing house. Carson digs out a clunky cordless phone and carries it around with him all morning as though expecting an important call. He doesn't hold it to his ear and simulate imaginary conversations, however; he isn't the least bit interested in pretending to be a daddy or a CEO, for that matter. He doesn't speak into the phone at all. Nor is he willing to share when any of the other children request a turn playing with the phone. On more than one occasion, the teacher pulls me aside to remind me that Carson needs to practise sharing his toys. "Only children often struggle with this," she says. And being an only child myself, I can't help but bristle at her words.

Part of me knows she's right, though. About the phones at least. They are becoming a problem. At home, Carson has amassed quite the collection: around 30 phones—some real handsets, some toy models. The toy phones are the worst. Their loud, chirpy beeps and constant buzzing set my teeth on edge. While Carson is at preschool one day, I crack. I dump all the phones into a plastic bag and drop them off at a nearby consignment store. What my son needs, I decide, is not a lesson in sharing but an intervention. The equivalent of AA for preschoolers. An opportunity to start afresh, a clean slate. Cold turkey.

Predictably, Carson is apoplectic when he gets home from day-care to find his stash gone. Partly to distract him (and partly to assuage my guilt), we drive to the big toy store where I allow him to pick something. Anything—other than a phone. The store is the size of a supermarket teeming with bright colours and fluorescent lights that instantly give me a headache. Together we wander up and down aisles crammed with games and puzzles, dolls and figurines. Dinosaurs. Play-Doh. Glow-in-the-dark stars. Tonka trucks. Duplo. Playmobil. Thomas the Tank Engine. Hot Wheels. There are so many choices, so much *stuff*; I point out various toys hoping something will ignite Carson's imagination.

Finally, he pulls a box from the shelf and hands it to me. "Mommy," he says, his hazel eyes pleading. "*Please*, Mommy." At first all I see is red plastic and the words *Fisher-Price*. A toy phone.

So much for fresh starts. Eventually I come to understand that it's not the phones themselves but the numbered buttons that hold the appeal for him. And numbers are everywhere. There is no escaping them. When we go for a walk around the block, Carson reads out every house number and every licence plate number of every car we pass. Sometimes he even stops to trace the numbers with his stubby index finger. Sometimes tracing the numbers isn't enough to placate him. One day he stops dead in someone's driveway. The house number is stylishly mounted on a sign at the end of the driveway. Carson touches the sleek digits. "Home, Mommy," he says. And at last I realize what he wants: he wants me to remove the numbers from the sign so he can take them home. He will not budge.

Crouching next to him, I patiently explain that the house number is screwed in place and can't be removed. I tell him house numbers have a very important job to do. And if we took them away, how would anyone find their home or have their mail delivered? And I am feeling smug about my ability to think on my feet. But Carson does not appear moved by my argument.

"But I *want* them," he insists in a voice that is squeakier than usual. His cheeks flush a shade deeper than usual. These are the telltale signs of his agitation. I need to hurry. I take his tiny hand in mine and attempt to lead him home, but he wrenches himself away. There, in front of the house with the stylish numbers, he drops to the ground and starts screaming and thrashing.

Numbers are everything to Carson. They aren't just symbols that serve a practical function in daily life; they are so much more. They are his favourite stuffed animal; they are his special blankie. It doesn't matter whether they are tacked to houses or printed on a keypad. He needs to hold them, to feel them. Everything changes once I understand how visceral this need is for him.

And so, the next day I capitulate and return to the toy store and buy him the Fisher-Price phone. I'm not a complete monster.

⌒⌐

When I arrive to collect my son from preschool, one of his teachers—a young woman of Indian heritage with long eyelashes and thick black hair—pulls me aside. She tells me how earlier that day she comforted a little boy by speaking her native language. Carson must have overheard because he later spoke back to her in Urdu. Her eyes widen as she recounts this story, and I smile with practised humility. By now I am growing accustomed to people telling me my child is so bright, so smart. Sometimes, though, in the sweetness of their compliments I detect the faintest trace of sourness. Like milk starting to turn bad.

The young woman hesitates. She arches a brow and glances at the other teacher, who has crossed the room to join us. So, Carson speaking Urdu isn't the reason for our little chat, it seems. Or not the only reason, anyway.

Out of the corner of my eye, I notice him then. My child. Sitting on the rug playing with a set of magnetic numbers and talking animatedly by himself, to himself.

I wait, looking between the teachers as they trip on each other's words in the most awkward dance.

Sometimes Carson . . .

We've noticed . . .

Carson isn't always . . .

Spit it out, I want to say, but of course I'm too polite for that.

"You might want to speak to his doctor," the one with the black hair finally blurts. Yes, that would be for the best, the other agrees. And they nod in perfect sync, finding their footing at last.

At least Nan is not like these women. She isn't one to pussyfoot around what she thinks. She gives it to you straight. Up until recently, this was a quality I admired in her. In myself. Her almost pathological inability to dish up bullshit in order to spare people's feelings. I used to love this about her.

"He's too smart," she said the last time I visited with Carson. "Something's not right. He's not normal." She shook her head. If anyone knew about babies, it was Nan. She'd had six of her own, after all. Seven counting me, her surrogate. With my father out of the picture for the foreseeable future, we went to live with Nan. She looked after me so my mom could work and eventually put herself through college.

If anyone knew what was and wasn't normal where babies were concerned, it was Nan. God damn her to hell.

⁓

In the pediatrician's office, you hold your breath. The room is small and stuffy and smells of antiseptic (at least you hope that acrid smell is antiseptic). You sit on the edge of your seat, too anxious to take your coat off and too repulsed to touch any of the dog-eared magazines. Doctors devote their careers to keeping people healthy, yet this waiting room is one of the most bacteria-infested environments you've set foot in.

Carson toddles over to an ancient abacus set up on a small table. As he slides the grimy beads around, you shudder. He will probably leave this appointment with a lollipop and a transmissible disease. Go figure.

The last time you were here, the doctor dismissed your concerns. At the time, Carson didn't have as many words as he should. He was late crawling and walking, and then he walked. Maybe it would be the same with talking. Maybe it would be fine. The daycare teachers were probably overreacting. And Nan (who was seldom wrong about anything) must be wrong about Carson.

But what if she's right? You are terrified that the doctor will confirm there is something wrong with your three-year-old. Yet you are equally terrified that he will think there is something wrong with you. It wouldn't be the first time. Yet another neurotic newbie mother worrying herself sick over nothing.

On this visit, though, he has a lot more questions about Carson's development.

Does he point?

Does he make eye contact?

How does he play with toys?

Does he line things up?

You hear the nervous falsetto in your voice. No, Carson isn't interested in stuffed animals—he prefers to sleep with the remote control! Your laughter booms in the cramped space. Your armpits are damp, yet there is no way you will remove your coat. Carson fidgets and squirms in your lap. You don't want to let him down because he will touch more grimy things.

"He cries a lot compared to other babies," you tell the doctor. "I mean, other people's babies. I don't have any other children. Carson is my first." You are babbling now. You hate how insecure you sound, how pathetic.

When the doctor scribbles on his chart, the bottom of your stomach drops out. He tells you he is referring Carson to a special clinic for further evaluation. You want to ask what kind of clinic, what kind of evaluation, but the words refuse to leave your mouth. You nod, take Carson by the hand, and get the hell out of there.

In a glass and steel tower, built with a sizeable injection of government money, it soon becomes clear. The special clinic is a far cry from the pediatrician's office. You take the elevator. The toys in the waiting area are pristine. There is a wall-to-ceiling fish tank housing tropical fish. You point out Dory and Nemo, the Disney fish, to Carson, who is beside himself with glee. While he undergoes observation in a room down the hall, you spend hours filling in questionnaire after questionnaire. Over an hour later, a woman in a lab coat steps in the room and closes the door. She sits across from you. It's officially official. There is a name for how your little boy is, and that name is autism spectrum disorder. Soon, she says, you will receive a full report in the mail. Sure enough, the report arrives. Ten pages long, printed on the clinic's fancy letterhead, the report is filled with jargon and terminology you don't pretend to understand. Visual reception. Interoception. Echolalia. Proprioception.

Carson has difficulty with communication skills.

His speech intonation is unusual.

Eye contact is limited.

Carson tends to wander around the room, and play is solitary.

He does not engage easily with other children and can become quite anxious, leading to physical or aggressive behaviour at times.

Carson covers his ears at the sound of toilets flushing or people talking in a group.

He is very focused on playing with phones.

You quit reading once the print blurs. Are you crying? The tears come as a surprise because the diagnosis itself isn't such a surprise. Not really. You knew Nan was right, even though you wished with every fibre of your being that just this once she was wrong. And yet there is something about reading "autism spectrum disorder" in bold typeface that makes you want to rip the words right off the page. You want to rip them off fast, like a Band-Aid, as though doing so might make them less painful.

These words don't belong anywhere near your baby with his peach-soft skin. At the same time, you know your child is different. He will be different whether you label that difference or not. Your child will struggle, that's a given. He will struggle whether you choose to name his struggle or not. And if you choose not to name it, others will step in and do it for you. He will acquire other labels, such as *stupid*, *lazy*, *rude* . . . And by the time you decide to explain this difference in the most simplistic terms you can think of, you do so because at seven he is already concluding that he is bad. That he is a "bad boy."

So, even though you want to tear those 10 pages into confetti and release them into the air—even though you want nothing more than to watch them flutter to the ground like fresh snow—you don't. Instead, you fold the report in three equal parts and carefully tuck it back into the envelope. Because you are an adult. You are a grown fucking woman.

There is a choking sound. It takes a moment for you to realize the sound is coming from your own body. A tsunami of emotions hits. Guilt, sadness, relief. You cannot settle on one. Ever since you brought Carson home from the hospital, you had the sense that you were going about this motherhood thing all wrong. Either you were doing too much or too little, or the wrong thing entirely. Your parenting track record thus far has been a comedy of errors. But now you're starting to think maybe that isn't the whole story. What if the way Carson is isn't your fault?

Then again, what if it is?

⌒

Historically, parents (particularly mothers) have borne the brunt of blame for autism—whether it was Leo Kanner in the 1940s who coined the phrase *refrigerator mother* to pin autism on "emotionally cold" mothers, or Austrian psychologist Bruno Bettelheim who later popularized the theory, claiming, "All my life I have been working with children whose lives have been destroyed because their mothers hated them."[14] In some cases, Bettelheim went so far as to recommend that autistic children be physically removed from their mother's care, a horrific procedure known as a *parentectomy*.[15]

Decades later, parent-blaming gave way to another baseless theory. In the '90s, an esteemed British medical journal published a paper linking the onset of autism spectrum disorder with the measles, mumps, and rubella vaccine.[16] At the time researchers desperately sought an explanation for the soaring rates of autism in children.

Although the original study was retracted, and its author found fraudulent, the conspiracy lives on in the minds of many. Time and again, the scientific community has disproved any connection between vaccines and autism. Yet that single paper did more damage on a global scale than any vaccine ever could, setting into motion a wave of vaccine avoidance all over the U.K. and other parts of the world, the impact of which is still felt today with diseases like measles staging a comeback.[17]

This debunked study also inspired in parents a kind of widespread hysteria. Charities resorted to fear-mongering campaigns. Autism became the bogeyman of our times, the worst possible thing that could happen to your child—a fate apparently worse than death or disfigurement from some hitherto-eradicated disease. Parents became fierce and outspoken opponents to vaccines and other supposed toxins in their children's diet or environment.[18] As usual, moms found themselves at the forefront of what appeared to be a moral crusade. After all, a good mother spares no cost, financial or otherwise, in the quest to "cure" her child of autism. Moms became warriors called on to protect their children, sparing them from one perceived harm (vaccines) only to subject them to potentially dangerous treatments such as chelation[19] and bleach enemas.[20]

If you are a good mother, it is understood that you will devote your life to working tirelessly and selflessly to "fix" your child by whatever means necessary. And if you are a good mother, you just might escape the clutches of guilt and blame.

⌣

It's 2012, and I'm deeply invested in the blame game. In the weeks and months following Carson's diagnosis, I routinely question what

I've done—or not done—to make my baby this way. During the last trimester of my pregnancy, I had a urinary tract infection. The doctor prescribed a course of antibiotics, and I stupidly took them. Is that what brought this on? Time and again, I cast my mind back and keep a running tally of all the ways I might have unwittingly brought on Carson's autism. My self-flagellation knows no bounds. Every week it seems there is a new study about causality. At the time of writing, the jury is still out. Experts believe autism stems from a marriage of genetic and environmental factors, including older parents, a problematic birth, and infections during pregnancy.[21] Untangling genetic variances is complicated. Genome projects, such as the Spectrum 10K study, court controversy among advocates who fear research may be used to eradicate autistic people from society.[22]

Eventually I come to realize that blame is a useless emotion. Blaming myself won't change the past, and it certainly won't help Carson, so I do my best to push through the fog of guilt and despair. There is no time to waste, the social worker tells me on the phone. There are long wait-lists for services and therapies. As usual, the onus is on me, as Carson's mom, to make things happen.

Nothing can prepare you for the bureaucracy that comes with an autism diagnosis. *Even organizing a transatlantic move with a newborn was easier than this*, I think as I wade through reams of paperwork. The rest of the time I read books and scour articles to learn more about this enigmatic condition. Although I am technically surrounded by professionals and so-called experts, I have never felt so alone, rudderless, drowning in a sea of red tape.

There are endless intake phone calls that stretch for hours in which I repeat the same information over and over. Conversations in which I must describe Carson as if he's the subject of a doctoral thesis and not a living, breathing little boy. My son is still there, somewhere, but with every phone call and every form, he becomes harder to see. Soon our calendar fills with appointments. Carson sees a behaviour analyst, a speech-language pathologist, an occupational therapist—all of which we pay for out of pocket. The fact that we can afford to pay for all these therapies is itself a luxury, an incredible privilege. Many families remortgage homes, dig themselves deep into debt, to pay for their children's therapies. Countless others must live with the certain guilt of knowing they cannot give their children the very things they are told will help them thrive.

Each new specialist we see sends a report outlining my three-year-old's supposed deficits in elaborate detail. Pages and pages listing handicaps and goals as though this were a sport and not Carson's life. Not all our lives. Therapy is helping, they say, but most days it feels like slow torture. All the appointments. All the driving to and from. All the goddamn forms. Carson is tired. I'm tired. Aidan is tired. He's working long hours, and when he's not working, we spend our nights after Carson is asleep talking and wondering how we will afford all these interventions. At night we lie awake next to each other in the darkness. Our pain is shared, yet somehow it feels private, individual.

Not for the first time, I imagine the scene playing out in a movie, a taut family drama. There is the requisite aerial shot of a woman in bed, her long brown hair fanned out on the pillow. Crying quietly so no one hears. Crying until she eventually passes out, her tears drying to salty blotches on her cheeks by morning.

If I had a remote control, I would grow impatient. I would fast-forward to the next scene and maybe even to the one after that. I would skip ahead to the good parts, assuming there are any. I need to know how this movie turns out in the end. I need to know that the therapy will help. That the little boy will be okay. That the couple won't split up or go bankrupt. That the family will be happy. For once, I want spoilers. For once—and even though it's not usually my taste—I want the Spielberg ending. I want someone to tell me it will all work out fine by the time the credits roll. Even if it means they must lie through their teeth.

The problem with empathy

When Carson is just over a year old, we pay a visit to our local community centre. I could say we go because I want him to play with other tots, but my ulterior motive is self-preservation. The main reason we leave the house, where my son has a perfectly good cache of toys (newer, cleaner toys than those at the centre), is to save my own slippery sanity. Since moving back to Canada, I have been slowly emerging from the abyss of a postpartum depression. As an only child raising another only child, I recognize that socializing is a necessary evil for both of us. After all, we are new to our leafy midtown neighbourhood, Aidan works downtown all day, and quite frankly I am as lonely as ever. Perhaps motherhood has made me more so because, let's face it, there are only so many hours a day you can spend watching *Peppa Pig* before things turn bleak.

As I sit stacking building blocks with Carson on the shabby community centre rug, my mind wanders. My version of pretend play means I sometimes pretend to be more engaged in this kind of play than I actually am. I want to stay in the moment, but I'm perpetually tired. I get bored easily. If there happens to be another woman around (most caregivers who come to the centre are moms or nannies), I might cast out a casual line about her baby's cute OshKosh overalls, let's say. And if she isn't glued to her phone, this other woman will take the bait. If we start chatting and hitting it off, I might even suggest meeting up at a nearby park sometime. I try not to come off as clingy or creepy. (I'm not always great at judging where friendly ends and creepy begins.) Sometimes the woman and I will swap numbers, and on the way home I'll try not to feel too sleazy about the whole thing.

I am a mom pickup artist. For the first time in my life, my social skills are on fire. Babies tend to make the work of making friends easier. Or at least easier than it has been at any other point in my life. Although I usually always have at least one friend, making those connections has never come easily. I either talk too much or too little. In groups I become a wallflower. A shape-shifter. A bore. Awkwardness oozes out of my visible pores. With babies there are always conversation points and common ground. When in doubt, you can always bitch about how exhausted you are, or coo over some unbearably adorable thing your baby did the other day.

In the dinginess of the local community centre, I routinely manage to strike up conversations without breaking into a cold sweat. And the moms I meet don't run away or make excuses to avoid me. It's taken 30 years, but I figure I must be doing something right. Trouble is, the community centre has drop-in hours, so you never know who will show up. Some days the space is deserted— just me and Carson surrounded by buckets of mouthed toys. One such day, resigned, I sling the diaper bag over my shoulder and head toward the lobby. Just as I am about to buckle Carson into his stroller, a little boy comes barreling down the hall toward us, screeching like a fire truck. His screams are so loud, I half expect them to set off the building's sprinkler system. Lagging behind him is a man in droopy jogging pants—the boy's dad, presumably. The man yawns and rubs his day-old stubble, not the least bit fazed by the screaming. Carson, on the other hand, takes one look at the boy's snot-streaked face and starts screaming. Now both little boys are wailing with everything they've got. Except for me and the bedraggled dad, the lobby is empty. There is no one at the reception desk.

Crouching in front of the stroller, I try to console an inconsolable Carson. The other tot, meanwhile, falls silent, watching us.

"See, it's okay," I say to Carson, "that little boy's fine now." I turn and see him leaning against his dad's thick leg as though it's a tree trunk. They both stand there watching us with matching expressions. *Well, that's rich.*

Carson carries on screaming at a pitch guaranteed to pierce my eardrums. My fingers fumble with the belt on his stroller; I can't get out of there fast enough. Once we step outside the community centre, I expect Carson to stop crying. But he doesn't. He carries on screeching all the way down the bustling street. And so, I keep my head down and walk as fast as I can. *Whatever you do*, I tell myself, *don't look up.* I can't bear the stares from the people on the street today. The same look of the boy and his dad. Curiosity bordering on contempt.

⌒

One of the most hurtful stereotypes about autistic people (there are many) is that we lack empathy. It's not that autists don't care about others. We care tremendously. It's more that we don't always enact empathy according to the world's standards. The relationship between autism and empathy is far more complex and nuanced than society would have us believe. If I so much as sneeze or cough, Carson will be the first to rush over and say, "Mommy, are you okay?" but utterly fail to notice when I'm sad or sick unless I tell him so explicitly.

Alexithymia is defined as a difficulty recognizing, expressing, and distinguishing emotions. While not all autistic people have alexithymia, it's estimated that around half of us do.[23] But struggling to interpret nonverbal cues is not the same as lacking empathy. Once we can correctly identify someone's emotional state, we tend to be as empathetic as anyone else. Research confirms that while autistic people exhibit less cognitive empathy (the capacity to understand other people's feelings), we exhibit typical levels of affective empathy (the capacity to respond to other people's feelings),[24] which, I would argue, is the more important element of the two. Quite often we miss signals and do not react immediately or appropriately (read: empathetically). We are immediately perceived to be heartless or indifferent when we are most likely simply oblivious and confused. A lag in processing means that by the time we understand and react to a situation, the moment has passed. And the damage has been done.

The trouble with empathy does not rest squarely on the autistic person. In 2012, British sociologist and social psychologist Damian Milton coined the term *double empathy problem* to refer to the fundamental difference in neurotypical and neurodivergent communication styles. Milton found that while autists may have trouble accurately interpreting the facial expressions of neurotypicals, the reverse is also true.[25] So, what is considered a lack of empathy in autistic people would more accurately be explained as a communication breakdown between neurotypes. What's more, one study found that neurotypical adults were more likely to form negative first impressions of autistic children than non-autistic children, which contributes to reported animosity, prejudice, and stigma toward autistic people.[26]

My own relationship with empathy is . . . complicated. From the outside, I can appear either melodramatic and reactive or cold and unfeeling. There is no middle ground. If anything, I feel too much. Like many autistic women, I am hypersensitive. I take on other people's emotional energy until it depletes my own. If I express empathy by sharing a personal anecdote (to show that I relate to how someone is feeling), that person may conclude that I am a narcissist trying to shift the conversation back to me. Other times I may be seen as aloof and standoffish because I tend to switch off when the emotional states of others overwhelm my nervous system. Research has found that empathic disequilibrium, or excessive empathy, is more prominent in autistic females.[27] Experiencing greater degrees of emotional empathy can cause overarousal and goes some way to explain emotional dysregulation in some autistic people. At times we may internalize the intense feelings of others such that it leads us to experience a meltdown or shutdown.

Growing up, I spent a lot of time with my grandmother. When Mom was working, I often stayed at Nan's place. We played cards and watched *The People's Court* and *The Price Is Right*. Sometimes I rubbed lotion on her feet while we watched TV. When it got dark outside, we took to the streets and "played" detective in our own version of the shows she loved, *Columbo* and Jessica Fletcher in *Murder, She Wrote*. We drove around town in her boat of a car, listening to eight-tracks of Kenny Rogers and Johnny Cash. A country girl at heart, Nan loved songs about downtrodden men whose hearts had been broken by cheap women. Having been divorced and widowed, Nan had been unlucky in love, but that never stopped her from trying to find the One. She was a hopeless romantic with a penchant for farmers and cowboys. It didn't matter if they were already taken. Those night drives were thrilling, mostly because I never knew where we were going or what we were looking for. Sometimes she'd park the car outside of someone's house. I had no idea that we were on a stakeout—checking to see if the man she was currently seeing was where he said he would be.

There was so much about my grandmother that I didn't understand until I was much older. To say she had trust issues only scratched the surface. The men in her life never stayed long, and I never asked why. According to Nan, men were "good for nothing" but also, confusingly, "only good for one thing," though she never elaborated. And I learned some things were better left unsaid. I learned early on not to ask about my father. His name was John, like the apostle. That's all I knew. That's all anybody in my family would tell me. My mom never breathed his name, and Nan never spoke of him, either. As far as they were concerned, he was as good as dead. Like a ghost, he was destined to remain mysterious and unknowable. And like a ghost, he haunted my childhood.

When it came time to sleep, I crawled into Nan's giant waterbed. She gave me a sloppy kiss goodnight. The waves made me queasy, but there was nowhere that felt quite so safe. Then she started snoring. Her gaping mouth in the dark frightened me. I wondered how a sound so deep and guttural could come from a woman's body. For hours I stared at the ceiling, willing sleep to come. I thought about John, my father. John, the ghost. In spite of myself, I wondered where he was and what he was doing.

Early one Saturday morning, your friend picks you up, and you drive north until skyscrapers give way to vast fields. As you sip coffee from a thermos, you peer out the window for sightings of cows and horses. You are headed to a weekend retreat for caregivers of children with disabilities. This *retreat* is really not your thing, but you agreed to go along to please your friend. Because you are in the business of people-pleasing. Some time ago, you met at a parenting workshop, and even though her son is a few years' older than Carson and your kids are very different, you understand each other. In her presence you don't feel the need to explain or to apologize, and that comes as a surprise and a great relief.

An hour later, she pulls onto a long gravel road leading to a cluster of outbuildings that look too rugged to be cottages. Your heart instantly races. All you can think is, *This is bear country.* Are there bears out here? Of course there are. Your friend tells you this place is a summer camp that in the off-season doubles as a venue for burned-out caregivers like the two of you. You laugh absently since you are too preoccupied with the threat of bears to fully take in what she is saying.

The woman who runs the retreat meets you in the parking lot and shows you to your cabin. You let your friend do the social heavy lifting while you trail behind, glancing at the deep woodland sur-rounding you. *Doesn't every single horror movie start this way?* you wonder. You would know, having watched so many of them growing up. A single bunk lines either side of the modest room you will be sharing with your friend. There is altogether too much pine for your taste. It smells of burial. Your friend tosses you the sleeping bag you agreed to borrow for the weekend (you would never dream of owning such a thing). And the mere act of unrolling the sleeping bag triggers some unresolved childhood camping trauma. Not for the first time you wonder why the hell you let her talk you into coming to this weekend retreat. Shouldn't you have gone to a spa instead? Isn't that what burned-out caregivers really need: a stiff drink and a massage?

The moment you enter the main hall and see the dozens of round tables, you know your instinct was right. You like people the way you like spicy food—in moderation. A handful at a time, and even then, there are only a handful in the world whom you actually like. Sartre was right about hell being other people. When did you become such a curmudgeon? Or were you always this way? After scribbling your name (and a smiley face, for good measure) on a sticker in black Sharpie, you suck in a breath and find your designated table. *It's just a weekend*, you tell yourself. *It's just a weekend just a weekend just a weekend*. But it stretches ahead of you like a sentence.

Gradually butts fill the many chairs. Nervous chatter echoes in the vast room. One by one, table by table, everyone stands and introduces themselves. Everyone here has a sob story. You are no exception. Aside from a few specifics, these stories are essentially the same. The organizer passes around boxes of tissues. Much hugging ensues. (These random acts of affection make you uncomfortable. You are not a hugger. As a rule, you do not appreciate being touched except by those closest to you—certainly not by people you met five minutes ago.) No one here seems to share your reservations, though. As the women take turns talking, you try to steel yourself against the emotion infiltrating the room, invisible and noxious as fumes. With each person and each story, you feel the grip on your stoicism start to slip. It is too much. There are mirrors everywhere you look. In their eyes you see your exhaustion reflected. In their words you hear your hopes and sorrows . . .

When your turn comes around, you rise on shaky legs. At first you cannot speak. This is nothing new. You often fall mute in times of stress, such as when a roomful of strangers stares expectantly at you. Eventually your mouth opens, and out tumble the facts. You say you have a son; you say his age and diagnoses. You point out your friend sitting at another table and tell them she dragged you here against your will. The other women all laugh, assuming you are kidding. You are a funny one; maybe that will make you more likeable or at least excuse some of your weirdness. You sit back down, pinning your hands underneath your thighs. You've done it. Now, mercifully, the spotlight shifts on to the next person. This continues for some time. You continue to sit at the round table, soaking up all the emotions of the room until you can soak in no more. You are saturated. Someone seriously needs to wring you out.

Whatever you expected from this weekend, this was not it. By early evening, the sessions end for the day. The first day. There is still a night and a full day to get through. For everyone else the party is just starting. As your friend uncorks the first bottle of Chardonnay, you make your excuses and escape. By then the air inside the hall is heady with so much sadness and hope, you cannot breathe. Head pounding, you search for the nearest exit. You don't stick around long enough to explain to your friend what you don't yet understand yourself.

Outside, you stumble along the gravel path, gasping. The air is fresh and beautifully cool. Alone. At last. At least you assume you are alone. A few feet away a goose screeches a warning and ruffles her feathers. Several goslings huddle around her. She is a mother. This stops you dead in your tracks. If you come any closer, she will attack you. You don't blame her. In her position, you would do the exact same thing.

Light dapples across the path. Your vision is kaleidoscopic. Even without the wine, you feel drunk, nauseous. It can mean only one thing. A migraine is coming. You reach in your purse for the bottle you keep on you at all times. Even as the pill sticks in your throat, you know it's too late. You know what will happen next because it's what's happened since you were a child. The deep shooting pain in your eye socket that will eventually radiate throughout your skull. A pain so intense, so pure, your entire body will convulse. You will vomit once, maybe more.

While your friend lets loose and drinks wine with other women, you head back to the cabin in the dark, alone. You want to cry, but you know that would only make it hurt more. By now the pain is so excruciating, so violent, you forget to worry about bears or, for that matter, serial killers. Cocooning yourself in the borrowed sleeping bag, you close your eyes and whimper in the dark. You imagine Sharon Stone in *Basic Instinct* stabbing you in the eye with an ice pick. That's the closest you have come to describing the pain.

As you lay alone in the cabin, you remember all the other times you have found yourself in a strange room, helpless like those goslings. This is the last thought you have while you wait for sleep to come and take you. Sleep is the angel of mercy. Sleep is the only escape.

At breakfast the next morning, you are the only attendee without a hangover. But you are also the only one who missed out on the drinking and camaraderie of the night before. You have the sense that you are outside the building looking in. Forever peripheral. The rest of the day you go from workshop to workshop in a haze, secretly counting down the hours until you can leave. After that weekend, you do not attend another retreat, and your friend knows better than to ask.

⌐

When I was little, my mother took me to see *E.T.* It was one of the few times we went to the movies together. Like the rest of the world, I found myself captivated by the funny-looking alien with the fat head and freakishly long index finger. When E.T. boards the spaceship clutching the little potted geranium, I lost my mind. On some level I knew he had to say goodbye to Gertie and Elliott and return home to his alien family. That was the whole premise of the movie. And yet, I couldn't accept this conclusion. As the credits rolled, I sobbed so hard I gave myself hiccups. "But w-w-hy did h-h-e have to leave?"

To this day, *E. T.* puts a lump in my throat. And yet my reaction went beyond the scope of what was reasonable, even for a sensitive little girl. Unlike boys, we were expected to cry and show emotion but, as I learned that day and over the course of my childhood, not *too much* emotion. I could already tell from my mom's shushing that my feelings were too big and that I should take them down a notch because the lights in the theatre were coming on and the people around us were staring. I was making a spectacle of myself, and one thing she hated was drawing attention. I could feel her growing impatient as she took my hand and pulled me toward the stairs. My mom was the centre of my universe then; the last thing I wanted was to upset her. So, I took a breath and tried hard to suck in all the feelings I had the way some people try to suck in their stomachs. It didn't work. All those feelings had to go somewhere.

My mother is a practical sort. She is strong. She trained herself to be. After putting herself through college while working, she went on to have a long career as a registered nurse. And yet the stigma of being a young single mother in the late '70s (a time when being a single mother carried considerable stigma) never quite left her. Over the years, the stain faded but never completely disappeared. And that stain rubbed off on me. To this day she worries about what people think of her. I worry about what people think of me. She wants people to like her and not judge her unfairly. I want people to like me and not judge me unfairly. Throughout my childhood, I tried hard to be normal—or at least not too weird—for my mom's sake as much as my own.

I had already been living in Toronto for a few years when she phoned one day. Her voice sounded different, strange. I hardly recognized her, and that scared me. Her voice trembled on the line when she told me Nan had died. Mom started to cry. Immediately I started to cry, too, but only after I heard her crying first. It reminded me of that day in the community centre all those years ago . . . how that little boy's wailing had set off Carson. They say laughter is contagious. Maybe grief is, too?

Nan had been at a hospice. Her passing wasn't sudden or unexpected. And yet the moment my mom hung up, I stopped crying. My tears dried. It made no sense. I loved my grandmother. We had always been close. And she had just died. So, what the hell was wrong with me? Was I that callous? I cried all the time for no good reason. At tearjerker movies, even at stupid commercials. My second mother was gone. I was sad but not sad enough, it seemed. Or not sad in the right way.

When our dog, Rosey, died a few years later, I was blindsided. We got her as a pup when Carson was five, so they essentially grew up together. She was his fur sibling and my fur baby. She was eight when she started seizuring. Over the course of that year, the seizures became more frequent and more intense. I knew she was sick. I knew we would lose her. Still, when it came, her death ravaged me. I did not sleep for days. My entire body shook. I could not stop crying. I threw up. Until then I hadn't understood that grief could be so physical. That it could lock you in its iron grip and not let go. The extent of my despair took me by surprise and only heightened the sense of guilt and shame I felt over Nan's death. That I should feel more broken up over my pet than my grandmother was seriously messed up.

What shocked me most about losing Rosey was how others reacted. In the weeks following her death, people apologized for my loss and in the next breath asked when we were getting another dog. As though we were replacing a broken appliance or worn piece of furniture. *Another dog?* I stood rooted to the spot, too dumbstruck to answer. I had no words to describe the hole blown open inside of me, a hole so much deeper and wider than it had any right to be. The truth was, I was not sure I could endure this kind of pain again. I was made of the wrong material entirely; I was too soft, too porous.

After a loss, there is a window of time in which you are expected to mourn, and that window stays open only for a certain period. Beyond that, your grief is deemed excessive, problematic. It is an inconvenient thing that no one wants to hear about, much less deal with. You need to move on with your life. The window has shut. It is hermetically sealed and cannot be reopened. And so, you sit on one side of the glass cradling your grief while on the other side the rest of world carries on.

⌐

Six months later. At dinner, Carson says he misses Rosey. I tell him I do, too. I doubt I will ever get over losing her, but by now I know better than to talk about this with anyone other than my family. At least I'm not alone. At least my husband and son are there with me, looking through the glass.

I keep on circling back to that day at the community centre. At the time, I took Carson's reaction as irrefutable proof that he was a sensitive little boy, an empath like his mother. Now I'm not so sure. I want to believe that he cares for others. I need to believe that he is good and kind, even if he doesn't always show it in the way that people expect.

Did he cry that day because he felt so moved by that little boy's hurt? Or was the piercing sound so physically painful that it overwhelmed his own nervous system? Was Carson crying for the boy, or was he crying for *himself*? I will never know for sure.

Daddy Elvis

Elvis is not dead. He is alive and well, apparently, in a small town north of Toronto. For one glorious weekend in July, fans and impersonators gather from far and wide. They don their best duck wigs and white pantsuits to pay homage to the late, pelvis-shaking great Elvis Presley.

Aidan and I pack our three-year-old into the car and decide to make a day trip of it. The drive takes just over two hours. It's the summer of 2012, yet we might as well have time travelled. The streets are lined with classic Buicks and T-birds, all gleaming chrome in the hot sun. Cafés and diners blast his music from jukeboxes, his baby face adorning posters and memorabilia in every shopfront window.

Elvis Presley, it seems, is omnipotent. He is everywhere, in his many iterations, all at once. There is clean-shaven army Elvis, all the way through to bloated Vegas Elvis. I worried the festival might feel macabre, given that the legendary American singer has been dead for decades, yet somehow it doesn't.

"Check out that one," I say, nudging Aidan. We wander the streets, nicknaming every Elvis we see. The scrawny one across the road, with the greasy hair and black velvet waistcoat, we call "Flea-Bitten Elvis."

I came late to Elvis. My mother never cared much for his music or, really, any music at all. He was not country enough for my nan, who remained faithful to the likes of Johnny Cash and Hank Williams. It wasn't until my last summer at university that I discovered Elvis Presley, and in the most unlikely place.

My plan had been to finish the last credit I needed to graduate and save up so I could travel around Europe in the fall with my friend Trish. That summer, I worked full-time at a women's clothing store in Montreal's west end. Two CDs played on rotation in the store: a best-of-disco compilation and Elvis Presley's greatest hits. My manager, Claudia, loved disco, but she loved Elvis more. Until I met Claudia, a pretty young mom with bleached hair and dark Italian roots, I thought only bingo-playing seniors with doilies on their coffee tables listened to Elvis Presley. I truly didn't get what all the fuss was about, but Claudia soon showed me the folly of my ways.

That summer Elvis was with me every minute of every shift. While I cleared out changing rooms or refolded the T-shirt table for the millionth time, I heard his voice, like warm caramel, in my ear. Whenever I rang up a sale or dressed a mannequin, I found myself mouthing the words to his songs, which I soon knew by heart. Working retail was often dehumanizing and monotonous. Not only was the pay terrible, the clientele could be incredibly shitty. At the end of a shift, my feet throbbed from the long hours on the shop floor. But Elvis was my saving grace. Elvis got me through that summer.

Now Aidan parks the stroller. He says he wants to pop into the costume store real quick to buy an Elvis wig. He can't resist those bushy black sideburns. I tell him I'll wait outside with Carson. Restless from the drive, my boy squirms in the stroller. No sooner do I unbuckle the belt so he can stretch his little legs, than he takes off. It all happens so fast, I don't know how to react. I press the stroller brakes, then run after him as fast as a woman in strappy sandals, who had no intention of running that day, can.

Fortunately, a three-year-old's legs can only carry him so far. I've almost caught up when I realize where he's headed: straight for one of the Elvises (or is the plural *Elvi*?). This one has on rhinestone sunglasses and dark blue jeans, and his jet-black hair—at least I *think* it's his hair—is styled into a quiff. He is not the least bit flea-bitten.

"Daddy!" Carson exclaims in his squeaky voice.

For a second Elvis looks up, clearly confused. Then just as my little boy races toward him, Elvis crouches down in his tight blue jeans, and Carson rushes into this man's open arms like it's the most natural thing in the world. As my son winds his tiny arms around a complete stranger—and an Elvis impersonator to boot—I am aghast.

"Carson," I say, breathless by the time I reach them, "your daddy went into the store, *remember*?"

Then I turn to Elvis and say, "I'm so sorry," my cheeks ablaze.

He chuckles and says in an accent that is as far removed from Nashville as you can get, "No worries." When he smiles at me, small craters appear on either side of his mouth. Dimples. *Wait, is he flirting with me? Is this what they call Southern charm? That would be very Elvis-y of him*, I decide. I wonder if he plans to stay in character all weekend long, or if it's just a ruse to flirt with women.

We stand there for a moment that stretches out in its unique awkwardness. This is the moment when I should probably make a joke or attempt some small talk to ease the tension. But even if I possessed those conversational chops, it's clear even to me that we have passed the point where small talk could save us. After all, my kid currently has his arms wound around this man's neck like a rhesus monkey. Instead, I hold up my phone and ask if I can take their picture. On cue, Carson and his "daddy" Elvis smile sweetly for the camera.

It will make a good story, I think, if anyone believes it.

⌒

I'd like to say this is the first time Carson has approached a strange man on the street and called him daddy. Alas, it is not. It is the first Elvis, however. Any tall man with dark hair can and is feasibly mistaken for Aidan, who is tall and dark-haired. It is no prank. Nor is it the kind of gag you see on those comedy shows. There are times when my child genuinely cannot recognize his own father.

Carson has what's known as facial blindness—or prosopagnosia. Although not exclusive to autism, prosopagnosia is more common among those on the spectrum, who report having difficulty both perceiving and remembering faces in everyday life.[28] To compensate, those with facial blindness sometimes latch on to identifying features, such as a person's clothing or voice. A sudden change to someone's hairstyle can therefore be deeply unsettling to a person with facial blindness.

It may seem funny, but believe me, prosopagnosia is no laughing matter. Facial cues play a critical role in social communication. Failing to put a face to a name not only leads to plenty of embarrassing encounters (as I can personally attest), it also contributes to feelings of social anxiety and isolation.

When someone calls Carson by name, he may appear mystified, even disturbed. "You know me?" he'll ask, and I will gently remind him of our connection to that person. Assuming I remember who they are.

Carson isn't the only one with facial blindness. Though my own social amnesia is less extreme than my child's, I have come to dread certain encounters. I've lost track of the number of times I've introduced myself to someone only to be told that we've met before. Ouch.

This happens no matter how attentive I am. There is a glitch somewhere in the system. Facial features blur and contort as in a Cubist painting. No trick or mnemonic works, and trust me, I've tried. Now I prepare for the worst. I warn the people I meet that I am bad at remembering names and faces. The ice is effectively broken, and everyone laughs. Except at this point, it's more of a caveat than a joke. Over the years, this affliction has cost me. It has happened with neighbours, acquaintances, people at grocery stores and parties, even folks I've had entire conversations with. When met with my blank stare, something happens. When someone realizes I do not remember them, their expression hardens. They are hurt. Indignant, even. And I get it. They assume they were not memorable enough for me to remember them. Or else they decide that I am too self-centred and stuck up to remember them. First impressions count for so much. *It's nothing personal*, I want to tell the people whose names and faces I've lost in transit. But I know it feels extremely personal. By then their minds are already made up about me and I've been written off as aloof, rude, or arrogant.

Between my emotional state and my facial expression lies a disconnect. A flat or vacant stare may make me appear bored or even hostile, when I'm simply concentrating. I may look downright pissed off when I am rapt and attentive. In other words: I have chronic resting bitch face.

Before Carson was born, I commuted from the village where I lived into London. At the time I worked as an executive assistant at one of the big law firms. The journey lasted just under an hour, so it was a popular destination on the commuter belt. After a time, I noticed one of my neighbours on the train, and soon we got chatting. She was easy to talk to, easier than most, and we sometimes carried on talking as we got off the train.

Despite living there for years, I didn't have many friends in England. So, I was excited at the prospect of a commuting buddy. When I told Aidan about the woman, he asked what she did for a living (travel agent). I rhymed off other details I remembered from our many conversations. That's great, he said. What's her name? I paused and cast my mind back. I had been a good listener. How else would I know all these facts about her? And we must have introduced ourselves at some point, but now for the life of me, I couldn't remember her name.

"I have no idea," I admitted, wincing.

What was I going to do? I wondered. Asking her name now was out of the question. She knew mine, I was sure of it. Her name would come to me, eventually. In the meantime, Aidan and I took to calling her Nameless. We had to call her *something*.

As the weeks wore on, and our conversations racked up, the situation grew more preposterous. Short of sneaking a peek at her licence, I was stuck. My only hope was that someone on the train would call her by name while I happened to be within earshot.

Eventually this exact scenario played out. A man said "Alright, Liz," as she stepped into the train carriage one day. But by then it was too late. Nameless (I mean, Liz) said a passing hello to me, but the chats stopped. Several weeks passed, and I noticed she wasn't on the train. Maybe she was away for work, or maybe her schedule changed and she now took a different train home. I tried to convince myself that it was nothing personal. She wasn't avoiding me, she was just busy with work or other obligations. But I wasn't convinced. Either I was being punished for my gaffe or else Nameless (Liz) had come to her senses and concluded that I wasn't friendship material, after all.

Maybe the name had nothing to do with it. Maybe it was some other thing I couldn't put my finger on that I had said or failed to say. I told myself it didn't matter. It was only a matter of time before I screwed up. I always screwed up.

⁓

After waving goodbye to Daddy Elvis, Carson and I head back toward the costume store. Just as I am buckling my son into the stroller, Aidan joins us outside. He proudly shows me the Elvis wig he purchased. Maybe Carson can wear it for Halloween. *Wouldn't that be hilarious*, he says. *Yeah*, I nod, *hilarious*.

Down the street a crowd has gathered around yet another Elvis. This one is considerably older and stockier, sweating profusely in an elaborate pantsuit. I worry that his thick sideburns will peel off in the heat. We stop the stroller and stand for a while taking in the performance. Before long, Carson starts to get antsy again. Before I can warn Aidan, he unbuckles the belt on the stroller and my boy climbs out. He wiggles around, shaking his bum to "Hound Dog." With his plump cheeks and floppy sun hat, he looks especially adorable today. No wonder Elvis couldn't resist him. Even I feel uncharacteristically pretty, in a blue strappy dress. I never wear dresses, not if I can help it. But the humidity makes you do crazy things. It makes Aidan grab my hand and start twirling me around until I'm dizzy.

And because I'm so busy spinning and laughing, I don't notice Carson edging ever nearer to sweaty Elvis. As he segues into the next song, a gospel number, he drops suddenly to his knees and serenades my little boy.

Here we go again, I think. Before I can interject, Elvis removes the yellow lei from around his neck and places it over Carson's head. The crowd cheers. They are loving the theatrics because of course. And I'm wondering how on earth I will extricate my little performer from the spotlight.

Toward the climax of the song, just as Elvis struggles to get to his feet in the skintight pantsuit, I recognize our cue. I elbow Aidan, who springs into action, deftly wheeling over the stroller. Carson climbs in. This time I take no chances. I click the belt loop and make sure the damn thing is securely fastened.

⌒

That's plenty of Elvis for one day. You have all had too much sun and much too much honky-tonk. Before heading back to the city that afternoon, you agree to stop and grab dinner. All goes to plan. And when dessert rolls around, you order vanilla ice cream for Carson. Except it's no ordinary ice cream. As the server carries it out, a plume of smoke rises from the small metal bowl. Dry ice. She sets it down, and you and Aidan applaud the magic trick. But Carson takes one look at the bowl engulfed in "smoke," covers his ears, and begins to scream.

Without missing a beat, you dip the teaspoon into the bowl and take a bite to reassure him. "It's just a trick, see. It's just ice cream." You then attempt to guide the spoon into his mouth, convinced that once he tastes the sweet vanilla he will calm right down and all will be well. Instead he jerks his head as though you are holding out a venomous snake.

"Mmmm," you say, shifting tactics. "Mommy will eat the ice cream then. Mmmm . . ." You pop a spoonful into your mouth and make exaggerated sounds to prove just how delicious it is when, in fact, all you taste is the cold clink of metal against your teeth.

At that point your child screams even louder.

Aidan races over and tries to lift Carson out of the highchair, but he swats his dad away. At the last second you grab the metal bowl and move it out of reach before Carson can throw it. You move the cutlery and the water glasses, too.

By now, the entire restaurant is watching. Forget Elvis. You have become the entertainment. Diners and wait staff alike pause what they are doing to gawk at your family. The heat of their stares alone could melt the ice cream, which has finally stopped smoking. The trick is up.

Aidan waves down the server and pays the bill—leaving an overly generous, apologetic tip. You throw your napkin down like a gauntlet. Even though half of your dinner is still on the plate, you scrape back your chair. You can't get out of there fast enough. The ice cream isn't actually on fire, yet you and Aidan move as though it is. You move like the entire restaurant, the entire town, is engulfed in flames because that's exactly how it feels.

You grab Carson and Aidan grabs everything else. Ducking down side streets and alleyways, you pick your way back to the parking lot. Instead of the dulcet tones of Elvis Presley, your ears are filled with Carson's screams. With his hot body pressed against you, you slowly lower him into the car seat while Aidan expertly folds the stroller and throws it in the trunk. He starts the car, and you tug on your seatbelt.

For a long time no one says a word. You stare out the window as you make your way onto the highway. The radio is off. No more Elvis. No more music. For the next hour, you drive in abject silence.

Soon the screaming stops, but your ears still ring with it the way your voice echoes when you shout into a canyon. You turn around to look at your child, who is now fast asleep in the back. His head is slumped to one side, his cheeks still on fire.

From that day on, you are primed for disaster. You keep a bag stocked with an arsenal of toys, crayons, and of course phones, at the ready. You don't leave home without your survival kit. At restaurants, you ask for the bill as soon as your food arrives. You conduct meticulous research before going anywhere, scoping out the nearest exits and escape routes. Despite your extensive preparations, things still sometimes go awry. Sparks ignite. The alarm sounds. Public places begin to feel booby-trapped, mined with unseen hazards and explosive devices. Going out under these circumstances feels too hard, too risky. So, you go out less and less as a family. You grab takeout instead of eating in restaurants. Download movies instead of going to the cinema. You go for walks around your neighbourhood instead of going to the playground.

Home isn't the most exciting place to be, but at least it's safe—a refuge from the screaming and the scorching glances of strangers. From the words they sometimes say to your face and those you know they say behind your back: *Control your kid or go home. You're ruining it for everyone. Leave. Don't be so selfish.*

⌒

Aidan and I have been married for 15 years. It's hard to believe. Time is a slippery, conniving thing. Just the other day we were in that café, devouring croissants and talking about starting a family.

My Irish Londoner is so much more than my partner. He is my rock, my person. No one understands me better. Rather than infantilize or shame me for my shortcomings, he builds me up for my abilities. There is no pedestal. He's not perfect. No one is, not even Elvis Presley.

At times I resent how much I rely on him—Aidan, not Elvis. But the truth is, we rely on each other. We play to each other's strengths. Aidan and I bring different things to the table. Where he is spontaneous and impulsive, I am methodical and sensible. As a neurodivergent person in his own right (Aidan has ADHD), he looks to me to ground him and organize our lives while he encourages me to take risks and step out of my comfort zone.

There is no denying that having a child with a disability puts a strain on relationships. The social, emotional, and financial stressors of raising a child on the spectrum often prove too much for some marriages to survive. Research has shown that parents of children with ASD are much more likely to divorce than those with typically developing children.[29]

In one study, divorce rates for both sets of parents were similarly elevated when children were young. However, in couples with typically developing children, the risk of divorce waned significantly as children reached adolescence and early adulthood. Whereas in couples with autistic children, the rate of divorce remained high throughout their children's lives.[30] This makes sense when you consider that many autistic children do not "leave the nest" and go on to live independently. Further, within these families, co-occurring behaviours such as aggression and hyperactivity in autistic children were more predictive of divorce than in children who did not exhibit these traits. Other factors increasing the likelihood of divorce were the parents' own coping mechanisms and psychiatric conditions.

In my experience, having an autistic child does one of two things to a relationship—it can tear you apart or bring you closer together. For Aidan and I, it's been the latter. It has not always been easy, but we have prioritized our relationship with each other. Often it felt like autism was a third, unwanted party in our marriage. There have been times where we risked losing each other. We disagreed, yet always circled back to each other. We were determined to stay aligned and united as partners and as parents. We never lost sight of our ultimate goal—to love and support Carson no matter what.

For our 15th wedding anniversary, we decide to go large. Go big or go home, they say, and there is no place on earth bigger than Las Vegas. My parents agree to look after Carson so we can get away. We decide to bypass the slot machines and head to the older, less glitzy part of the city, where the famous Little White Chapel is located.

The morning is surreal. We arrive at the Chapel and head next door to the public washrooms to change into our wedding attire. So far, so not glamourous. I can't believe how many celebrities have married here. By some miracle, after all these years years my wedding dress still fits. In honour of the occasion, I had the crinoline removed and the hem taken up to the knee. Aidan brought along of his work suits. Just as we are about to head inside, a pickup truck swings into the parking lot. A man with jet-black hair steps out, suit bag slung over his shoulder, and disappears into the washrooms. *Could it be?* A moment later, out struts Elvis, all dark glasses and blue velvet, exuding cool confidence. The King has arrived.

The Little White Chapel is every bit as kitsch and seedy as I hoped it would be. In between ballads, Elvis flirts shamelessly with me and cracks jokes. He sings "Love Me Tender" and "The Wonder of You." Aidan and I renew our vows. All over again, we swear to love each other through thick and thin, for richer and poorer, through all the seasons under the sun. In the 15 years we have been together, we've seen quite a few seasons already, and I have no doubt there are more storms ahead. There is no one I'd rather weather them with. I guess that is the secret of marriage, if there is one. Find the least annoying person on the planet, and then hunker down. I rarely know my own mind enough to trust my judgment, yet of this one thing—this one person—I have always been sure. I married Aidan a few days shy of my twenty-third birthday. We had only been together a few months. Everyone we knew thought we'd lost our minds. I can't blame them. I would have thought the same in their position. There was probably a sweepstakes on how long our marriage would last. Smug as it sounds, there are few things in life more satisfying than proving people wrong.

That day in the Little White Chapel, Elvis Presley works his singular magic, and I fall under Aidan's spell all over again. Finally I understand what my manager, Claudia already knew all those summers ago in Montreal. With all my heart, I believe. *I believe I believe I believe.*

No alarms and no surprises

My son's teacher is a lovely man who speaks in a camp counsellor's singsong voice that must be a job requirement for all kindergarten teachers. I decide to be upfront about Carson's autism to give the school ample time to prepare for his entry. No alarms and no surprises, like the song by Radiohead. At least that is the intent.

When I take my four-year-old to meet his teacher a week before school starts, I am relieved to find the man is small and unthreatening. He sits at the little table next to Carson as though he is one of the kindergarteners. He tells my boy to choose a book from one of the overflowing bins. There are colourful pandas and classic caterpillars. After rooting through the many board books on offer, Carson returns with an alphabet book. No surprise there.

He sits back down and recites the book, clearly and fluently, from cover to cover. Like many kids on the spectrum, he is hyperlexic—

meaning he learned to read early and without being explicitly taught.[31] We found out by accident one Sunday when Aidan took Carson out on a coffee and pastry run. While he waited for our order, our three-year-old began reading aloud from a discarded newspaper on a nearby table. Heads turned, jaws dropped, including my husband's. It's not every day that you hear about rising interest rates or trouble in the Middle East in a squeaky preschooler's voice.

When Carson finishes reading the alphabet book, the teacher claps enthusiastically (another kindergarten teacher prereq), then asks how high Carson can count. Carson happily obliges, and when he hits 100 and shows no sign of stopping, Mr. Kindergarten glances over at me with a raised brow.

"Bravo, Carson," he says, cutting him short. "That was *wonderful*!"

Usually this is the point in the story where someone gushes about how bright my child is, and I graciously receive their praise. Except by now I am somewhat hardened to such plaudits. The memory of being pulled aside by daycare staff who voiced their "concerns" about Carson feels all too recent and raw. So, I simply nod and carry on standing stiffly next to the little table.

Nothing about this meeting feels good. Recently the province has introduced full-day kindergarten, and I have no idea how Carson will cope. Or how I will cope, for that matter. Preschool was one thing. Having my baby gone all day feels too sudden and excruciating to bear. I will miss him too much, the sounds of his *pitter-patter* and inane chatter throughout the house. It doesn't occur to me to postpone kindergarten for another year. That such a decision is even within the realm of possibility. After all, Carson is already reading and counting well above grade level. Won't he be bored out of his little skull if he stays home for another year? And besides, he needs to be around other kids. He needs—as people keep stressing to me—to learn to take turns and share and all the other kinds of social learning I can't give him at home because he is an only child. This separation is all normal, I tell myself. All part of the process. Kindergarteners go to kindergarten. And working moms go back to work. None of this makes me feel any better.

For the past year, I've been working part-time from home. When I applied to be a staff writer at a popular online parenting magazine, I never expected to get the job. Even when the call came offering me the position, it didn't seem real. I was beyond excited. Finally I would get paid a salary to write. It was a dream come true. Then the anxiety set in. How the hell would I meet deadlines with a two-year-old at home? And not just any two-year-old but Carson. My colicky baby had grown into a tricky toddler, prone to explosive outbursts that went beyond your run-of-the-mill tantrums. Friends told me not to worry, I'd figure it out. So, I did. While Carson napped, I scanned headlines and wrote hot takes on stories of interest to moms like me. Anything from recalls and current events to the latest studies and celebrity gossip. I wrote in a fury, fuelled by Tim Hortons coffee and ambition. Every weekday, I wrote 10 short posts, then emailed them to my editor, who loaded them in something unfortunately dubbed "the back end" and ran them on the magazine's website the next day.

The best kind of work does not feel like work at all—so the cliché goes. But that's exactly how it felt for the five years I worked as a staff writer at the parenting site. During that time, I worked like a dervish, churning out a crazy volume of output. But for first time in my professional life, I was enjoying myself. I had almost complete control over the stories I would cover, how I would cover them, and when I would cover them. Provided I filed by a certain time, my editor was happy. And if my editor was happy, I was happy. Throughout my time at the magazine, my boss treated me like a force of nature. And like any woman who against all odds manages to juggle motherhood and a career, I felt like just that. A force of fucking nature.

Part of the reason I managed to be so prolific and disciplined in those years was because my working arrangement was so unconventional. The parenting magazine operated virtually. There was no bricks-and-mortar office as such, which in 2012 was still something of a novelty. Once or twice a year, my boss would throw a party, and the members of the team would fly in from all over the country. Even though I was glad to finally meet with my colleagues in person, I struggled at these events. Group settings have always been my social Achilles heel. For several nights leading up to an event, I battled insomnia. As I got ready for the party, I caked on concealer hoping to hide the evidence of several sleepless nights. My stomach was in knots, and I literally shook with nerves. Nothing had changed since high school. I often hid in the bathroom for at least part of the night. To combat my anxiety, I had started knocking back one or two glasses of wine the moment I arrived. Wine helped take the edge off; it also fooled me into believing I was the life and soul of the party. In reality it probably just made me oblivious to my own awkwardness.

Alcohol eases inhibitions in everyone, but in autistic people it also eases some of the acute sensory and social difficulties many of us experience. In fact, neurodivergent people face an increased risk of dependency and addiction, particularly those with high IQs and/or ADHD.[32] In my case, booze made for a wonderful social lubricant, except it also had the unfortunate side effect of making me seriously ill. All it took was half a glass of Riesling to land me in bed with a migraine, puking all night. Of course the migraine might have been merely a side effect of stress and autistic overwhelm.

Aside from those office parties, working remotely suited me for reasons I didn't grasp or fully appreciate at the time. No longer did I have to contend with the inherent stressors of an office environment, which had never failed to make me sick in the past. The commuting, the noise of an open concept, the fluorescent lighting, the pressure to socialize and engage in banter with colleagues, and the need to perform for bosses whose minds I could only second-guess. It's little wonder that I fell ill so frequently when I worked in London. I never knew exactly when my migraine attacks would occur, but the fallout was predictably messy. I would call in sick, then spend the next 12 to 24 hours in bed vomiting. For a brief spell I worked as an administrator for a tiny publishing company. Since the job was on the other side of London, I had to change trains twice during rush hour. I was only 22, and I got sick so often my boss must have assumed I was too hungover to show up. When I called in sick yet again one morning, he outright accused me of faking it. I never went back. I had no idea why I couldn't seem to cope. I just knew that I couldn't.

As the prevalence of autism continues to rise, some large corporations are striving to make workplaces more accessible to neurodivergent employees.[33] However, navigating the job market remains a challenge for autists in particular, who for various reasons are more likely to be unemployed or underemployed. For one, the interview process still caters to neurotypical communication styles and many working environments are far from "sensory friendly." Things like dimmed lighting, noise-cancelling headphones, alternative seating plans, written instructions, advance meeting agendas, and flexible work schedules can make all the difference. Disclosing a diagnosis or requesting such accommodations may place neurodivergent employees at risk of discrimination and stigmatization.

It's worth noting that in the five years that I worked remotely for the parenting magazine, I rarely if ever called in sick. There was no need. Although I worked incredibly hard, my environment catered to my sensory needs, there were no social requirements, and my role afforded me ample flexibility and creative freedom. Even though I had a toddler at home and competing demands to juggle, I felt physically and mentally healthy for the first time in my working life. My boss routinely marvelled at my productivity. With my support needs met, I not only performed well, I thrived. I was an entirely different employee than I had been at 22. My London boss would not have believed it. My younger self would not have believed it, either.

If there is a silver lining to full-day kindergarten, it's that I will have more time, with fewer distractions, to write. Then I can devote my full attention to playing with my son.

When I arrive to pick up Carson one day, the teacher asks for a "quick word." Since school started a few weeks ago, I've noticed a sharp decline in the exuberant clapping. And Mr. Kindergarten's voice is decidedly less singsong as he recounts my four-year-old's various transgressions that day: Carson snatched another child's toy; Carson hid under the table and covered his ears; Carson refused to join the others on the rug during "circle time;" Carson would not touch the sand at the sand table or the water at the water station.

"He has autism," I gently remind Mr. Kindergarten. It sounds redundant and obvious, as though I'm stating the fact that my child has brown hair. But I say it anyway. The teacher nods to show his compassion, or rather to *show me* that he's showing his compassion.

The next day, the principal calls and asks—or rather tells me—I need to come and pick up Carson again. I arrange to come in and see her. I'm perturbed by all these calls. After all, I've been upfront about my son's autism and how it affects him. I have shared with the school all the reports and assessments we have on file and even brought my son in to meet the teacher and see the classroom before the first day of school. I was proactive and laid it all out on the table. I did my due diligence as a parent precisely so there would be no surprises. And in spite of all this, the teacher keeps sounding the alarm. The alarm sounds continuously.

The principal is a middle-aged woman with neat short hair and a brisk manner. When we meet later that week, she tells me about her golden retriever whose framed photo sits on her desk. She tells me she named the dog after one of the characters in *The Lion King*— Simba or Pumbaa maybe. Despite having a young child at home, I've never seen the movie and I frankly don't give a single shit right now about *The Lion King*. What I do give a shit about is my little boy and the fact that he needs more support than he's getting. The principal laces her fingers together while I plead my case. When I finish, she says that Carson is a wonderful boy. And while she is sympathetic to what we are going through, she says it's not fair or realistic to expect his teacher to manage my son's needs when he's got 30 other kindergarteners to look after in his class.

I grit my teeth, feeling as though she's somehow missing my point. And I get the feeling then, as I often do, that there are two conversations going on concurrently: the one that I'm hearing and another that I cannot understand. I imagine this is how it feels to be a dog, to be the principal's own beloved retriever, understanding only occasional words. Sometimes, if I tune in to the right frequency, I get the gist of this secondary conversation. The rest of the time, though, it's just noise. This is one of those times. I feel myself growing flustered—by her lack of transparency as much as by my own lack of understanding. *What should I do*, I ask her, exasperated. *Should I quit my job so I can help Carson in the classroom?* The principal sits back in her chair, no doubt taken aback by my directness. She shakes her head. *No, no, of course not.* Me volunteering in the kindergarten class, she insists, is not "in Carson's best interest." So, what is in his best interest, exactly, I want to ask. But of course I don't. I can't make a scene, that wouldn't be good for Carson. But I feel the fire spreading through my body and I know I have to leave her office, I have to evacuate the building, before it's too late.

Once I have calmed down, I decide to go about things a different way. If I can't get the school to educate my child, then maybe I can educate my child's school. With the principal's blessing, I arrange for an outside agency to provide a primer on autism spectrum disorder. The workshop will be held over lunch break, and I order in several pizzas to entice school staff to come and learn more about autism. If nothing else, they'll get a free lunch out of it.

Another morning, I make a guest appearance in the classroom while Carson is occupied with the resource teacher. Mr. Kindergarten claps enthusiastically and tells the children sitting criss-cross on the rug to welcome "our new friend," Mrs. Green. I pinch myself. It feels as though I've landed a cameo on *Mister Rogers' Neighborhood*. *Should I change my cardigan for the occasion*, I wonder. The kids listen attentively as I tell a story about difference and how although we may look different on the outside, we are all the same inside and we all want to be treated with kindness. The kids are adorably receptive. They raise their hands and wave to get my attention. They ask things like: Why does Carson scream and cover his ears? Why does Carson hide under the table? Why doesn't Carson answer when I say his name?

I do my best to get through my presentation without crying. My one-woman mission to build autism awareness at my son's elementary school doesn't hurt, but ultimately it doesn't help much, either. The phone still rings most days. And most days I drop whatever I'm working on. I rush to the classroom and find Carson splayed on the rainbow rug, screaming and flailing, while 30 kindergarteners stare from across the room like he's Linda Blair's character in *The Exorcist*.

When he sees me, Mr. Kindergarten can only apologize. I'm not sure what he's sorry for exactly. After all, autism is no one's fault. It just *is*. Or maybe he's apologizing for his own impotence, the fact that despite his training he is clearly not equipped to care for a child like mine.

Crouching on the rug, I scoop Carson into my arms and carry him out of the classroom. In the thralls of a meltdown, it's like he's not there. It's as though his body has been inhabited by other-worldly forces, so maybe like Linda Blair, after all. His arms and legs windmill. He throws kicks and punches that he won't remember when it's over. And I will be left with bruises, bitemarks. It's worse when there is an audience. If the call comes near pickup time, throngs of moms and nannies are gathered outside, rubbernecking. These are the times I dread the most. Cutting across the playground to the parking lot with my head down so I won't see their expressions of pity and revulsion.

As I wrangle Carson's thrashing body into the car seat, none of the moms and nannies come over to see if we're okay. To see if we need help. I'm not sure I blame them; I'm not sure I would do any different in their position.

It's not until I've secured Carson in the back and buckled my own seat belt, not until I round the corner away from school, that I allow myself to exhale fully. By the time I pull into the driveway at home, my heart is pounding, so is my head. I steal a glance at my little boy in the rear-view mirror. Whatever force occupied his small body only a moment ago is long gone. I unbuckle the car seat and carry him, fast asleep, upstairs and set him down.

For a long time, I stay sitting on the edge of his bed, watching him and listening to the steady hum of his breath. Then I close the blinds and lay down beside him. I tuck myself into him and wait for the pounding to stop.

One morning while I am working at a nearby café, I get an email. It's from a mom whose daughter is in Carson's class. I don't know her, but all the parents are on a class mailing list set up by Mr. Kindergarten. I half expect a request to bake cupcakes for a fundraiser or attend a PTA meeting—neither of which are in my wheelhouse. In the end, I couldn't be further off the mark. As I scan the first line, a hard lump forms in my throat. *You'd better do something about your son.* Ever since *your son* hit my daughter in the playground, she no longer feels safe going to school. Olivia has been having stomach aches and night-mares thanks to *your son.* Even though she clearly knows his name, this woman keeps on saying *your son.*

A taste like battery acid floods my mouth. For a second, I think I might throw up—right there in the café. Instead, I start to cry. Tears come easily now. They no longer have the power to surprise me. I don't even care that I'm in a public place. But the hurt still catches me off guard, the way it keeps taking on new forms. And this particular strain—the kind that comes when a stranger vilifies your child—is one I will never get used to.

The principal is copied on the email, and to her credit, she reacts quickly. She tells Olivia's mom in no uncertain terms that she is not to contact a parent, that is not the purpose of the class list, but to direct such concerns to her. I appreciate her coming to my defence. But it's too late. The damage is done. The proverbial writing is on the school's brown brick wall. Carson is woefully unprepared for school, and school is woefully unprepared for Carson. My son has a right to an education, though. He has as much of a right to learn as Olivia and any other child in any other family in our neighbour-hood. The onus is not on me if the school cannot teach him. He is highly verbal, gifted even. He is too autistic and at the same time not autistic enough to warrant the level of support he needs. The education system is broken, irreparably broken, everyone agrees, and yet one seems to know how to fix it.

There are no more threatening emails from parents. Still, the phone calls to pick up Carson come thick and fast. When we meet next, the principal says her "hands are tied," painting an image of her that I don't want in my head. We go from sending him to school half a day to half a morning to a couple hours a week. This can't go on. It's not fair to keep putting my boy through this. It's like taking a camel out of the desert and throwing it into the ocean, thinking that if we just keep doing it the camel will eventually learn to swim.

⌒

Your own introduction to school is a nightmare. "*Parles-tu français?*" Kids keep coming up to you and shouting these strange words in your face. Except to you they are not words but just sounds. You stand frozen in place. It feels like you've been dropped into a foreign country, and a war zone at that.

Although your mom can't speak French herself, she wants you to have more opportunities than she did. When you live near the Quebec border, that means being bilingual—which means sending you to a French Catholic elementary school on the other side of town.

At recess, the nuns patrol the playground like militia. Anyone caught speaking English is dragged in to see the principal, Sister Marie-Hélène. She is a fearsome creature, from what you can tell. Once you witnessed her march over to a boy caught talking during assembly. Everyone sitting cross-legged on the gym floor was too scared to breathe. They watched her mighty hands hover over the boy's head. You wondered whether she had special powers and might perform a miracle, like the one Jesus pulled off at Cana. Instead, she gripped the boy's skull and rattled it as she raved incomprehensibly.

By the time you start kindergarten (circa 1981), the nuns are no longer allowed to mete out punishments. In your stepdad's day, the nuns regularly cracked his hand with a pointer stick on account of him being left-handed. Left-handedness was thought to be a sign of the devil. So the nuns kept smacking Mitch's left hand in the hopes that he'd become right-handed. No such luck. Fortunately for you, you are right-handed. Not that it matters. You are doubly cursed as the daughter of an unwed mother and an anglophone, to boot.

You learn to keep your mouth shut and your head down. Over time, you begin to recognize certain sounds and certain clusters of sounds in French. Often it's enough for you to get by. School remains a hostile land in which you have no friends or allies.

To add insult to injury, the Christmas recital is coming up, and your mom has inflicted a haircut that makes your head look like a mushroom cap. You don't have a big part in the production—that always goes to Sylvie who hails from a good, god-fearing francophone family. (Sylvie, who once handed out prayer cards instead of Valentines to the entire class. You threw yours in the garbage as soon as you got home.) Sylvie is the real star of the show. She looks so pious in her blue veil with her hands pressed together, you could scream. If nothing else, the girls in your class are united in your hatred of Sylvie because you all wanted to play the Virgin Mary. Despite the fact that none of you yet knows what a virgin is.

You do not have a part in the nativity scene. Instead, cast as one of several nameless children on Christmas Eve, you get to wear pyjamas and hide inside a giant gift-wrapped box. When the teacher gives you the sign, you are supposed to pop out, jack-in-the-box style, and perform some action. Your action is playing violin. But since you can't actually play violin, you must pretend. You aren't even sure what the point is, but your performance has magnitude in the way everything does when you are very young and very small. On the night of the recital, you step inside the big box and wait. Inside the box is dark and cramped. Your heart beats too fast, like the wings of a hummingbird. Finally you feel a tap on the box; that's your cue. You fight your way out of the cardboard flaps and stand on wobbly legs. In the dim you see the rows of fold-out chairs and scan the silhouettes looking for her. But you can't see her anywhere.

You remember the violin as an afterthought. You grip its slender neck in one hand while the bow dangles uselessly in the other. Only then does it dawn on you: you have no idea how to hold a violin, let alone play one. Unlike many of the kids in your class—unlike *Sylvie*—you've never had violin or piano lessons, for that matter. You've never had music lessons of any kind because your mom doesn't have that sort of money. So now you're stuck because you have no idea how you're meant to position the instrument, and everyone is watching and waiting for you to figure it out.

Paralyzed, you stare out into the black of the gymnasium, too afraid to cry. Any second now Sister Marie-Hélène will come for you. She will stomp over to where you are standing in your oversize carboard box. She will take your skull in her powerful hands, and she will crush it like a melon. You squeeze your eyes shut against the vision. *Don't cry don't cry don't cry.* But it's no use; you are such a baby. Your cheeks are already soaked. A moment passes. Suddenly there are hands resting on your hands, fingers on top of your fingers, feverishly arranging them on the violin's frets.

You open your eyes to see—not Sister Marie-Hélène but your nice teacher, who drops her hands and retreats into the dark. You stand there, inert, holding the violin. After some half-hearted applause, you crumple inside the box where it is dark and warm and safe.

Like so many late-diagnosed women, the signs of my autism were missed, glossed over in childhood. In the early years, my social and communication difficulties were partially explained by the language barrier I faced at school. Then when I learned to speak and understand French, I was regarded as incredibly shy. Then I was simply an only child who liked playing on her own, in her own little world. Then again, I was a spoiled girl who acted out when she didn't get her own way. Time and again, my differences were either excused or overlooked because I did not get in trouble. I worked hard at school and didn't draw any attention to myself.

Unlike many boys on the spectrum, autistic girls typically show fewer externalized behaviours such as meltdowns.[34] If we struggled socially, we often managed to keep it hidden by watching and copying our peers. In other words: masking. The majority of us didn't give our teachers or parents a hard time. If anything, we were so meek and mild-mannered, we barely existed. In many ways, we fit the ideals of our parents' generation: that children should be seen and not heard.

To this day, autism remains a developmental condition that predominantly affects boys, since girls are believed to "carry protective genetic factors."[35] This is changing, with growing awareness about the different presentation of autism in females. Long held as four-to-one, the boy-to-girl ratio is now thought to be closer to three-to-one. The demographics of autism are also shifting, with more Black and Hispanic children being diagnosed.[36] Marginalized communities have traditionally reported cultural barriers to autism assessment and resources.[37] The spectrum, it seems, is no longer the mainstay of white boys.

For the rest of the year, I go out of my way to avoid driving past Carson's school. Most days I take detours that add time to my journey. Sometimes, though, I have weak moments. When I round the corner and the brown brick building comes into view, I lurk like a stalker. I slow right down so I can get a good look at the artwork taped to the windows. Fingerpainted masterpieces of horses and dogs, flowers and hearts. These are from the kindergarten class, I just know it—Carson's class. *His artwork should be up there, too,* I think, gripping the steering wheel too hard. And it doesn't matter how many weeks or months have passed, my heart hurts all over again. Past leaks into present. The levee breaks, and it all comes flooding back: the picture books, the rainbow rug, the nuns, the goddamn violin. My little boy is still so young. How much of this place will he remember in years to come? Will he remember hiding under the table during circle time? Will he remember the guppy-eyed stares of his classmates?

As I creep past the school, I scan the yard for faces I might recognize. I live in fear of seeing Olivia's mom. Still, I keeping coming here. I can't help myself; I creep and creep. I never stop.

Friend is a four-letter word

In anticipation of our move to Toronto, we make an appointment with a real estate agent. As he ferries us around town showing us different places for sale, he points out enclaves where the "Jamaicans are at" and "where the Hasidic Jews live." My jaw sets as he narrates the tour. In all my life, I don't think I have encountered a more racist asshole. In the backseat of his fancy silver car, Aidan and I exchange glances. I bite my tongue hard enough to draw blood. It's not until much later, once I've been in this city awhile, that I understand what the agent was getting at—the fact that people here tend to stick to different ethnic pockets of the city. Nonetheless, I decide the guy is probably still an asshole.

"This is where the WASPs live," I imagine him saying of our new neighbourhood. And it bothers me that he'd be right. Our ramshackle home is located on a leafy crescent in the middle of the city, yet it feels every bit like the suburbs. There is a ravine at the end of the road with a brook running through it and a park with an elaborate play structure and walking trails. The space is idyllic, a haven for runners, dog walkers, and young families like mine.

We don't know our luck. In our new neighbourhood kids still play in the street like they did when I was growing up in the early '80s. In those days we roamed in packs, practically feral. There was safety in numbers. My cousin Jess and I knew enough not to get into strange cars or to accept candy (supposedly laced with razor blades) from people we didn't know. Anything else was pretty much fair game. And we were not expected to return home before dinnertime unless there was blood involved. It was clear that no one would rescue us; we kids had to figure shit out ourselves. People tend to get nostalgic about that era. In a way that kind of upbringing represented the ultimate freedom, but at other times, it felt like neglect. Aside from a fractured wrist (or two), I was lucky to escape childhood unscathed. Many did not.

Now I spend most afternoons gazing out my bay window as the neighbour kids tear up and down the sidewalk on trikes and scooters. I watch them draw chalky rainbows and happy faces that will be washed away with the next rainfall. These children are never truly alone, never truly unsupervised the way we were growing up. There's always someone in the wings, ready to swoop in should little Jacob or little Isabella get a boo-boo. In spite of myself, I like how safe and protected this nook feels, cushioned from the crime that plagues other parts of the city. It's not fair. It's not right, either. But I'd be lying if I said my privilege didn't afford me some comfort as a parent. All parents deserve peace of mind, but staggeringly few of us get it. Such is the uncomfortable reality of my new life back in Canada, one I was largely oblivious to before becoming a mom.

That's not to say I fit in. The women in this neighbourhood all share a certain aesthetic: designer yoga pants paired with cardigans that hug their gym-toned bodies. The dads are a less homogenous bunch—in suits or golf shirts and cargo shorts. They stand in each other's driveways talking about hockey and the stock market, while the moms dish about the PTA and each other. Having never been one for gossip, in their company I am awkward as ever and don't have a lot to say.

When I see the kids outside playing, though, my heart warms. I hurry outside with Carson for a while before I need to start preparing dinner. These are good kids, I sense. They talk to my son, and include him, even if he doesn't always respond. Even if he doesn't understand the rules of whatever game they are playing. Adults could learn a lot from these kids, I think.

⁓

When I was around four years old, my mom and I moved out of my nan's house into the upstairs apartment of a duplex. The family who rented out the bottom level had a daughter my age, a heavily freckled girl also named Julie. That coincidence may seem uncanny or fated somehow, but Julie was one of the most popular girl names then. Other Julie and I were thrown together out of convenience, yet I'm not sure we ever really clicked. And maybe that was intentional. I was never invited to play in their apartment—a fact that didn't occur to me until now. We were either sent to play outside or down in the basement. Some basements are converted rec rooms, with plush carpets and smooth plastered walls. That was not the duplex basement, which was dank and cold and mildewy. The sort of place to which children in fairy tales are banished or sent as a punishment.

Being down there should have terrified me, given the proliferation of smells and cobwebs. But I didn't mind; I liked being surrounded by our stuff. Since we didn't have a lot of space in the apartment, the landlord let us use a corner of the basement for storage. My crib, a hand-me-down, was there. For a long time I would secretly climb into it, and the crib's ancient, rickety legs threatened to buckle under my weight. Because we didn't have room for it upstairs, the doll-house was down there, too. It was beautiful: Victorian, painted teal with ornate-looking windows. Another antique, the house was a gift from the British widow across the street. She had no grandchildren of her own—at least none that came to see her. Mom felt sorry for her, so she sometimes brought me along for visits. I thought she was fancy because she served cookies out of a cookie jar and tea out of a teapot with roses on it. She had a helmet of white hair and papery skin that barely covered a lattice of royal-blue veins that freaked me out. To avoid looking at her, I helped myself to more stale cookies from the jar and focused on her voice, which was soft and polished like Her Majesty the Queen. She could have been part of the royal family for all I knew.

Next door to the British widow lived two kids in a sprawling white house with bright green shutters. Kelvin was the same age as me, his sister a few years older. Kelvin had tight blond curls and an arrogance that I assumed came with living in a big house. I didn't like him or his curls one bit. I'm not sure how old I was when he invited me and Other Julie to his place. I only went because I was nosy. I wanted to see what that big white house looked like inside. I had spent so long at that point looking over at it from my bedroom window. I needed to know: was there an indoor tennis court and a swimming pool? An arcade, a movie theatre, a snow cone machine? I would never find out because after answering the door, Kelvin led me and Other Julie straight to the basement. Could he tell I was crestfallen? But my disappointment was short-lived. Kelvin's basement had thick, cozy carpets and shelves chockful of toys. I'd only ever seen that many toys in one place—Kmart. He asked if we wanted to play doctor, and I nodded eagerly. I was game and even volunteered to be the doctor because I figured with my mom being a nurse I had some expertise in the area. I even had a medical kit at home stocked with real gauze and a tongue depressor.

Kelvin offered to be the patient. No sooner had I asked him to "show me where it hurt" did he drop his pants, revealing the whitest pair of Y-fronts. I had never seen a boy in his underwear before, and my jaw dropped. I didn't hang around long enough to complete the examination. Without a word, I raced out of that big sprawling house and up the stairs of the duplex, my cheeks hot with some feeling I couldn't identify. Shame? Anger? Embarrassment? Or something else entirely? Once inside the apartment, I hid inside my bedroom. My mom assumed there was a squabble with Other Julie, and I didn't bother to correct her.

It was better when my cousin Jess came over. She was the closest I had to a sister. Since we were the same age, our family treated us like we were the same person. I fantasized about being one of the blonde, blue-eyed identical twins in *Sweet Valley High*. Except Jess and I had both inherited the brown hair, brown eyes gene. Jess and Julie. Julie and Jess. At times, it did seem like we were interchangeable. At Christmas, we learned to open our presents at the exact same moment because every single toy and every single outfit we received was identical except for the colour. One year we got the same dress—with a black velvet bodice and puffed sleeves. Except she got the one with the gold sleeves while I got silver, and I was beside myself. Everyone knew which position came first in the Olympics. And I cried because I had desperately wanted gold.

Although she only had eight months on me, Jess seemed so much older. She was the fun, outgoing twin, while I was destined to be the quiet and sullen one. She knew how to be around other people in a way that I didn't. She knew things about our family that I had no hope of figuring out. For years I followed her around like a besotted puppy. She joined Brownies; I joined Brownies. She joined baton; I joined baton. She joined softball; I joined softball. And despite being terribly uncoordinated, I persisted season after painful season. It wasn't that I consciously ignored my own interests—more that I had no idea what they were.

When Jess wasn't around, I was bereft. I hated that she lived in a different part of town and went to a different school. I couldn't understand why I had to go to a French Catholic school and she didn't. I counted down the days until the summer break when we could spend almost every waking hour together in our matching jelly sandals, eating Popsicles and swimming at public pools. We made collages out of old Sears catalogues. We played dress-up and ran through sprinklers. When we were together, we were never bored.

When we were together, I forgot the way I felt when she wasn't around. Weird, sad, lonely . . . She didn't mind when I freaked out for no obvious reason or refused to let her touch certain things in my room. She didn't laugh when I had trouble learning to ride a bike or blow a bubble with my Hubba Bubba gum.

When she wasn't around, time felt stretched thin and drawn out. I undressed Barbie and Ken and pressed their plastic bodies together joylessly. Without Jess, I had no scripts for what they might say or do. That was her thing. If my mom wasn't working or too exhausted from working, she might get down on the carpet in my room and play with me. Such times, Barbie and Ken remained chaste and fully clothed. As much as I loved time with my mother, she wasn't Jess. And every so often, my mom would get this terrible notion that I needed "fresh air" and shooed me off to the park. *By myself.* No amount of whining would persuade her to come to the park with me or, better yet, let me stay home.

The kids at the park were wild and unpredictable. I gave them a wide berth. I spoke to no one and prayed no one would speak to me. I wandered around the perimeter singing a Belinda Carlisle song on a loop under my breath, waiting until enough time had passed that I could return to the duplex. To the sanctity and sanctuary of my room. Everything I needed or wanted was there: my collection of records and books and pins and trading cards and marbles and dolls. I loved my mom so much it made my chest hurt. But sometimes I wondered if she loved me back. Because if she did, she never would have sent me to the park alone.

⌒

At school, you aren't bullied in any major way, although in junior high a girl you've never spoken to tells one of your friends that she "doesn't like your face" and wants to beat you up at recess. Terrified, you make up a new reason every day to stay indoors. You don't know this girl, and yet she wants to smash your face. Up until that moment, you thought you had to provoke someone for them to want to smash your face. Up until that moment, you thought that if you just kept your head down and your mouth shut, you could steer clear of trouble. Somehow trouble found you anyway. Luckily your strategy paid off; the girl got bored and moved on.

You aren't bullied in the way that Natalie is bullied. Natalie is—it has to be said—mouthy and annoying and pays dearly for her visibility. One fateful day someone decrees that Natalie has "cooties," and from that point on no one goes near Natalie. You feel bad for her, but not bad enough to befriend her and risk catching some indeterminate yet highly transmissible social disease. As long as she remains the target, you figure you are immune.

When you're in elementary school, birthdays are a big deal. It's not uncommon for the entire class—even Nasty Natalie—to be invited to a party at someone's house. Having the entire class show up at the duplex is out of the question. But one year your mother has a brainwave. She hosts your party at the local Burger King. A few classmates come, so does Jess and Other Julie. For one day you are a queen in a cardboard crown. Kids whose birthdays fall during the summer months throw pool parties and have barbecues. Not even the sprawling white house across the road has a pool. It occurs to you for the first time that you are not like the kids at school, and this difference must be concealed. The kids in your class live in houses, not apartments. The kids in your class live with two parents, not one. No one you know has parents who are divorced or even separated. Nan says it's better to have one good parent than two rotten ones, but you aren't convinced. You worry that the kids in your class will find out you live in a shabby upstairs apartment. That you don't have a pool, much less a father.

You make up for these shortcomings by being an impeccable guest and a perfect friend. On the rare occasions when you are invited to a girl's house, you play whatever she wants to play, even if it's Monopoly (you prefer the Game of Life). You lip sync to Madonna (you prefer Cyndi Lauper). You agree to watch *Dirty Dancing* and pretend to find Patrick Swayze sexy (you secretly think he looks like a greasy old man). The fact is, you are so grateful for the invitation, you don't want to screw it up. You learn to swallow your opinions so often that you aren't sure what you think unless someone else tells you. There is nothing especially funny or interesting or charming about your personality. But because you're so quiet and easygoing, so utterly pliable, you usually get invited back.

When two girls from your class ask if they can come over, you are so stunned you have no idea how to react. Great, they say, taking your silence as an invitation. *I'm having friends over.* You say the words over and over in your head all the way home from school that day. In the days that follow, you feel queasy with excitement. You spend hours organizing and reorganizing your room in anticipation. You tell yourself it will be okay if they touch your stuff. You can always put things in their exact places as soon as your friends leave.

Then the day comes, and you hear their footsteps on the duplex stairs. You study their faces as they step through the front door directly into the kitchen, which is crammed with a table and chairs and washer and dryer. You study their faces for signs of disapproval. You tell yourself it will be okay.

You let them into your room, and you hold your breath while they touch everything. Then one of girls pipes up and says she has an idea. How about we give each other makeovers? *Yes!* Makeover shows are all the rage in the early '80s. Your favourite is *The New You* for its radical beauty transformations. People are assigned a season and told to dress according to their colour palettes. Since your hair has reddish undertones, you decide you must be an Autumn. The hairstylist wears a cowboy hat and speaks with a sophisticated Parisian accent that may or may not be an affect. His name is Fabio or Fabian. And like the guests who appear on the show, you long to be transformed by Fabio or Fabian.

The girls agree you can go first, and they rummage through your mom's used eyeshadows and Avon lipsticks. You close your eyes and offer up your face to the makeup artists. You cannot wait for the big reveal. You have grand visions of the Before and After. You will be one of the ugly-ducklings-turned-swans you see on TV. One girl dusts your eyelids with powder, while the other instructs you to "pucker up" so she can apply colour to your lips. Every so often, the girls coo at each other and their handiwork. Like Fabio or Fabian, they seem utterly pleased and convinced of their genius.

"Can I look now?" you ask, growing impatient.

"Hold your horses," one of the girls says a bit crossly.

So, you close your eyes again and wait. You wait for what seems an eternity. Of course, what you really want from this makeover isn't strictly possible, you know that. What you want more than anything is to look glamorous like the actresses on *The Young and the Restless*, the soap opera Nan watches every day. You want to look like the pretty girls in your class, who are blonde and blue-eyed, not dark-haired and dark-eyed like you. What you want isn't strictly possible, but that doesn't stop you from wanting it.

At last one of the girls claps her hands, and you flinch. "Okay," she says, "you can look now."

She passes you the compact mirror from your own dresser. Nothing can prepare you for what you see reflected there. Monstrous green shadow slathered over eyelids and cheekbones. Lips a hideous, unnatural shade of coral. You wanted glamour; instead you got Halloween. You wanted *Y&R*. Instead, you got *The Incredible Hulk*. Watching your reaction, the girls can't keep it together any longer. They burst out laughing. You don't get what's so funny, but you smile anyway. You want to be in on the joke. You always want to be in on the joke.

Shortly after the "makeover," the girls say they have to go. Their parents are picking them up. But you haven't even had a snack yet, you think. You listen to their footsteps barrelling down the duplex stairs. The minute they are gone, you run into the bathroom. You sit on the closed toilet seat, rocking and sobbing so hard your body shakes.

Your mom comes in and says, "Oh honey." She fills the sink and soaks a cloth in warm water. She scrubs and scrubs your face until your skin feels raw. Until the white cloth turns green.

⌣

One day while I am outside with Carson, a few of the neighbour kids rush over. I am forever luring them over with bubbles and chalk. Forever aspiring to be the fun mom, the cool mom. I am extra friendly and sweet as pie; I am duplicitous for the best possible reason: so these kids will spend time with my son. Carson doesn't have friends or an aptitude for making them yet, so I do what I can to facilitate these encounters.

The day is perfectly mild, which in this land of extremes is a rarified thing. The sun is out, yet the air still carries a slight chill. The leaves on the maples flanking either side of the street are just starting to seduce with their changing colours. One of the littles asks if he can have a turn blowing the bubbles. "Sure," I say and hand over the bottle. No matter how many times, in how many ways I try to teach him, Carson can't seem to get the hang of it. But he is content to join the others chasing after the bubbles and poking them till they pop. The odd bubble escapes their reach, and I follow its wobbly ascent as it rises toward the treetops and street-lights where it inevitably bursts into a soapy blob.

After a few minutes, the boy gets bored and hands me back the bottle. "Who wants to see me blow the biggest bubble ever?" I ask, and the littles cheer like I'm some kind of bubble-blowing rock star. That warm, familiar feeling spreads across my chest. I like how the children congregate on my small front lawn. With each passing season, I like this neighbourhood more and more, the coziness that I draw around me like a shawl. This is home.

The girl next door, Chloe, is the same age as Carson. She moves past me on the lawn and climbs the couple steps of our front porch after Carson. She says something to him, but I don't catch it. I am too focused on producing the next bubble, on expending the exact right volume of breath so the bubble will grow and grow without bursting. Behind me comes a thud followed by a shrill cry. I spin around to find little Chloe splayed at the foot of our porch. Her thick navy tights are bunched, her hands a little scraped maybe, but there is no sign of blood.

"Chloe," I shout. But before I can even set down the bottle of bubbles and go to her, the girl's mother appears out of nowhere and swoops down and wraps her arms around her daughter. Chloe mashes her face into her mom's designer sweater.

Chloe draws back and in between sobs says, "Carson pushed me."

"Oh my god, I'm so sorry," I say, the words gushing from my mouth. "I'm so sorry."

But her mother doesn't look at me. She knows about Carson. Probably everyone on our street does. You tell one mom, you tell them all. People have been nice and supportive. They love to tell me their nephew / friend / second cousin / colleague's kid has autism as if that proves something.

Without a word, Chloe's mom scoops her up, carries her into their house and shuts the door.

The remaining littles on my lawn stand perfectly still as though playing a game of dance-freeze. They have stopped chasing the bubbles because I have stopped blowing them. They seem to understand that the fun is over, it's time to go. So they do. One by one, they flee, zigzagging to and fro back to their respective homes.

Stunned, I glance down at my feet. The bottle of bubbles has been knocked over and is steadily dripping out onto the driveway. I pick up the bottle and place the wand inside. I tighten the lid to conserve what's left, even though the bottle is practically empty. Even though I know there will be no more bubble-blowing, no more littles gathered on my lawn.

Finally, my fingers sticky from the soapy liquid, I turn and face the porch. Carson sits on the bench, his chubby legs dangling. In my throat, there is a chalky taste. I'd take bubbles over chalk any day.

I hate chalk, always have. The dusty feel of it between my fingers. The press of it against the pavement sets my teeth on edge. And my son is never content with a simple hopscotch. No, he always begs for more elaborate variations: prime numbers, multiples, the fucking Fibonacci sequence. Yet I do it because it makes Carson happy. I do it because that's what good mothers do.

"Did you push Chloe?" I ask now in a low voice. In my mind I try to run through possibilities. Maybe she got too close to him on the steps? Maybe she touched him when he wasn't expecting it. I wait for my son to answer me. I know it can take him a while to process language. But I'm in no mood for waiting.

"*Carson*," I repeat, growing impatient. "*Why did you push Chloe?*"

My boy stares down at his small Velcro running shoes and shrugs. My tone of voice has no doubt scared him. He has no idea why he did it. I immediately know he is telling the truth. And this, quite possibly, is the worst part.

⌒

Right before I started junior high, my mom met Mitch, and we moved out of the duplex into a small bungalow down the road from where Jess lived. My cousin and I finally lived close enough to walk to each other's houses. We could hang out whenever we wanted. It was a dream come true, except it came too late. Without either of us noticing, Jess and I had drifted apart; the sleepovers stopped, and we hardly saw each other except at family get-togethers. We were getting older, I guess. We no longer wore matching jogging suits and jelly sandals. Jess was still as outgoing as ever, and I was as studious and painfully shy as ever. Jess had a slew of boyfriends—actual human boys— while I had crushes on hockey players and boy-band members. The time was ripe for a new friend, and that new friend was Carrie.

We quickly bonded after learning of our shared obsession with New Kids on the Block. They were all we ever talked about at school. And every weekend we poured over *Teen Beat* magazine as though researching PhDs. We grilled each other about the band members—"What's Joey's favourite food?" and "What's Donnie's favourite colour?"—and answered quizzes like "Do you have 'The Right Stuff' to be Jordan's dream girl?" We watched music videos, memorized dance steps, and talked about how hot Donnie, Jordan, Jon, and Joey Joe were (all but Danny, whom we agreed was too simian-looking to be hot).

NKOTB was a safe bet because the boys in the band weren't *real*. I mean, they were real insofar as they were mortals. But they existed only in the realm of our collective imagination. Fantasy boys were perfect precisely because they were rooted in fantasy. The boys in New Kids on the Block were really no different than the Easter Bunny. At 14, I was in no way prepared to talk to a real boy, let alone go out with one. Besides, wasn't Nan always saying that men were "good for nothing"? And by men, we both knew she meant one man in particular: my father. At least boys you only dreamed about could never leave or disappoint you.

⌒

Every weekend Carson attends a special program downtown. Learning social skills is one of the most common forms of "therapy" for autistic children. In these sessions, kids learn how to greet someone, how to ask someone to play, how to be a good sport. They are taught certain stock phrases and practise through role play. Carson's memory is formidable. Trouble is, human interaction doesn't work in this rote way. It's similar to learning a foreign language from a guidebook. You may learn how to say thank you or ask where the bathroom is, which will no doubt come in handy. But you won't learn how to have a real conversation because real people rarely stick to a script. If you rely on guidebooks alone to learn a language, then you will arrive at your destination unable to understand a damn thing anybody says. And no one will understand a damn thing you say, either.

Perhaps unsurprisingly, Carson makes little progress in these social groups. It's disheartening, yet we keep on attending year after year, group after group. Well-meaning therapists encourage us to host playdates in our home. So, I invite friends who have kids the same age as Carson to come over. Even though I loathe baking as a rule, I make cupcakes and cookies for the occasion. I spend all day cleaning. When my friend and her child show up, I'm exhausted. Carson either ignores our guests or has a meltdown. The play date ends abruptly, with my bewilderment and profuse apologies. It's not that my son dislikes other kids *per se*. Being around them is just not something he craves or actively seeks out. I remember all the hours I spent in the duplex basement or in my room alone, lost in my own world. When I wanted connection, I had Jess and if I couldn't have Jess, I had Other Julie. Later, I had Carrie. My child has no one. There are no cousins his age on either side of the family. Aidan's relatives all live in Ireland; most of mine are still in my hometown several hours away. I feel responsible for Carson's isolation, which is tied to my own isolation. I feel guilty, but not guilty enough to bring another child into the world. Every time the topic of having another baby comes up, Aidan and I skirt around it. Maybe once things get a little easier with Carson, we say. But things never get easier.

And anyway, we only ever planned on one. I'm not sure I have what it takes to look after another baby. After the depression I went through postpartum, I am right to be concerned. I would not want Carson's needs to overshadow those of another child. Not least of which, there is the strong possibility that other children we have could also be autistic. I try not to be naive about what a second baby might bring to our family. Besides, Carson never asked for a brother or sister. He seems most content in his own company. I need a lot more time alone than the average person. Autists are, by nature, loners. And I don't mean that in any pejorative sense. The term *autism* comes from the Greek word "autós," meaning *self*. It was used in 1908 by psychiatrist Eugen Bleuler to describe a schizophrenic patient who had withdrawn into his own world.[38] Being around people (even people I love) for long periods of time is exhausting. I need time to recover. I have learned the hard way that if I don't allow myself this time and space alone, the stress will build up in my nervous system, leading to either a meltdown or a migraine. In 44 years, that has not changed.

When Carson turns five, we decide on a compromise. We get a puppy.

⌒

Social skills are just one of the therapies Carson is offered. In time I come to resent these so-called "interventions," the most common and widely available of which is applied behaviour analysis or ABA. It is also the most controversial. In the 1960s, Norwegian-American psychologist Ole Ivar Lovaas drew on classical behaviourist techniques to pioneer a treatment for autistic children.[39] The goal of ABA (then known as the Lovaas Method) was to teach new skills and modify behaviours to make autistic kids "indistinguishable from their peers."[40] ABA is known for being extremely intensive and repetitious, with children as young as five undergoing up to 40 hours of therapy a week.[41] Touted as the "gold standard" in autism treatment, ABA is often the only therapy endorsed and funded by governments and insurance companies. Although aversives such as punishments and reprimands are no longer used as part of the treatment, at its core applied behaviour analysis remains rooted in compliance— that is to say, in making its subjects comply. Autistic self-advocates have long decried ABA as being unethical, even abusive, claiming it causes lasting harm by suppressing natural autistic behaviours like stimming and enforcing unnatural behaviours like eye contact.[42] Critics maintain that ABA simply "trains" autistic children to behave like neurotypical children, at the expense of their autonomy and self-esteem.

We carry on the therapies. Throughout elementary school, I enroll Carson in a variety of classes and programs—drama, *Minecraft* coding, yoga, tae kwon do—hoping he will meet and click with some like-minded kids. He does not. And though it makes me sad, I eventually quit forcing the issue and recruiting prospective playmates for him. My friends' kids naturally go forth and forge friendships of their own. After all, relationships take shape organically, not in a colour-by-numbers manner. It is shortsighted and ignorant to assume that we have no desire for connection. Autistic people can and do make friends, although our way of interacting may look different.[43] We may engage in parallel play or bond over shared interests. There is synchrony and acceptance among our neurokin. However, it is not always easy for us to find our people. On the surface, girls seem to fare better, yet we still struggle with conflict, rejection, and bullying.

Long after I have given up on developing Carson's social "training," he meets another autistic teenager in an online forum for language and writing systems. Unfortunately, this other boy lives in Oklahoma, more than 2,000 kilometres away. But thanks to the wonders of technology, the two boys talk for hours every day about linguistics.

It seems obvious now, but I was slow on the uptake. My son wanted connection all along. But he didn't want to be friends with just anyone; he was selective. And why shouldn't he be? It's one thing to sit chatting with someone you just met at a dinner party. But when that same person, with whom you have nothing in common, insists on staying in touch after the party is over? *No thanks very much.*

Loneliness is a killer. Contrary to popular belief, autistic people get lonely, too. In fact, there is a disproportionately high incidence of depression and anxiety tied to isolation in autistic populations.[44] Being lonely is not the same as being alone, mind you. We do need and want connection, but only when it is on our terms.

~

By high school, Carrie had outgrown both boy bands and me.

Every hour was comprised of 60 minutes. I knew this rationally, yet I did not always experience time in a linear fashion. Some hours raced past while others dripped by with painful torpor. Lunch was the longest hour of the day. The crash of voices and wafts of grease in the cafeteria left me nauseated. Rows of shouting, high-fiving, swearing, and laughing kids made my head explode. Every table was its own continent, with its own distinct dress code and dialect. Cliques abounded. It was like living inside a John Hughes movie, only I possessed none of Molly Ringwald's quirky, self-assured style or red-headed beauty. In grade nine, all I had going for me was a smattering of acne, a mouthful of braces, and buckets of insecurity.

Every day I scanned the long tables in the cafeteria, searching for a space where I could feasibly insert myself while attracting the least amount of scrutiny. If I caught a glimpse of Carrie, I might sit at her table alongside the new friends she'd wasted no time making. She didn't exactly welcome me with open arms, but she didn't turn me away either. Hunched, I nibbled the corner of my peanut butter and jam sandwich while the conversation swirled around me. Fashion, celebrities, boys, teachers they hated, did you see so-and-so's hair that day, ohmygod, yet more boys, yet more celebrities . . . Gone were the days of NKOTB, when Carrie and I talked over each other, breathless and giggly. I was the same, frozen in time, while she had moved on without me. It was like being back at school with the nuns, having to learn a language everyone but me could speak.

Most days I sat stony faced and mute in the cafeteria. Other times I laughed too loud or too late at a joke I didn't get. Thanks to my apparent slow-wittedness, one of Carrie's new friends nicknamed me "'tard." Derived from the French, "en retard" means slow or delayed and typically refers to a late arrival. As in, you are *en retard* for the party. I was late arriving to the party in a different sense. In English, the word with its prefix is used to describe someone with an intellectual disability—a word so derogatory, it is no longer used in polite company. But the company I kept in the early '90s could hardly be described as polite. The nickname stuck. *'Tard*. Despite being on the honour roll year after year, I was earnest and painfully gullible. I took everything anyone said at face value and rarely knew when Carrie and her friends were being sarcastic. Either I was the smartest stupid person alive or else the stupidest smart person. *'Tard*. Sometimes Carrie and her friends passed around notes. Sometimes they looked and me, then muttered to each other and laughed. I wished I could time-travel back to the simple days of NKOTB videos and drooling over Donnie and Joey.

I had a sense that Carrie and her friends were mean, but I had nowhere else to go. Some days I spent the entire lunch break wandering the halls, staring straight ahead as though I had purpose and a fixed destination. Other times I barricaded myself in the girls' bathroom to kill time before my next class. Inside the stall, I breathed through my mouth and read the graffiti about who was sucking whose dick and other words that made me wince. At least I'd never read my name there. But there was still time.

⌐

Drama was a bird course, everyone said so. An easy credit. And maybe it was . . . for everyone else. But I wasn't everyone else. I was no Meryl Streep. And I sure as hell wasn't Claire Danes, who played Angela Chase on my favourite show, *My So-Called Life*. I couldn't act my way out of a paper bag (whatever that means). What was acting anyway but a socially acceptable form of lying? Which, incidentally, I was also terrible at.

Despite my best efforts, I couldn't seem to be anyone but myself. I knew this. My teacher, a man with orange spray-tanned skin and an irritating nasal voice, knew this. Since it was a split-level class, he paired me with a student in the next grade to perform a one-act play. Melanie played the (male) captive, and I played her (female) captor. The play essentially consisted of her monologue; I had all of three lines in total. My part was extremely physical and involved a lot of grunting and shoving her with the butt of a rifle—a prop her father made from old lumber. The rest of the time I pretended to look tough by chain-smoking unlit cigarettes, not as easy as it sounded. (I'm not sure where we got the cigarettes. Clearly this play would not be performed nowadays.)

Even without a speaking part, I was godawful. But Mel was a star. To this day, I have no idea how she memorized all those lines. Since I lived in town, we rehearsed at my place after school. At first the rehearsals were as awkward as the play itself. Mel and I didn't know each other, we'd been thrown together for this assignment. To make matters worse, Melanie's character spends the entirety of the play trying to flirt his way out of captivity. So, Mel had to pretend to flirt with me. The play was supposed to be subversive, a shifting of gender norms or maybe I still don't get it all these years later. We rehearsed and rehearsed so Melanie could get her lines straight. And I had to pretend to rough her up with the pretend rifle and make it look real. There was a line she had to say, "Hey, baby" in a sleazy drawl, and every time she said it we busted a gut laughing. We couldn't seem to get past that line without losing it. We rolled around on my living room floor in fits of giggles, clutching our guts. The play was not meant to be funny. But Mel's wooden delivery killed me. Our grade depended on a solid, serious performance. We were obviously doomed to fail.

One day at lunch, Melanie waved me over in the cafeteria. Since she was a grade older, I didn't know any of her friends. I hesitated, intimidated. As a clique, they were hard to categorize according to the usual groupings. They weren't jocks or nerds, misfits or metal-heads. There was no defining feature I could see that united them except the fact that they didn't fit anywhere else. They were a bit quirky, artsy a few of them. I joined them at the table. Mel introduced me, and for the longest time, I hovered on the edge of every conversation, saying nothing. Old habits die hard. I was afraid that once they got to know me, they wouldn't let me sit with them. Once the play was over, Mel and I would never talk again.

After rehearsal one day, Melanie asked if I wanted to hang out that weekend. Her friends all had their licences, so a bunch of us drove to 7-Eleven for Slurpees. Another weekend, we ordered some fries, then loitered for hours in the mall food court. The next week-end, we dressed in weird, mismatched outfits and threw gutter balls at the bowling alley. We were bored but never so bored that we got into any real trouble.

My mom loved my new group of friends precisely because they weren't especially into boys or partying. Because they weren't like Jess, who got pregnant in our senior year of high school.

When the day finally came, we were to put on our one-act play on a makeshift stage at the mall. Live. In front of people. I was so nervous during the performance I accidentally knocked Mel in the mouth with the butt of the prop rifle. So much for acting. By some miracle, none of her teeth dropped out. Another miracle: I passed. Drama was my lowest grade ever, a blight on my stellar grade-point average. But it was worth it. I never sat with Carrie and her friends again.

Thirty years on, Mel and I still shout, "Hey, baby" whenever we meet.

⌒

Some afternoons I see the neighbour kids playing in the street. Chasing after each other in T-shirts, their coats and backpacks dumped and strewn haphazardly on various lawns. But I no longer race outside to court them with bubbles and chalk.

Instead I watch from the bay window as they kick up piles of fallen leaves. There is a healthy blush in their cheeks from all the fresh air. My mother would approve, I think as I imagine them holding secret conversations and making up nonsensical games. Some days the sight of them makes me smile, and that warm, familiar feeling spreads across my chest.

Other times I watch them howl with laughter, the black Os of their small mouths gaping obscenely. I watch them tearing up and down the street like jackals. Some days—even though it's early afternoon and the most amazing honeyed light pours into our living room—I draw the curtains so I won't have to see the carefree joy on their little faces. So I won't need to explain to Carson why he can't go out there with them.

Sweet sensory child o' mine

It's the most beautiful beach in the province, so say all the guidebooks. And they are not wrong. I will always remember that beach but not for its beauty.

The logistics of the trip are all mapped out. We will drive east, my parents will drive west, and we will meet on the peninsula—in the middle, as it were. Instead of renting a cottage, we have opted for a bed and breakfast. That way no one has to worry about cooking, and there will be plenty of hands on deck to look after my five-year-old. Set on a big plot of land, the B&B has a pool, a swing set, even a coop with fresh eggs. I can already picture Carson running around chasing the chickens.

If all goes well, this road trip might become a summer tradition. Who knows, one day we may even feel confident enough to venture to the U.K. and on to Ireland to see Aidan's family. Most of his relatives haven't seen Carson since he was a baby, before we moved to Canada. He deserves to know his aunts and uncles and cousins, and they deserve to know him. But the reality is complicated. My boy is too anxious to board a plane, and we are too anxious to risk a meltdown midflight. I don't expect Aidan's family to understand. They don't know Carson well enough to understand. And how could they? They haven't spent enough time with us to know him. On some level, I know that is my fault for dragging Aidan to live in a country far away. He travels to Ireland on his own for a week or two every year. But we have not been back to visit as a family in five years. I imagine they view my reticence to travel with Carson as a cop-out. I don't blame them. Still, I'm hopeful this long weekend will be a step in the right direction.

Aidan parks the car. We step out and follow a winding path through the sand dunes. Sand dunes in Ontario—nothing could be more surreal. It's an ecological whoopsie. Like mother nature got the hiccups. When we reach the beach, I let out a gasp. The guidebooks are right; it's spectacular. We waste no time unfurling towels and unpacking drinks from the cooler. I drag Carson's T-shirt over his head and slather industrial-strength sunscreen all over his margarine-white chest and arms. Then I unpack a bucket and shovel and the hordes of colourful plastic sea creatures I bought from the dollar store specially for the occasion. If my child won't set foot in the water, then at least he can play in the sand. And as far as sand goes, this stuff is premium: soft and golden as demerara sugar. A baker's dream.

I shimmy off my jean shorts and sit next to Carson in my two-piece. When was the last time I was on a beach? When was the last time I wore a swimsuit for that matter? The shock of air on my body makes me suddenly self-conscious. It's not the fact that my body has changed since giving birth; it has, immutably so. It's more that I feel overexposed. After so many months concealed under layers of winter clothing, being in a state of partial undress feels jarring.

Now a veil of cloud obscures the late morning sun. It's not exactly beach weather, yet I try not to let that dim my mood. The sun may burn through yet, leaving us with a glorious summer's day.

"Hey, Car," I say in my perkiest voice. "Want to build a sand-castle with Mommy?" I grab the bucket without waiting for his reply. We are together on this beautiful beach, it's finally happening. And the kid in me is raring to go. *This will be so much fun,* I think. I imagine us all pitching in on the sandcastle, and after that, a burial. I am already smirking at the thought of us burying Mitch up to his neck in the sand. Carson would find it hilarious—seeing his grandfather's floating head, like the headless horseman in reverse.

A woman on a mission, I spring to my feet and head toward the shore to gather water in my bucket. I'm acting like an authority on the matter, when in truth I have only the vaguest idea of how to build a sandcastle. At 36, I've never actually done it. There were no beach holidays when I was growing up. My parents were devout campers. There was no such thing as "glamping" then. The roadside sites we visited were derelict and ominous-looking, places where someone might feasibly dump a body and then have the good sense to keep on driving. If I was lucky, the nicer places sometimes had a pool—that is to say, a concrete hole in the ground with peeling paint and dead leaves floating on the surface.

When it came to camping, my mom and Mitch were old school. They pitched a big orange tent that all three of us slept in. But we were never alone. No matter how fast we zipped the screen door, mosquitoes got in. So many nights I spent drenched in sleeping-bag sweat holding my pee till it hurt. The campsite washrooms were invariably down a dirt road, far from our lot. I was too scared to go alone, and I didn't dare wake my mom because I knew she wouldn't be thrilled about the prospect of escorting me there in the middle of the night. For hours I lay awake, my bladder a swollen balloon, listening to the sounds of the "great" outdoors. Except as far as I could tell, there was nothing great about them. Then came a noise like twigs cracking underfoot. A bear—it had to be. In my mind's eye I heard the lumbering steps, the heavy bear breath right outside our tent. I saw the shredded orange canvas. All it would take was one swipe of its massive claws.

By morning, I awoke doused in sweat inside my sleeping bag, unsure of whether I had slept at all. I stepped outside and checked the tent for claw marks. Just in case. There was no evidence of bears, but I was hardly unscathed. Every inch of my body was covered in what looked like welts. Against Mom's advice, I scratched and scratched the mosquito bites till they bled.

While she boiled water for coffee, Mitch stood at the picnic table, humming as he fried bacon on the portable grill. He was so perky, I wanted to stab him in the eye with a fork. They were both in their element. They *loved* camping. I was miserable. Why anyone would willingly subject themselves to worse conditions than they lived in at home, I couldn't fathom. Surely travel was about upgrading your quality of life, not downgrading it. My parents couldn't understand why I didn't share their enthusiasm, why I was practically allergic to the outdoors. It wasn't just the mosquitoes, though they definitely factored, with their sadistic gouging. It was too hot to sleep, and the constant stickiness of sweat on my skin. Then there was the sharpness of the grass (they are called "blades of grass" for a reason). I never, ever walked around barefoot. The only part of camping I could stand were the nightly bonfires. In the warm glow I sat in a lawn chair, staring transfixed as orange flames licked at the air like so many tongues. Every year Mom roasted marshmallows to a charred crisp on the end of a stick, and then tried to cajole me into eating them. And every year I reminded her that I did not like marshmallows on account of their gooey texture. Even in the dark I saw her frown. I was being difficult. I was a spoiled girl who complained too much and enjoyed too little. *Any other kid would be having a ball out here.* But I was not any other kid, was I?

If I had my way, I stayed inside the shade of the tent reading and listening to mixtapes on my Walkman. I could only get away with this for so long. It was only a matter of time before I was told to go for a walk and find other kids to play with. All I wanted was to bide my time until we went home. The last thing I wanted to do was "find other kids to play with." But there was no use arguing with them. It was now two against one, at least that's how it felt. Mitch had this authoritative air; it was always his way or the highway. And the worst part was, Mom backed him up every time.

Vacation was not at all like the Go-Go's song; it was an orange canvas prison from which there was no escape.

⌣

As you traipse back from the shore carrying a bucket of water, you vow to never subject Carson to something he hates as much as you hated camping. You set the bucket down and sit next to your boy in the sand. If you had any idea what would happen next, you would freeze the moment right there. You would not instruct Carson to dig a well in the sand. You would not pour water from the bucket into the well and mix it with the shovel until the sand formed a grainy batter.

At this point, you are improvising hard on the sandcastle-building front. You are shooting from the hip. But your five-year-old can't tell the difference. He does not know you are an amateur when it comes to sandcastles and so many other things. None of it matters because you never get a chance to pack the wet sand into the bucket. You never get to the part where you invert and carefully lift the bucket, hoping the sand would hold its shape. You never find out how your sandcastle would have turned out, had you carried on building it that day.

Oh no oh no oh no. Carson sinks his fingers into the sand. But it's not the same sand from a moment ago. It has undergone a transformation. The consistency has gone from a soft demerara to a coarse and lumpy gravel. You watch his mouth twitch. The new sand clings to his fingers. It sticks to his bare thighs. You take his hands and try to brush the sand off his tiny fingers. It's no use. He starts to scream. Grabbing a nearby towel, you frantically swipe at the clumps of sand on his thighs. Carson only screams louder. He screams as though you are rubbing sandpaper against his skin, which is exactly how it must feel to him.

Switching into panic mode, you pitch the bucket at Aidan and bark at him to grab more water. You think if you can just rinse off some of the sand, the situation—and the day itself—might still be saved. Dutifully your husband races toward the shore, but by the time he returns Carson's arms are flailing, and you see that it's impossible to pour the water over his hands without soaking the rest of him. His screams carry down this pristine beach that stretches as far as the eye can see. Heads swivel. And with them, like clockwork, the hard stares to which you have grown accustomed.

Your parents hover in the periphery, wanting to help but not knowing how exactly. You can't bear any of it. Without a word you begin throwing the plastic sea creatures back into the bag you unpacked only moments ago. The red crab, the purple octopus. The green shovel. The yellow bucket, now tipped on its side, slopping out what's left of the water. Tears burn as they track down your cheeks. Roughly, you yank on your jean shorts and hoist Carson onto your hip. He struggles in your arms, screaming all the way back to the car. Aidan calls after you, but you don't slow down. You don't stop.

Stumbling back through sand dunes, you finally arrive at the parking lot, your whole body shaking with adrenaline. You try the door handle. Of course. Aidan has the keys. Eventually he emerges from the dunes, followed by your parents.

On the drive back, you lean your head against the window and cry quietly, so no one hears you. For once, even your parents are quiet. In the car seat, haphazardly covered in a beach towel, your child is fast asleep. When you arrive at the B&B, Aidan lifts Carson out and carries him to your parents' room. He does not stir. You head straight for your own room, and Aidan knows not to follow you. You draw the blinds, then curl into the fetal position on top of the covers. You grip your knees to your chest and rock like a baby.

You are 36, and you have never built a sandcastle. But you came close once.

⌒

The rest of the weekend on the peninsula is a bust. My heart isn't in it. Not anymore. But I go through the motions for my parents' sake—for Aidan's sake, for Carson's sake—trying to salvage the unsalvageable. The beach didn't work out—so what? Any other person could move on and make the best of what's left of the long weekend, but I am not any other person.

Time marches on. We eat ice cream and visit a park with a giant wooden play structure. We order meals from restaurants I have carefully vetted with my son's limited palate in mind. At the end of the day, I turn the scene at the beach over in my mind and I realize my son and me, we are not so different, after all.

I tolerated the sand on the beach that day, yet I will not walk barefoot on grass or even on the hardwood floors at home. Every night I wear socks to bed because I don't like the sensation of the sheets on my feet. Shoes are a tricky thing. Heels are off limits, as are most sandals. Clothing tags are razors; bras, medieval torture devices. When it comes to the fabrics I wear and the foods I eat, I am just as selective as my son. The difference is, as an adult I have agency. I can eat what I want and wear whatever I choose. Carson can only express his distress and hope that someone will listen.

For autistic people, the world is often too much. No one quite knows why we experience such sensitivities, yet sensory process-ing differences are a hallmark of autism, affecting most of us on the spectrum.[45] The particularities vary from person to person. We can experience discomfort—even pain—from stimuli such as loud noises, bright lights, and certain textures of food and clothing.

A person may seek out or avoid certain sensations, or they may fluctuate between extremes. Many autists are hypersensitive to touch, for instance.[46] Grooming routines such as hair washing and nail trim-ming are agonizing rituals and the source of much hand-wringing for parents. Unlike Carson, I love having my hair washed and brushed. My aunt believed hair should be brushed every night to keep it healthy. When I stayed overnight at Jess's place, we took turns sitting on the floor while my aunt brushed our hair (exactly 50 strokes) before bed. The sensation of bristles being dragged across my scalp was nothing short of ecstasy. But to another child—to my own child—this routine would have been nothing short of torture.

For those with such sensitivities, many childhood rites of pas-sage are off the table. I once knew a boy who became triggered when guests sang "Happy Birthday." The loud chorus of voices, followed by the crescendo of clapping, was too much for him. We were under strict orders from his mom not to sing at his party.

Although I understood, it made a happy occasion feel like a very sombre affair. At the other extreme, a boy seeking sensory input rode the same roller coaster repeatedly. (Fortunately, this family held season passes to Canada's Wonderland and were able to visit the park almost every day.)

Today sensory toys are big business. From poppers and fidget spinners to tag-free clothing and noise-cancelling headphones, there are many products nowadays that make living with sensitivities more bearable. I have learned certain tricks I can do to keep sensory assault to a minimum. Even on overcast days, I wear sunglasses to lessen the glare. I watch TV with the captions on and wear noise-cancelling headphones in airports and malls. The problem isn't noise but certain types of noise; it's echoing and overlapping sounds. If Aidan is talking to me while the radio is on, I find it impossible to understand what he is saying. If I eavesdrop in restaurants or shops, it's not because I lack decorum or that I am nosy (well, maybe a bit), it's because I can't tune out other conversations even if I wanted to. Everything comes in at the same frequency. I hear things others can't. I smell things others can't. The smell of my husband's "plain" bagel makes me gag. Some days it feels like an army of bugs are crawling over my skin. Convinced I'm going crazy, I'll ask him to inspect my neck or back. Most of the time, there is nothing there. On bad days, I will take to my bed in the middle of the day like some haughty aristocrat. I will do what I have to do to shut out the world until the feeling passes. Earplugs in, eye mask on, a weighted blanket pinning me to the mattress. On bad days, I wish I had no body whatsoever. I wish I could unzip my skin and remove it like a coat.

When have issues with sensory processing, intimacy is . . . complicated. Not all autists are touch-averse (though of course some are). Each of us has our quirks and personal tastes, in sex as in everything. Sometimes touch is overwhelming. Other times it's a sensual feast. Certain types of touch may be jarring, even unbearable, one day and tolerable—even highly erotic—the next. Sensory hot buttons cannot be turned on and off at will; they can only be carefully managed and respected. For those in relationships, having a sympathetic partner is a must. Having the courage to talk openly about sensory preferences is another must.

The older I get, the better I understand myself. This understanding is a gift, an upper hand if you will. If I am lucky, I can sometimes engineer my sensory environment to my liking (or remove myself from it altogether). Other times, there is no fix, or else I arrive at it too late. The computer screen freezes, then goes dark. All I can do is wait for my nervous system to reboot. It can take hours for my operating system to return to normal.

A few years ago, Aidan and I went to the cinema on a date night. He chose the movie, which I later learned was no ordinary movie. It was shot in 48-frame IMAX 3D, and over three hours' long. Aidan was excited. He'd read all about the amazing special effects, so I went along. Half an hour into the show, I realized I was in for a rough ride. The "special effects" were an egregious visual assault. Closing my eyes for stretches of time was not enough to stave off the flashing colours onscreen, the relentless smashing sounds that hurt my eardrums. I stole glances at my phone, counting the minutes until the onslaught was over. I know I should have said something to Aidan, but I couldn't bring myself to do it. He was so engrossed in the movie. And if he suspected I was in any way uncomfortable, he would insist on leaving.

Date nights were precious, and I didn't want to ruin it for him. The night was ruined anyway. By the time we finally left the theatre, three and a half hours' later, I sat catatonic in the passenger seat of the car. It might have looked like I was sulking, but I wasn't. Aidan knew there was something wrong. I couldn't speak; my words were gone. We drove home early. I closed my eyes the entire way, and by

7 p.m. I crawled into bed and stayed there for the rest of the night. The next day once I was able to articulate what had happened, Aidan felt awful. I told him it wasn't his fault. He had no way of knowing what was happening inside my body.

Some people believe the way to "cure" autists of sensitivities is through exposure. If you don't like bananas, keep eating tiny pieces of banana until you do. Eat bananas in pies and smoothies and fruit salads. When all is said and done, you will probably still hate bananas—you will probably hate them more than ever—but you might learn to suppress the urge to gag when you eat them. Repeatedly subjecting a person to something that is painful does not make the sensation less painful over time. If anything, forced exposure makes the anxiety more entrenched. Desensitization is an exercise in trauma; it is cruelty wrapped in a pretty box. There must be a better way.

⌒

You leave home at 17. You leave as soon as you possibly can. You cannot wait to be free of your small-town shackles and far away from your stepdad, Mitch, with whom you lock horns almost daily. Despite your honour roll status and all-around good girl reputation, there is no pleasing this man. And it's not like you haven't tried. Unlike many of the kids in your class, you don't get wasted beyond recognition every weekend. You don't sleep with questionable boys. You don't have a boyfriend. You don't even have a curfew because you've never stayed out late enough to warrant one. There is something about you, though—maybe it's just the fact that you are not his daughter. You will never be his daughter.

You cannot wait to set out on your own, for your life to begin. But instead of the immense freedom you expect to feel once you leave home, all you feel is terror. A ticking bomb inside your chest.

Your previous life was stifling, unbearably small. Every day you completed the circuit from home to high school to the nursing home next door, where you worked part-time as a dietary aide, then back again. Rinse, repeat. Once at university, unmoored from everything that once grounded you, you drift like tumbleweed down Saint Catherine Street. This is unexpected. The only time you feel truly free is on a nightclub dance floor at 3 a.m. For many people dancing feels self-conscious. But for you, it has the opposite effect. It's only when you move that you feel in control of your limbs; you become your own puppeteer. Only when you are dancing do you fully inhabit your body. Your breath quickens and heart rate soars, and for that brief exhilarating moment you feel utterly alive.

After a blow-up with your roommate during second year, in which your friendship ends prematurely, you decide you are better off living alone. Sharing your space with someone—even someone you like—is too messy and complicated. For your final year of university, you rent a cheap studio apartment (what Montrealers call a "1½") downtown. It is a claustrophobic space, but the ceilings are cathedral high. Best of all the space is your own. Most of the time, you are content in the solitude you have carved out. But some days it's as though a sinkhole has appeared under your apartment, ready to swallow you. Sundays are the worst, those amorphous afternoons. To kill time, you might go to the Blockbuster Video around the corner and rent a bunch of Cronenberg movies on VHS. *Rabid. Scanners. Videodrome.* If you have no assignments due and no carefully constructed plans with a friend, the hours stack up in front of you like bricks.

One Sunday morning you wake up immediately feeling off. Your hair is bothering you, although "bothering" is an understatement. Every single hair on your scalp, every follicle, feels *wrong* somehow. And that wrongness won't leave you alone. You yank and twist segments of hair; you work the strands between your fingers compulsively. You drag your hair into a clip and fasten it. Then, when that doesn't help, you try tucking the strands behind your ears to force it into submission. But the hair falls just short and refuses to stay in place. If you had one of those skintight swim caps, that might help, but you aren't a swimmer. Nothing you do can distract you from the wrongness, from this feeling that goes beyond mild irritation. Not the clash of pots and pans from the next-door apartment. Not even the revolting sound of your neighbour coughing up phlegm. Like an animal in captivity, you pace back and forth, back and forth, all the while clawing at your scalp.

Wait, you have an idea. Your mother's sewing scissors are long and razor-sharp, specially designed for cutting fabric. (She hates sewing—still, she'll be pissed once she realizes the scissors are missing.) You'll just take a little off. A bit of a trim might fix the wrongness, then you can move on with your day. Inside the bathroom, which is little more than a crawlspace with a toilet and a narrow shower stall, you stare at yourself in the chipped vanity mirror. The long blade of the scissors catching the light. *Snip snip.* Filaments of brown hair fall on your shoulders and into the small sink. The young woman in the reflection looks determined. *Snip snip.* Tufts of hair land on the cheap lino. The blade feels cool as it slices through the hair, again and again.

When it's over, you shiver and take a step backward. You step out of the room without glancing in the mirror or sweeping up all the hair on the floor and in the sink. Dropping the scissors on the desk, you grab your keys. You lock the door to your apartment, your heart beating too fast, and head toward Saint Catherine. There is a place around the corner . . . you vaguely remember the red-and-white-striped pole outside. It's still early, and the streets are dead. The bars here close a lot later than those in your home province, and the students are still sleeping off the night before. But not you. The door chimes as you enter, giving you a jolt.

A burly man, of Greek or maybe Italian heritage, gives you a once-over, his dark brow creased. You can only guess at how you must look to him. Like a wild animal. Beautiful, yes, but also unpredictable, perhaps even dangerous. You ask awkwardly if he can finish what you started. Are you sure, he asks, and you nod. He ushers you to a leather chair so worn it is cracking, then drapes a black cape around you. He gets to work. You close your eyes. The low buzz and vibration of the clippers on your scalp makes you sleepy. When you open your eyes, it is like that time with the girls in your room. A chrysalis. You hardly recognize the creature in the mirror. You run a hand over the circumference of your scalp, which feels soft and strange and cool as the moon itself.

After he removes the cape, you rise in a daze. Already the relief feels like a watershed. You feel free but free of what, you cannot say. In a timid voice, you thank him. The barber nods, the same wariness in his expression. Although now you suspect that maybe it was sympathy all along. You have never been good at reading people.

You hand him some cash and step out onto Saint Catherine. It isn't until you are back in your studio apartment, with the deadbolt locked behind you, that you realize what you have done.

The following weekend is your grandmother's birthday. Your mom is throwing her a surprise party at one of the few restaurants in town that Nan likes. The whole family will be there. Aunts, uncles, cousins. There is no getting out of it. So, you don a pair of gold hoop earrings and bright red lipstick. You don't normally wear makeup or jewelry, but you make an effort so as to avoid looking like one of Charles Manson's groupies. You think you look okay. Not pretty or fierce-looking like the Irish singer with the shaved head (whom everyone will assume you are trying to emulate with your new look) but okay.

When your mom sees you for the first time, she breaks down.

At the party you sit with your shoulders hunched, sipping iced tea. You can tell people are deliberately avoiding the topic of your hair or lack thereof. Everyone but Nan.

"It's only hair," she says, then rubs your scalp with her knuckles *for luck.*

After the party, when you finally have a moment in private, your mom asks what possessed you to shave off all your hair. "Possessed" is an apt way to put it. You shrug because you don't have an answer. Or at least not one that won't make you sound bona fide crazy. And maybe you are a bit crazy. Your mom, convinced that you are depressed, sends you to see a shrink in town.

⌒

It will be years before I hear the word *autism* and many more years before I learn about sensory processing and stimming. When I do, I will remember that Sunday morning in Montreal in the late '90s when I held my mom's sewing scissors.

Self-stimulating behaviour, or stimming, are repetitive movements that can take many forms, though hand flapping is likely the most noticeable among autists. Stims may involve small movements, such as finger flicking and toe tapping, or whole-body movements, such as rocking and spinning.[47] Stims may be visual (staring at rotating objects), tactile (stroking or rubbing items with a certain texture), olfactory (smelling objects), or auditory (squealing or repeating certain sounds or phrases).

Until recently, I didn't think I stimmed. And because Carson didn't flap his hands or walk on his toes, I figured he didn't stim, either. When I was little, my favourite blanket was robin's egg blue and bordered with a satin hem that I rubbed between my fingers.

I sucked my thumb while rubbing the satin. I rubbed the hem so much that the material wore out. I did this for hours. Thumb sucking is a common form of self-soothing, but most babies eventually give it up. I didn't. I carried on sucking my thumb for so long that I needed retainers and braces to reverse the damage done to my teeth and palate. I no longer suck my thumb. And the blanket is tucked away in a trunk somewhere. Yet in its place I often find myself rubbing the hems of my shirts between my fingers.

Thumb sucking has also given way to a less innocuous stim: skin picking, known as dermatillomania.[48] Even now, I am rarely conscious that I am doing it until it's too late. Blood beads around the cuticles, the half-moons of my fingernails ripped down to the quick. Even the sight of my own blood is not enough to deter me. Some days several of my fingertips end up covered in bandages. Carson does it, too. I've noticed him sitting on the couch, absently peeling layers of skin from his lips until there is an open wound. Seeing him hurt himself in this way hurts me. Maybe because I see so much of myself whenever I look at him . . .

Not all stims are self-injurious. In many cases, stimming is a harmless activity. A joyful expression, a bubbling over. Oftentimes, stimming serves a purpose. Without understanding that purpose, many professionals have sought to extinguish stims like hand flapping simply because they seem odd or draw unwanted attention. While some stims admittedly look strange to an observer, these repetitive behaviours may provide necessary sensory input or a release of energy that might otherwise build and result in a meltdown.

Although I never again shaved my head, I still have "bad hair days" in which the sensations of my hair and scalp feel all-consuming. Nowadays I know not to take drastic measures like I did all those years ago in Montreal. I tend to wear my hair short and make a point to keep an elastic or bracelet around my wrist that I can rub or twirl between my fingers when the compulsion is there. And I keep my nails short and painted to help me resist picking at the skin. It doesn't always work. There are still periods when the urge is too powerful.

When my mother-in-law learns of my diagnosis, she isn't the least bit surprised. And frankly, her lack of surprise surprises me. *But how did you know?* She suspected I am autistic, she says, because of "the thing you do with your hair." What *thing?* Until that moment I am genuinely unaware of my stims. *You are forever doing this thing with your hair,* she says. She might have said something sooner. I wonder how many autistic people are the last to find out they are autistic.

Now in my 40s, I am actively trying to unmask because it's healthier. Part of unmasking involves embracing my stims rather than suppressing them. Now that I am more attuned, I realize I stim much more than I realized. There is the slight nodding of my head and the circular motions of my wrists. These movements feel both involuntary and liberating. As though my body is acting of its own volition. It feel good to let it move the way it wants. At first such motions feel self-conscious, then I figure my stims are less noticeable when I'm out walking with headphones on. As far as anyone can tell, I am just some middle-aged woman who's really into her music. Stimming openly feels like an act of bravery, of defiance, even—much like not dyeing my greying hair. But I am leaning into it. If people give me funny looks, so be it. I tell myself I am too old to care what people think, and I wish this was always the case.

⌒

We don't return to that beach — or any other beach — with Carson again. The beach, I come to realize, is my son's version of camping. Why did I not see it before? If I linger on it too long, the thought depresses me. I'm still not sure why I reacted the way I did. Was I frustrated that we couldn't enjoy a simple day out together as a family without it blowing up in our faces? Was I sad that my boy was missing out on a fun activity, or was I sad for myself?

My reality regularly fails to live up to my expectations. It's something I still struggle with. Experience is what makes life worth living, after all. I want a life that is rich and textured. I don't want autism (Carson's or mine) to limit how we live. But the fact is, it does, time and again. My son and I are made from the same stuff, yet we are distinct people. I seem to forget this because he came from my body. Who am I to ascribe value to his experiences? Some people love swimming; others love skiing. Some people love sleeping in a canvas tent under the stars. Others love reading in the shade. No one way of being is right or wrong. Above all, no one gets to decide what feels right or wrong for another person.

For years I obsessed over the things I imagined we were missing out on. Happy families do happy things together, so I believed. They take trips together. They go out to dinner together. They swim or bike or bowl or *whatever* together. Happy families invite friends and family over to visit. The fact that we did none, or very few, of these things was not lost on me. Such times waves of longing and self-pity crashed into me, their sudden force threatening to bowl me over. I couldn't let that happen. I had to find an alternative, a different way to live or else I would surely go under. And I would never get back on my feet.

In order to hold on, I had to let go. I had to rip up the crystalline picture I had in my mind of how a "happy family" should look. I had to remind myself that we are not some cute stick-figure decals on the rear windshield of a car. Happy families are not defined by what they do but by how they feel in each other's company. Happy families can eat pepperoni pizza from the same takeout place every Saturday night. Happy families can watch the same game show while curled up under a blanket together on the couch. Happy families can play Monopoly every single time the grandparents come over. (They can even buy the exact same property sets and build the exact same empires out of plastic hotels.) Our life will probably always appear less exciting than that of another family, but we can still be happy.

The dreidel game

We are not a religious family—though we were for a spell. By the time Carson reaches fourth grade, he has attended three different schools, none of which has been able to provide him with a remotely adequate education. Toward the end of the term, his last school politely expels him. Disgruntled, I decide to home-school him for the remaining few months. *How hard can it be*, I wonder. It's third grade.

Springing into teacher mode, I purchase curriculum workbooks and print out a daily schedule that factors in lots of breaks for snacks and trips to the park and local library. I find I am just as eager to read the middle-grade biography series called *Who Was?* We learn about the lives of various noteworthy figures—from Bob Marley and J. K. Rowling to Jesus Christ and Bill Gates—then Carson types (because typing is easier than handwriting) a report about what he's learned. So far my child doesn't seem to be actively hating the experience of "Mom School."

But it quickly becomes apparent that I can't meet deadlines with Carson at home full-time, so I give notice to leave my job as a staff writer. Five years is a good run. My boss is disappointed, but she's a mom. She understands that my son must, and does, come first. Quitting the online parenting magazine breaks my heart, yet I can see no way around it. Carson is eight; he won't be eight forever. This time with him is precious, and I can always find another job. But will I ever find another job that fulfils me the way this one does? That's the burning question. Over the next few years, I transition into freelance work. I write occasional articles for magazines and newspapers and copy for a handful of corporate clients. The income is patchy, but at least my boy seems more settled and less anxious.

A couple of months into our foray at home-schooling, it becomes plain that I cannot comfortably wear these two hats. Playing the part of both mom and teacher eventually takes its toll. There is no clocking off at the end of each shift; I'm always on duty, perpetually spread thin. I long for the days when I was *just* Carson's mom, when I was just a writer getting paid for my labour. Come fall, I am more than ready to hand over the educational reins to the experts. I am not a trained teacher. Home-school was fine for a time but I can't see doing this indefinitely. Besides, a new private school for kiddos with developmental disabilities has recently opened across town. The more time Carson spends in a traditional school setting, the more convinced I become that it's not a good fit for him. Inclusion is a beautiful goal, but to work it must be done right. And I've yet to see it done right.

The directors of the new school are a young married couple: she a behavioural therapist, he a business administrator. They seem knowledgeable and passionate about supporting children like Carson.

(Most of the students enrolled are autistic, the director tells me on the tour, but some have Down syndrome and other disabilities.) On paper, the place sounds amazing. My heart sinks when I realize the school occupies the lower level of a synagogue. The thought of sending my child off to learn in a basement, where there are no windows and natural light, leaves me feeling pissed off and resentful. Other kids get to walk a short distance to schools with windows and gyms and playgrounds like the one where Carson went for kindergarten. Other parents send their kids to school and manage to go to work without worrying every single minute that they will be called. I want nothing more for Carson than what every other family takes for granted.

Instead I suck it up and write a cheque for tuition we can scarcely afford. And every morning, in all kinds of weather, I grudgingly pack my boy into the car and drive 45 minutes across town in rush-hour traffic. There is no sense in brooding about it. My bitterness at our situation changes nothing. The fact is we are incredibly fortunate. Not many families can afford to home-school their child, let alone pay for private tuition. But even our privilege has limits. We agree to try out this school, hoping a year might make all the difference and maybe he'll be able to return to the public system next year. For one year, I place all my faith in this young ambitious couple. After all, where would we be right now without them and their fledgling subterranean school?

Unlike me, Carson has no qualms about going to school in a basement. In fact, he is gaga over the fact that there is an elevator in the building that carries us down to the lower level. The hallways and classrooms are plastered with colourful posters in Hebrew since on weekends children from the synagogue come to learn the language. Within a matter of weeks, Carson is singing songs in Hebrew and watching alphabet videos on YouTube. Within a matter of weeks, my son becomes completely enamoured with all things Jewish.

When we sit down to dinner one night (pork chops, I kid you not), the conversation goes something like this:

Carson: "Our family is Jewish."

Me: "What's that?"

Carson: "We're Jewish."

Me (sawing into my pork chop): "No, we're not."

Carson: "Yes, we are."

Me (gently): "Car, I think it's great that you are interested in learning Hebrew. And I'm really glad that you are liking your new school, but that doesn't mean we are Jewish—"

Carson (interrupting): "Yes, I am, Mommy. I'm *Jewish!*" He delights in saying the word.

Me (setting down my knife and fork): "Look, you don't just decide to belong to a religion. It's something you are usually born into, depending what your parents—"

Carson (interrupting again): "And I'm *Jewish!*"

Aidan (barely stifling laughter): "What Mommy is saying is that we were both raised Catholic. So, if anything, you would be Catholic. But we don't go to church anymore. We don't practise any—"

Carson (hopping up and down in his chair): "But *I am*! I am *Jewish.*"

Me (shrugging at Aidan): "Okay, honey. Okay."

⌒

The subject of faith and religion soon becomes taboo in our home. As with all my child's prior obsessions, we assume this one too will run its course. There is nothing for it but to sit tight and wait it out. And so, we lapsed Catholics play at Judaism like tourists. The whole thing is grotesque. The truth of the matter: I lost my religion many years ago.

I dropped it somewhere along the way like a stray glove or hat and never found it again. The story is long and convoluted, in any case too long and convoluted for my eight-year-old autistic son to understand.

In the beginning, there was a farmer's daughter who gave birth to a daughter of her own. That daughter spent a lot of time with a neighbour who took her along to church and taught her stories from the Bible. Eventually this girl was baptized, and when she was too young, much too young, she had a baby girl of her own. And even though the church held strong views about unwed mothers, the girl baptized her child in the name of the Father, the Son, and the Holy Spirit. That girl in turn was sent to a French Catholic school . . .

Though they no longer beat children with sticks, the nuns who ran my school were neither meek nor mild. The principal, Sister Marie-Hélène, was a force to be reckoned with. As a painfully shy anglophone, I had no intention of reckoning with her, or any of the nuns for that matter. There was already one strike against my name (two, if you counted my unwed mother), which was plenty. Early on, I learned that fear was just as potent as faith. Fear carried me through elementary school and middle school, through all the blessed sacraments, from First Communion to Holy Confirmation. I came to dread Holy Confession. I never knew what to say. I tortured myself, almost wishing I had something vaguely salacious to share. Talking back to my stepfather, Mitch, was the extent of my sinful behaviour. Nothing a few Hail Marys couldn't remedy. By the time high school rolled around, my reputation as a "good Catholic girl" was cemented. I attended mass at school during the week and every Sunday with my family.

My grade ten religion teacher (another nun) enjoyed initiating debates. However, the questions were loaded, and there was always only one correct answer according to God. During a "debate" about sex before marriage, the teacher told us to stand on either side of the room according to whether we were for or against premarital sex. I wasn't totally stupid. I knew on which side of the classroom to position myself if I wanted a decent grade. Around the same time I agreed to take part in a pro-life charity event. You didn't kill babies, and you didn't have sex before marriage. Simple as that. My religion held no shades of grey. That's what I loved about it. There was none of the nuance that so often left me feeling lost and confused. Much like my then-hero, John Lennon, Jesus Christ had a message, and it was crystal-clear: love is all you need. There was a purity and simplicity to Catholicism (post–Vatican II, at least) that I found deeply comforting. All I had to do was follow the rules (aka the Ten Commandments) and I would be guaranteed my parking spot in heaven. And God knows I was good at following rules.

Eventually my parents quit going to Sunday mass. Like a lot of families, they still showed up for special occasions like Christmas and Easter, but the rest of the year their attendance turned sporadic. For a period, I woke, dressed, made my breakfast, then made the pilgrimage to church myself. Despite the contempt I felt for many of the nuns at school, I briefly considered becoming one myself. I was no Mother Teresa and yet I pictured myself working for the Peace Corps or some NGO. At 15, my faith—not to mention my idealism—was stronger than ever.

The turning point didn't come when I sat alone in the church on Sunday mornings. Or when I accepted the Body of Christ and let the papery wafer dissolve on my tongue. No, the turning point came later.

⌐᠍

In the lead-up to the winter break, the kids at Carson's school learn about different holiday traditions: Christmas, Diwali, and, of course, Hanukkah. At home, we google "menorah" and learn about the ritual of lighting candles. One day Carson brings home a spinning top from school. It is made of wood, and each of the four sides is carved with Hebrew letters. *It's called a dreidel*, he says, then he teaches us how to play. Depending on how the spinner or *dreidel* lands, you either put in a token (שׁ shin), get nothing (נ nun), get half the pot (ה hei), or the entire pot (ג gimel). Traditionally, gold coins are used as tokens. We improvise using Skittles. It's no wonder Carson likes this game so much and begs us to play every night after dinner.

While walking past the toy store one day, I notice a familiar shape in the window display. My first mistake is telling Carson that maybe we can buy a dreidel from the store and return the one he borrowed from school. When we head inside the toy store that weekend, I ask the woman behind the counter if I can buy a dreidel like the one in the display. She shoots me a funny look.

"The dreidel isn't for sale," the woman says sharply, and I know I have offended her. Everything about her is severe—from the cropped hair to the metal frames of her glasses. For someone paid to work in a toy store over the holidays, she is distinctly lacking in mirth and good cheer.

I apologize and immediately start backtracking. But I don't even get to finish explaining the reason for my unorthodox request before she storms off. *Ouch.*

Stunned, I turn and steady myself against the counter. Now I have to break the news to Carson that he cannot have the coveted dreidel, after all. I'm bracing myself because it's Sunday morning and I haven't had nearly enough coffee yet and am in no way equipped to handle any drama. Just as I'm wondering how to let him down gently without crushing his soul, the mirthless worker returns. She holds two hands behind her back and gets Carson to pick one. Then she opens her palm. Inside is the dreidel from the store window. Cherry-red wood with gold-stencilled Hebrew characters, the dreidel is exquisite. Carson squeals with delight as he takes it from her.

"Wait, are you sure?" I ask, incredulous.

She nods without smiling or baring teeth. She's not mirthless after all, but possibly autistic herself. Of course this won't occur to me until years later, when I am writing this scene. Just as it never occurred to me that the reason the dreidel in the window display was not for sale was because it was hers. It belonged to her.

I can't thank her enough. I buy a pack of Crayola markers we don't need just to have something to ring through the till. As we leave the store, I thank her again and together, Carson and I step out into the December frost. I don't feel the cold, though. Not immediately. For the briefest moment, I am the star of a Hallmark movie, suffused with the warm, fuzzy spirit of Christmas—or is it Hanukkah? *'Tis the season*, I think. Whatever you choose to call it.

⌒

Maybe a week later, a mysterious package arrives on my doorstep. The postmark says Brooklyn, and it is addressed to "Master Carson." Strange, I think. I don't remember ordering anything from New York. I'll ask Aidan about it. Most of the address is correct, but the postal code is missing. It's a miracle the parcel even made its way to us. Inside is a set of brightly coloured foam alphabet floor mats—in Hebrew. Ah, so it is for Carson. Aidan doesn't know anything about it. So I check in with my parents to see if maybe they ordered an early Christmas gift for their grandson. They did not. Then I ask Aidan's mother if she or one of his aunts ordered something online and forgot to mention it. They did not.

Well, letter mats from Brooklyn don't just order themselves. Someone somewhere paid for this present, whether they realize it or not. It's a mystery worthy of Agatha Christie's Poirot. Preliminary inquiries at school turn up empty. No one we know knows anything about this parcel. Now that you mention it, says the director, Carson has been using a school iPad. *Aha*. Maybe whoever owns the iPad must have their credit card details stored on the device.

When Christmas rolls around, we hand over the parcel to "Master Green." Carson is tickled by the mystery gift. Aidan and I talked about withholding the mats, but what good would that do? Though we can't help but admire our son's chutzpah, we sit him down and explain that you cannot just go around ordering things online without permission. But we stand corrected. Our eight-year-old did exactly that. It's not our finest parenting hour. Better to have donated the Hebrew mats to the synagogue . . .

When school resumes after the holidays, I offer to refund the director for the mats. I don't know what they cost. And anyway, she still isn't sure if her theory is correct or if any charges were made through the iPad. She says she'll get back to me. But she never does. The mystery remains unsolved, a cold case. The culprit is never caught. Justice is never served.

⌒

The turning point is Stephanie. One Sunday, you notice her at mass. You are alone as usual, and she is sitting with her perfect nucleus of a family: two parents, one brother, one sister. She wears a pretty floral dress, and her long blonde hair is woven into an immaculate French braid. No one has ever braided your hair like that. You can't stop staring. At school Stephanie is so different. Forever flanked by an entourage of disciples who laugh when she laughs, whisper derisively when she whispers derisively. And it's just like it was with Carrie. You never know who they are laughing at, who they are whispering derisively about, though it happens too many times in your vicinity to be a coincidence. At school, Stephanie is powerful and popular, yet here, on Sunday, kneeling with her head bowed among her younger siblings, she is the poster girl for piety.

In the early '90s, your Catholic high school has yet to implement a uniform policy, so for now everyone is free to wear what they want. But Stephanie and her disciples all dress the same. They wear shirts imprinted with the names of men—Calvin Klein, Tommy Hilfiger, Ralph Lauren—while you wear whatever you find in second-hand stores. You thrift long before thrifting becomes trendy. You wear clothes worn by other people in other decades: velvet jackets and pinstriped suits with receipts and tissues balled in the pockets. You imagine weddings and funerals. You wear polyester shirts with butterfly collars from the '70s. The material feels silky against your skin, yet it makes you sweat.

Even though you live in a house now, your mom and Mitch still can't afford designer brands, and you don't want them, anyway. Stephanie might wear men's names, but you wear their entire history. Outside of school, you never cross paths with her. Why would you? Stephanie captains virtually every team. You've never attended a game, let alone tried out for a place on a team. Even if you had any desire to, you are far too clumsy and uncoordinated for athletics. You aren't jealous. Yet when you see her at mass that Sunday, sitting pretty near the front of the church with her perfect family, something in you that you hadn't realized was pulled taut, snaps. Who the hell does she think she is, Nan might say. You know it's not your place to assume the role of judge and jury. You are all just guests in God's big house, after all. But that particular Sunday, you can no longer bear it. You cannot stand to sit under the same roof, breathing the same oxygen, as Stephanie and her perfect family. You cannot idly stand by as she smiles sweetly, showing one face to God and another to everyone else. Her hypocrisy eats away at you; it pecks and pecks at your faith until all that's left are crumbs.

To make matters worse, a story blows up about a pedophile ring that puts your hometown on the map for all the wrong reasons. The scandal attracts national attention and is further mired by allegations of payoffs. Hush money. Even though you are not personally affected, the news feels personal. One by one, the headlines shatter your carefully constructed belief system. In a fury you draft a letter to the editor and fire it off to the local paper, the one where you will eventually write your own column.

As you put pen to paper, the solution seems clear. If Catholic priests were allowed to marry, then maybe scandals like the one poisoning your town would not happen. If priests were not forced to take a vow of celibacy—an unnatural, impossible vow—then perhaps they would not molest children. Even though your logic is flawed, your argument peppered with holes, your letter is published in the paper. People do not molest children out of sexual frustration. You are 15, and you have a lot to learn about the workings of the world. Still, your heart is in the right place. You are desperate to piece your faith back together by any means possible.

If something isn't right, then it must be wrong. Like many autistic people, you thrive on absolutes. Religion provides moral certainties in a world of uncertainty.[49] This is why your faith provides such solace. Or it did. But now you see that it's all a lie. If girls like Stephanie are allowed to exist with their two faces; if men of god can hurt children one day and then stand on the pulpit preaching the gospel the next, then you cannot continue to believe.

You never go to mass alone again.

The longer Carson stays on at the basement school, the more deeply entrenched his belief becomes. My child is convinced that he's a direct descendent of the Israelites. That he is one of the original Chosen People. I don't think Carson intentionally fetishizes the Jewish faith; he simply becomes infatuated with it in the way that he becomes infatuated with any number of arbitrary things. There is no persuading him otherwise.

For now we try to shrug off his religious appropriation, trusting that it will pass in its own time, until the director pulls me aside one day. The way her mouth is pursed tells me it's serious. She says Carson has been stealing a classmate's kippah. The boy's father is rightly upset, as is the boy. Playing with a dreidel is one thing; coveting a religious head covering is another.

On the drive home from school, I put on my sternest voice. "You can't take that boy's kippah."

"But it's not fair, Mommy," he says. "I want a little hat, too."

"The thing is, Car, it's not really a hat. I mean, I know it looks like a hat . . ." I pause and check my wing mirror before changing lanes. "Do you know what a symbol is?"

I glance over and see him shrug. He has no idea what I'm talking about.

"A *symbol* is something that looks like one thing but actually means something else. Like how a red octagon means stop."

I brake, impressed at my ability to pull that analogy out of the bag. But when I look over at Carson, I can tell he still has no idea what I'm talking about, although the mention of a red octagon has him intrigued. He can't wait to tell me that an octagon has eight sides, and he has been alive for eight years. There are some conversations you expect to have with your child, and then there are those we have with Carson. Parenting him is a constant improvisation, a perpetual exercise in making-it-up-as-we-go-along.

"So this kippah, it's not just a hat, it's a symbol . . ." I say, trying to get back on track. The drive I can do on autopilot, but this conversation is another story. "To this boy, it's a way of showing how he feels about his God. Like, say that Dad gave you a special hat and you wanted to wear it every day to show how much you love him. Does that make sense?"

Carson nods enthusiastically. "So, Dad will get me the hat?" he asks.

"No, no, Dad is not going to get you the hat. It's just an *example*."

Carson's features scrunch up, and I worry about what will come next. I can't have him losing his shit while I'm driving across town in rush-hour traffic. *Sweet Jesus, please help me out here.*

My own religion was inherited like a birthmark. A birthright. Same with my husband, Aidan. We had no choice in the matter, no agency whatsoever. We wanted something different for our son, something special, something intentional. Was that so crazy? Much to the consternation of both sides of the family, we refused to baptize him in the church. Even my parents, themselves practically heathens who had long forgone Sunday mass, were hell bent on having Carson christened, lest we doom his soul to eternal damnation. Alas, we would not be hypocrites. We would insist that our only son choose his own faith, or no faith at all. Given our respective indoctrination, we figured the greatest gift we could give our baby was the freedom to determine his own spiritual path.

We figured wrong, it seems. Now our eight-year-old is hell-bent on his right to be a Jewish boy, and it's cause for mutiny.

"Okay, Mommy," he says, seeming to compose himself. And I wonder if my words are finally starting to sink in. "We can go to the store after school tomorrow. I will get a little hat, and then I won't have to keep taking that boy's."

Exasperated, I want to pound my head on the steering wheel. Then I remember how the woman handed him the little red dreidel with the gold letters. The unexpected kindness of that day set a precedent in Carson's mind. All I need to do now is find an excuse or a distraction that will carry us through tomorrow, and the next day and the day after that. Until we can all move on with our lives, which, my prayers answered, is exactly what happens.

Twice exceptional, once shy

I don't recognize the brunette standing at the podium. She's five, maybe six, years younger than I am, with an effervescent quality like a carbonated drink. Whereas I am flat, she sparkles and fizzes. I can feel her energy all the way from the back of the gym, where we sit on metal fold-out chairs, wilting in shirts and blouses on this humid June afternoon.

Her energy makes me feel tired. Suddenly, overwhelmingly tired. And I'm hoping before it even starts that this ceremony won't drag the way these ceremonies generally do. *Graduation*. My baby is headed to middle school. *How is this possible*, I wonder as I rake my fingers through my hair, cross and uncross my legs.

"The student I am about to introduce," the brunette says, leaning into the microphone, "only joined us in October and had never studied French. Now, normally language acquisition takes repetition; it takes all kinds of practice. Not for this student." She shakes her head and smiles broadly. "When it comes to language, this student's brain is wired in a very special way—in that you need only say it once and before long he is correcting the teacher."

The audience chuckles. I elbow Aidan in the ribs and shoot him a *Is she talking about who I think she's talking about?* look.

"This year's award for excellence in French goes to Carson Green. *Bravo*, Carson!"

My jaw hinged, I rush to cover my mouth while my son shuffles toward the brunette at the podium who, it finally dawns on me, is his French teacher. "Merci," Carson says, formally shaking her hand as he accepts a small brass plaque.

Aidan reaches into my lap and squeezes my hand, which has gone limp and clammy. I turn toward him, but his features look smudged. It's as though there is petroleum jelly smeared across my eyes. I am crying, and so is he. We both are crying because we have been railroaded by this moment. This happy, completely unexpected moment.

⌣

My son's infatuation with languages does not stop at Urdu, Hebrew, or at French for that matter. While we are visiting my friend, an immigrant from Taiwan, Carson spies a children's book in Mandarin on her shelf, and she graciously says he can keep it. For years she's been trying to teach her native language to her own kids. *Maybe you'll have better luck*, she says with a shrug.

And Carson takes to Mandarin the way he takes to learning any foreign language—like it isn't foreign at all. While other parents sign their kids up to swimming and gymnastics, I find a language centre a short drive away and decide to enroll my seven-year-old in Mandarin lessons. I share his diagnosis with the Chinese-Canadian instructor ahead of the classes (no alarms, no surprises), and she seems flattered by his interest.

Every Sunday morning, we head to the second floor of a commercial plaza where we are met with perplexed stares. Towering a full head over the other kids, and with no Asian heritage whatsoever, Carson is an anomaly here. I smile at the caregivers dropping off their charges and usher my boy into the room. He takes a seat at the little table alongside the other children and opens the green folder that contains his flashcards. Every week, he learns new vocabulary in Mandarin and painstakingly traces the characters with a black Sharpie. Writing is incredibly hard for him. He has trouble gripping the marker, so his letters look like chicken scratches. But he is undeterred. Hunching over the index cards, his mouth pursed in concentration, he takes such care with each stroke. In time the chicken scratches transform into an ornate calligraphy.

From the moment he acquires my friend's board book, Carson embarks on a passionate love affair with Mandarin. For the next several months, he lives and breathes the Chinese language. There is no room for anything else. As usual, Carson has no interest in doing what his peers are doing. Not baseball. Not piano. Not karate. Not Scouts. Carson is his own person. And even if he could be persuaded to try a more conventional hobby, I am in no position as his mom to steer his interests or decide what he does for fun. And right now Carson's idea of fun is learning pinyin.

As I watch him sitting at the little table with his flashcards, I am awed at his ability to absorb language as if by osmosis. I remember the first time he tried to teach me the Cyrillic alphabet. He found it hilarious that I couldn't tell the difference between the vocalizations of Ш (sha) and Щ (shcha). To my hapless, untrained ear, both letters sounded the same. He was four years old.

At the time it never occurred to us to approach an organization like Mensa. Carson had psychoeducational testing done in kindergarten. If he was formally identified as gifted, then maybe it would inform the way he was taught.

At five, Carson was too young to be assessed. But the school psychologist went ahead and tested him anyway. While the other kindergarteners were busy finger-painting next door, he sat in the resource room across the hall spelling a series of random words. *Laugh. Watch. Turtle.*

Eventually he complained that he was "tired of spelling" and wanted to stop. He tapped her hand with his pencil. The psychologist smiled patiently, her rimless glasses perched perilously on the edge of her nose. "You must keep going, Carson, until you make a mistake."

Her report, when it came, revealed glaring disparities in his cognition. In some areas (working memory, verbal comprehension, visual-spatial processing, fluid reasoning), Carson scored in the highest percentiles; whereas, in others (processing speed, receptive vocabulary, visual-motor integration) he ranked among the lowest. These discrepancies made perfect sense to me. After all, my son could name every element of the periodic table and identify the flag of every country in the world but forget to drink or use the bathroom. He could direct you anywhere in our sprawling metropolis but could not throw a ball or hop on one leg. He knew a nonagon from a dodecahedron but couldn't make a friend. He could recite the value of pi to a hundred decimal places and sing the alphabet in a dozen languages but often fail to communicate his basic needs.

Kids like Carson are what's known as "2e" or twice exceptional—simultaneously intellectually gifted and developmentally challenged.[50] Many autistic people have what's known as spiky learning profiles. Despite what many TV shows and films would have us believe, not all autists are savants. In real life, we are not all prodigious surgeons (*The Good Doctor*), genius card counters (*Rain Man*) or theoretical physicists (*Big Bang Theory*). Many of us have gaping imbalances in terms of our abilities, possessing areas of both exceptional strength and exceptional weakness. Carson might read fluently and be able to recall all the facts of a story but have no idea what the main plot is about. It's no wonder so many children slip through the cracks. The term *gifted* is not only archaic; it is often a glaring misnomer. Being gifted is seldom a gift. Twice exceptional kids fool everyone with their brilliance while their struggles largely go undetected. Teachers may talk about students with "so much potential" yet lament that they're "not trying hard enough." Not only are 2e kids largely misunderstood, many wind up trapped in education systems that don't quite know what to do with them.

Carson has experienced this educational limbo first-hand. Over the years, he has cycled through various school settings, yo-yoing from public to private, from special education to home-schooling, and back again. Going to school for my son was, I imagine, like being stuck in a changing room where the sales associate keeps offering you different outfits. At first you are impressed by the selection. *Wow*, you think, *such an array of styles to choose from!* But the moment you start trying things on, the initial excitement evaporates as you realize not a single outfit fits. Everything is either too baggy or else skintight. Nothing is right for you because none of these clothes were made with your body in mind.

⌣

Unlike my son, I was a late bloomer academically.

Pulled out of a grade 11 history lesson by a woman I did not recognize, I could only panic. My first thought was that a family member must have died—it was the only plausible explanation. I never got called out of class. I was a good Catholic girl who never stirred up trouble of any kind at school, aside from a minor dress code infraction involving a Pink Floyd T-shirt. (A uniform policy was instated shortly after my high school graduation. Coincidence?) For all intents and purposes, and in all the ways that mattered, I was a card-carrying rule follower, a straight-A shooter, repeat honour roll offender, and perpetual pleaser. In other words, a principal's dream student.

But no one I knew had died that day. I followed the teacher (was she a teacher?) down the hall. Did she even tell me who she was? If she did, I immediately forgot her name. I was too busy noticing her eyes. It was unusual to see someone with eyes that were actually green, and not some muddled version of hazel. Her eyes weren't the only unusual thing about this woman. Her hair was an explosion of frizz, dyed a shade of burgundy not found in nature, that made her head look twice the circumference of a normal head. The way she spoke suggested she wasn't from my hometown but from a distant planet. In other words, she was educated. I followed as she led me to a room tucked beside the guidance counsellor's office. How come I'd never noticed this room before? Was it a portal to somewhere?

Once inside, she motioned for me to sit.

"Am I in trouble?" I asked right away, my skin itching with worry.

The alien woman chuckled heartily, as though the idea of me getting into trouble was somehow hilarious. "Of course not," she said. "I just want to run a few tests, if that's okay with you."

It was not okay with me, as a matter of fact. Not that I had the nerve to say so. The word *test* wasn't helping. Nervously, I sat on the edge of the seat watching as she removed an elastic from a deck of flashcards. One after another she held up a card and asked me to describe what I saw. Blob. Another blob. A fatter blob.

I hesitated.

She said, "Don't worry, there are no right or wrong answers."

I took a deep breath and did what I was told. I always did.

Cloud. Sailboat. Dachshund.

"Good." She replaced the elastic on the deck of cards and moved on to the next test. Eventually Alien Woman explained that I was being considered for a special program.

Antsy, I shifted in my seat and glanced up at the clock on the wall. The red hand pulsed forward insistently. History was not my strongest subject. I was terrible at remembering dates. Skip one critical event, and the whole timeline fell apart. I had to get back to class before I missed too much and fell behind.

Just because I was a straight-A student didn't mean I loved school. The truth was, I couldn't wait for summer. With both my parents working shifts (my mom as a nurse, my stepdad as a firefighter), I was often left to my own devices for stretches of time. It was amazing. Mom left Tupperware containers in the fridge and little handwritten notes on the kitchen table before her shifts. If my heart so desired, I could spend all day reading or drawing or listening to music. And yes, my heart desired it very much, thank you.

Books and music have always been my chosen creature comforts. They offered an escape route at a time when I most needed it. When Mitch married my mom, my life changed overnight. That's not hyperbole. I went from living with my mom in a little upstairs apartment to living in a bungalow on the other side of town. Suddenly there was this man with us who was strict and cold. And for a brief time, my step-brother came to live with us. There was a lot of friction, and sometimes shouting matches, as the four of us struggled to find our places within this new hierarchy.

Allegiances shifted. For the first time in my life, my mom wasn't guaranteed to be on my side.

So, I withdrew to my room to scribble angry verse. For hours, I lost myself in a particular Pink Floyd album, imaging myself exiled by *The Wall*. Other times I disappeared into a book and forgot who or where I was. Reading was the most blissful form of amnesia. Some autistic people prefer nonfiction to fiction. For me, novels like *Cat's Eye* and *Catcher in the Rye* were so much more than entertainment; they were manuals for living. Blueprints on how to be a "normal" person. Sometimes I became Elaine Risley, baffled and tormented by girls who only pretended to be my friends. Other times I became Holden Caulfield, an outsider with an abhorrence for phoniness.

It's a myth that all autistic people are into trains. Or sports stats. Or superheroes. Or video games or manga, for that matter. Some of us are into psychology and '80s music and dogs and literary fiction. When I wasn't diving into the worlds of Atwood and Salinger, I checked out library books about serial killers, witchcraft, and reincarnation. Back at school in the fall, I wrote papers on cults and incest. Atypical psychology fascinated me—anyone whose mind was basically weirder, darker than my own. By rights, the Children's Aid Society should have come knocking on Mom's door in the early '90s, but I guess they had better things to do. Besides, I was only reading about Jeffrey Dahmer. It's not like I was out mutilating cats in my spare time.

⌐

At the start of class one day, your sociology teacher parades up and down the row of desks, handing back the papers he has just graded. There are audible moans and sighs as people look at their marks. You are still waiting for your paper to land on your desk when he starts reading aloud. Your heart somersaults as you recognize the words. You sink deeper in your seat, convinced that everyone knows. When he finally finishes reading your conclusion to the class, he walks over and places the essay face down on your desk. "Well done, Julie," he says.

Everyone is looking. You imagine the heat of their stares melting the back of your skull, as though you are one of those wax figures at Madam Tussauds.

"Sir," a voice pipes up, plaintive and whiny. You know exactly who it is. You can see her teased bangs, her folded arms over her polo top, without having to turn around. She is what you would call (if you were being polite) *opinionated*. And today she's not holding back. She accuses the sociology teacher of showing "blatant favouritism," and she's not wrong. Meanwhile, your face burns.

You want to die.

You want to disappear.

Long after the bell goes—long after papers are gathered, textbooks are slammed, and bodies dispersed—you don't move. Then, just as you are about to stand, the teacher says your name. *So much for disappearing.*

You don't look up as he approaches your desk. "I just wanted to say—" He clears his throat, suddenly nervous. "I never should have singled you out like that. I'm sorry. I wasn't thinking."

You nod because you still cannot bear to look up at him. You cannot face eye contact at the best of times. You know his apology is sincere. You know he feels terrible about what happened in class. What he wants, what he expects now, is for you to tell him it's okay. But you can't do that. Because it's not okay. He made you visible, after all this time. After how hard you worked to stay hidden. He made you a moving target for the likes of Hairspray Girl. And who knows how that will end.

He is standing too close now, as in the Police song. He tells you again how much he enjoyed the essay. Again, you nod. Maybe you are being unfair. You are being a bitch, even. He's not a bad guy or a bad teacher. And for whatever reason, he clearly has a hard-on about this paper. You know if you turn it over on your desk, you'll see an A+ scrawled at the top, along with some superlative and a surfeit of exclamation marks. But you don't turn the paper over. Frankly, you are tempted to leave it there for him as a souvenir. You don't care if you never look at it again. That sounds harsh but it's the truth. Even if you could find the words, you are not sure how you could begin to explain in a way that he'd understand. How it is when you're writing. Calling it a spell isn't quite right, but what then? The act consumes you such that you disappear completely. Your *self* recedes into the background. Time itself melts and drips into meaninglessness, like in that famous surrealist painting. You forget to eat or drink. You hold your bladder until it hurts. Your single-mindedness turns you into someone else, someone who is likely not the nicest person to be around. It makes you *self-ish* and self-absorbed. Maybe it's the way with all writers. You assume that's what you are, or at least what you are on your way to becoming—a writer.

This state of hyperfocus is a feature of your autism, except you don't know that yet. You don't know how to tell any of this to the man still lingering next to your desk and staring expectantly at you. So, you get up and walk away.

⌣

I looked up to find Alien Woman watching me. Had I zoned out again? Had she asked me something? Oh yes . . . A gifted program. Did I want to go down that road? Drawing that kind of attention would be like going around with a Kick Me sign on my back. No, not really. What I wanted was a stack of library books and long succession of summer days all to myself.

When she called me back to her office a few weeks later to go over the results of the testing, I wasn't all that surprised by the findings. Superior range in language, average to below average in numeracy. *Well, no shit, Sherlock.* She rambled about having to find something stimulating for me to do because clearly high school wasn't cutting it.

"How would you feel," she asked, "about writing for the local newspaper? It wouldn't be for credit, obviously, but it could be fun."

I looked up at her big alien face and burgundy frizz and said, "Sure, I guess," because I just wanted to get back to class.

Later she arranged a time for me to meet the editor. The newsroom was downtown, next door to the old county jail that was supposedly haunted. A thin, balding man showed me around and introduced me to men and women whose names I instantly forgot. He set up a workstation for me across from the paper's one sportswriter, a younger guy with a booming voice. I was terrified. We agreed that I would write a weekly column about the "youth scene" and report on things that my generation supposedly cared about. The idea of there being a "scene" at all in my hometown was laughable. Kids my age either loitered in the mall food court or drank Slurpees at the local 7-Eleven. Or they ended up in detention centres. The minute we could flee, most of us fled—to places where things happened: Montreal, Ottawa, and Toronto. Or father afield, out West, the States . . . we fled as though our lives depended on it.

For my first story, I decided to write a profile of our local punks. I knew most people in my town viewed them as druggies and delinquents, and I had no idea if either was true. But I wanted to find out. With their blue or pink or green hairstyles, they were easy to spot in the mall. The thought of approaching them was less straightforward. At 15, I was terrified to talk to anyone of the opposite sex—with or without a spiky hairstyle. So, I brought along a friend for moral support. I went up to them in the food court, notebook in hand. Within a few minutes of chatting, I relaxed. They seemed like mellow enough guys. The most intimidating thing about them, from what I could tell, was their hair.

For the rest of the afternoon, we hung out. We watched the punks skateboarding in a municipal parking lot. People stared and gave my friend and I dirty looks by association. *Had anyone taken the time to talk to these guys*, I wondered. Had anyone asked the kinds of questions I asked that day: What does your culture stand for? Do you think people judge you unfairly? And, most importantly, how do you get your hair to stand up like that?

I scribbled their answers in my notebook. I transcribed my copy on foolscap, then typed it into word-processing software called WordPerfect. I wasn't naive enough to mistake my column for serious journalism. But as I had my headshot taken, I felt—*stimulated*. Alien Woman was right. Then the day came. My profile of the punks ran in the paper. My first ever byline, and I wasn't prepared. No one knew except the friend who'd been with me that day. I hadn't told anyone about the column except my parents. I felt conflicted. On one hand, I was proud of what I had written, yet at the same time deeply embarrassed by my pride. I still feel that strange mix of pride and embarrassment, even when I write for a national publication. I seem to forget that anyone will actually read my words after I've written them.

Toward the end of the school year, Alien Woman pulled me aside in the hall. She told me there would be a gala for the gifted program. I should have known there'd be a catch. Turns out, *gala* was a gross word for a gross affair. A show-and-tell in which her troupe of prodigies performed like pet seals. Parents, school staff, and bigwigs from the community were all invited to attend. I'm pretty sure the newspaper editor was there, though I honestly can't remember.

I had trusted Alien Woman. Now I felt conned, betrayed, just as I had with the sociology teacher. She had set me up at the local paper, done me a favour. Now she wanted her pound of flesh. Being a pleaser, it never occurred to me to say no, I would not perform for an audience. I was not her fucking seal.

When it was my turn, I recited a poem called "Ode to the Weak." It was a rally call to underdogs, like the punks I had interviewed for my column. The misfits and miscreants with whom I had aligned myself, having long known I was different without knowing the specifics of that difference. The poem might well have been called "Ode to the Autistic." In my mind, I had come to equate difference with weakness. I guess I had already internalized self-loathing and ableism.

As I took the stage in the school auditorium, my hands trembled. My biggest fear—aside from bears—was public speaking. I opened my spiral notebook. I cleared my throat and read:

> *You wake each day within hollow glass*
> *Your potential and your voice bottled.*
>
> *You examine and dwell in the beauty*
> *Others cannot seem to fathom.*
>
> *You are the one whose name is lost . . .*
> *The being indifferent in some memory.*
>
> *You are the last of gems to be plucked,*
> *To be remembered.*
>
> *Your voice is my secret compulsion.*
> *Your potential I have long recognized.*
>
> *You are not so minor.*
> *Your courage keeps me alive.*

In my head, I sounded like Patti Smith. But in reality the poem was lame. My abysmal performance at the gala may have spelled the end of my stint in the gifted program. But it marked the beginning of my burning ambition to become a writer. I wasn't sure if I had Alien Woman to thank or to blame for that.

⌒

In the 1930s, an Austrian pediatrician and professor named Hans Asperger worked with a group of children. Asperger noticed that while these children exhibited social difficulties and obsessive traits, they also possessed significant expertise in certain areas.[51] It wasn't until the 1990s that this eponymous subset of autism, known as Asperger's syndrome, was included in the *Diagnostic and Statistical Manual of Mental Disorders* (*DSM*). For a time, history looked favourably on Asperger for his role in saving children from the Nazi eugenics program during World War II. However, it has since come to light that although he spared some children who fit the "Aspie" profile, he sent countless others with more "profound" autistic traits to their certain deaths.[52]

Hans Asperger remains a controversial figure. By 2013, Asperger's syndrome was scrapped from the *DSM* as a distinct disorder, subsumed under the umbrella term of autism spectrum disorder. Many autists have since distanced themselves from any affiliation with the name Asperger.

Although he was simply diagnosed with "autism," my Carson fits the textbook definition of an Aspie. Socially awkward and precocious. Orating on his specialist subject (linguistics) in a flat monotone. That hardly makes him special. That doesn't make him superior to anyone else on the spectrum. The entire idea of a spectrum is misleading because it suggests a linear path—with a mild presentation at one end and a severe presentation at the other. The spectrum is more like a colour wheel of varying hues and gradients. It's been said that no two autistic people are alike; even within the same families, there is infinite variability in how it shows up from individual to individual. The one thing that is not variable is our dignity and intrinsic value as human beings. Something Hans Asperger clearly did not understand.

⌒

When I was young, I wanted to be an astronaut, a teacher, or a dancer—like the ones in shimmering stilettos and leotards on the 1980s TV show *Solid Gold*. Instead, I became a writer when I found I couldn't always trust myself to speak. For the longest time, it was easier to take a vow of silence, especially at school where I didn't speak the language and where the nuns scared me into submission. But then I grew older, changed schools, and left the nuns behind. Still, I sometimes found I could not speak. Speaking at times left me crippled with shame and insecurity. Selective mutism is a form of social anxiety affecting some autistic people, predominantly females.[53] I was continually accused of being shy as though shyness was a mortal sin or fatal flaw. My reticence wasn't borne out of fear; I did not stutter or have any noticeable speech impediment. Often I fumbled for my words. Or else I rambled, taking long detours from the carefully mapped-out route in my mind. To this day, when I open my mouth, what comes out is seldom what's intended. Like errant soldiers, my words frequently step out of rank, refusing to line up in the correct order.

When I write, I have better control. I can carve, whittle, and shape words until they resemble the picture in my head. Autism is essentially a communication disorder, though it is not as clear-cut as that implies. After all, many of us are hyperlexic—early readers. I don't flatter myself into thinking I'm the next Atwood or Salinger.

On the page I can be my true self, not the one gagged and tongue-tied whenever I open my mouth.

Being a writer is a forgiving occupation for someone who struggles with public speaking, or for that matter, private speaking. But sometimes writers are asked to make media appearances based on material they have written. Once my freelance work started taking off and I was contributing regularly to newspapers and magazines, requests for interviews came in thick and fast. Radio was a forgiving medium since I could forgo eye contact with the host; I could fidget and pace the room, and no one was the wiser. Movement helped the flow of my words but only marginally so. Still, I frequently blanked mid-sentence, when the connection between thought and vocalization fritzed. And my head filled with a kind of white noise.

This happened once during a live segment on morning TV. I agreed to the interview because how could I turn down national television? But that meant driving to the studio before the sun had come up. That meant sitting in a chair as a makeup artist powdered my face. At one point, I considered excusing myself to be sick. Not very showbiz. All I could think about while I sat in the green room moments before my segment was how to escape. Maybe there was an exit I could sneak out of. Maybe I could make my way to the parking lot without the producer noticing.

Too late. Someone was fitting a mic in my clothes, then someone else led me onto the set. So many bodies buzzed around. So many cables snaked in every direction along the floor. In the dark I tried not to trip on any of the wires as I walked toward the couch where the host sat waiting for me. Then we were live in three, two, one . . . The host nodded and glanced over at me with pretty, heavily made-up eyes. The look she gave me was gentle but imploring. *Speak. Speak.* A second on live television stretches out like five. My words fought behind the gate, tripping to get ahead of each other.

The host was gracious. But the second my segment ended, her smile fell like a dropped anchor. An assistant swooped in, unplugged my mic, and led me back through the tangle of wires. In a sweet, mechanical voice, she thanked me for my time, then handed me a mug with the network's logo on it and promptly showed me to the exit. When I stepped into the parking lot, it was still dark outside.

⤻

Sunday morning. I work on my laptop in the café while Carson attends his Mandarin lesson upstairs. Since I finish up a bit early, I decide to wait outside his classroom, listening in on the last few minutes of the lesson. Eavesdropping is a guilty pleasure. I know it's socially frowned upon, but the writer in me can't help it. I love being a fly on the wall, observing others. If people are out talking loudly in public, then I figure their conversations are fair game. For me, it's the equivalent of reading a novel. The equivalent of a reality show that predates actual reality shows. I glean so much insight from what people talk about, from their mannerisms, and whether they swear or use slang. It's as much about what they say as what they don't say. You can learn a lot from a snippet of conversation. At least I do. I've been doing it since I was a child because I've always found people fascinating and confusing.

The instructor asks the class a question, and a child blurts the answer in a squeaky voice. I know that voice. I can picture him right now bouncing in his seat.

"Shì, Carson," the instructor says. Give the other children a chance to respond. There is a trace of annoyance in her voice—or am I imagining it? I can't always trust my own judgment. I am the classic unreliable narrator. I often miss crucial subtext, or else I invent subtext that isn't there, all of which makes me second-guess myself.

It's better when Aidan is around to play translator. He checks my incoming emails, vetoes my drafts before I send them out, to make sure I say what I mean to say. My native language may be English, I may even call myself a writer by trade, yet I need an interpreter for this other language that runs just below the surface of every conversation.

Is the instructor annoyed with Carson? If Aidan was here right now, he would know. But Aidan isn't here. Aidan can't always be here to figure things out for me. I hate how lost and juvenile I feel without his help. But by the end of the lesson, the answer is clear, even to me.

The classroom door cracks open, and all the little girls and boys file out quietly. All except my Carson who remains seated on the small chair, shuffling through his scattered flashcards. He seems unaware that I am standing in the doorway or that the lesson is over.

When the instructor notices me, her expression darkens. She ushers me inside the classroom and tells me to wait. After the last child has been picked up, she closes the door behind her.

"Carson." She says his name like it's a bite of food she finds gross but is too polite to spit out.

"He touched another student's hair and cut a piece with his scissors." At this the instructor makes a snipping motion with her fingers. What's most perturbing is how easy it is to imagine Carson doing this—petting the girl's sleek hair as though she were a prized pony. How easy to imagine him wanting a lock of her beautiful raven-coloured hair to take home and keep as a souvenir.

Eyes downcast, I shape my mouth in such a way that I hope conveys shock and sadness. I mean, I am shocked and saddened, yet I also have the sense that I've played this part before. That of the mother whose child has been accused of some wrongdoing. Haven't I been here before, in another time, in another place?

"I'm so, so sorry," I say, fully prepared to plead forgiveness and to ask for a second chance on my child's behalf. I will talk to him, make sure Carson understands that what he did was wrong. I will give her my word that this sort of thing will never happen again. But the second I open my mouth to speak, the instructor holds up her hand like a stop sign. She is shushing me, as though I'm one of her students disrupting the class.

"No more Mandarin for Carson," she says, shaking her head vehemently.

I nod slowly, a sudden heaviness bearing down on me. It seems to emanate from the top of my skull moving through my shoulders and back. My laptop bag suddenly feels unbearably heavy. I adjust the strap and walk over to the little table where Carson is still fully absorbed in his flashcards. He hasn't even noticed I'm there, let alone registered a word of my conversation with the instructor. Just as well.

"Time to go, Car," I say, carefully rearranging my features and pitching my voice to sound outrageously cheerful, like one of the children's presenters on *Treehouse*. I want him to think that everything is hunky-dory when it so clearly is not. At last Carson looks up at me with his eager hazel eyes. He still has the chubby cheeks of a toddler. Even now his fine curls barely cover his scalp. He is seven, yet in many ways he is so much younger.

"Mommy!" he shouts, waving a flashcard for me to see. He sounds out a brand-new word he has learned. His pronunciation, as usual, is on point. It still amazes me that his mouth can make these unfamiliar sounds, that he can make learning a new tongue look so effortless. Since I can't command my own mouth to speak, I flash him my biggest mom smile.

"Come," I manage to say, "you can show me at home." As I start gathering the flashcards and placing them inside the green folder, I wonder what became of the lock of hair. I forgot to ask the instructor. Did she confiscate it as evidence? Did she hand it over to the girl's parents at pickup, or will I find it later, tucked away in one of Carson's pockets when I do the laundry?

I try to imagine what the instructor said to the girl's parents—the selection of words she used to describe my son and what he did. Then I try to summon my own words, the ones I will use to tell my child that he is no longer welcome here. That he is no longer allowed to do the one thing in the world that brings him pure joy. I use words for a living. They are my tools, my implements, and sometimes my weapons. There are so many of them at my disposal, and I know how important it is to choose them wisely. Sometimes, though, words and language abandon me altogether. And I revert to that girl in the playground, mute, powerless.

Tucking the green folder into my bag, I take Carson's small hand in mine, and together we head down the stairs, one painfully slow step at a time.

Maybe when I'm 64

The year he turns nine, Carson discovers the Beatles. He discovers their music much in the way that Columbus "discovered" the Americas. As in, he discovered what was already there. But that's the thing about the Beatles. Everybody stumbles upon their music for the first time and feels like those songs were written just for them.

It's a wonder Carson is interested in the Beatles at all. For the first eight years of his life, he was utterly unmoved by music. It didn't matter whether it was Mozart or The Wiggles, music left him stone cold. *Who even is this child*, I wondered. In desperation, I joined a mom-and-tot music class. Every week I sat on a rug in a damp church hall. Every week I bounced him up and down on my lap and duly sang nursery rhymes through gritted teeth. My son yawned and looked around the room, his disinterest palpable. Okay, so maybe I didn't blame him exactly.

I didn't mind if he never picked up a hockey stick or a violin. But if my baby didn't appreciate a good guitar riff, where did that leave me? By the time I gave birth, my CD collection warranted its own storage facility. Some bands, like the Smiths and Depeche Mode, required entire drawers. To keep track of our substantial inventory, I created a spreadsheet—alphabetized by artist. Aidan teased me mercilessly about my spreadsheet. I didn't care. I could no more fathom a life without music than I could fathom a life without sight or taste.

Once Carson was diagnosed with autism at age three, his aversion to music made a lot more sense. We learned that he was hypersensitive to noise. Certain sounds caused him distress. Hand dryers in public washrooms blasting hot air. Even the flush of an automatic toilet could trigger a meltdown. His chubby little hands raced to cover his ears, and Carson would scream as though he was being stabbed.

In the car we learned to leave the radio off, knowing he needed the quiet. And in time, silence became our family's soundtrack. I missed cranking up the tunes, singing and dancing around the kitchen while preparing dinner. But I did what any parent does: I subverted my own needs for my child's.

Where did Carson first hear the Beatles, I wonder. On a TV commercial or at a supermarket? Or maybe it was in the bathtub . . . I used to sing "Octopus's Garden" to Carson because he had this bath toy, a purple octopus, that spouted water when you turned it upside down. That purple octopus might have been to blame for everything that followed.

⌒

I don't remember the first time I heard the Beatles. Their songs are as woven into my childhood as the blue Dodge Dart we drove around town in, our arms dangling out the window because there was no air conditioning. No seat belts, even. "Penny Lane" was sticky Popsicle fingers and jelly shoes that cut into my feet and gave me blisters. "Ob-La-Di, Ob-La-Da" was the acrid chlorine smell from the public pools where my cousin Jess and I swam all summer long.

My first prized possession was a portable record player that I carried around like a briefcase. Even then music was serious business to me. I would have been around five years old. The first record I owned was a 1979 compilation called *Super-Sonic*. Excavated from a clearance bin at Kmart, the record had songs by Earth, Wind & Fire; Toto; Joe Jackson; Amii Stewart; and Blondie. On the cover was a giant pair of headphones with wings sprouting from them. That image was apt. Music really could make you fly. Some songs had the power to transport me from my small bedroom in the upstairs apartment to places faraway in my mind.

That was how I experienced music. Certain songs seemed to demand certain rituals. Every morning I made my bed to my .45 of "You Can't Hurry Love" (Phil Collins—not the original by the Supremes). The lyrics of every song that played on our local radio station, CJSS, were burned into memory. Even the songs I didn't like I knew by heart.

In 1984, while everyone was busy fawning over a dancer named Madonna, I mooned over another pop singer, Cyndi Lauper. Kooky yet beautiful as a porcelain doll, Cyndi existed on the fringes, a mishmash of punk and pixie princess. Her vocals alternated between throaty and powerful one minute, chirpy and impish the next. With her half-shaved bleached and orange-streaked hair, she swanned around in Converse high tops and lacy vintage dresses. If Cyndi was so unusual, then so was I. To emulate my idol, I wore neon-coloured shoelaces in my hair and sashayed around the duplex apartment in a flowing skirt.

That year my mom surprised me with tickets to see Cyndi perform live at the old Forum in Montreal. Our seats were in the nosebleeds. Before the show, I crawled the steep stairs in the engulfing black, equally petrified of heights and the dark of the stadium. Then I heard the opening bars of "When You Were Mine," and the world fell away. Transfixed, I watched as my idol came down from the rafters in a metal garbage can—part trapeze artist, part Oscar the Grouch. It was 1984. I was eight years old, and I had never seen anything like it.

Cyndi Lauper was my first crush as well as my first autistic special interest or SPIN. Up until recently, I didn't think I had a special interest because there is nothing "special" about being into music. I assumed everyone loved music the way I did, but I came to see that wasn't the case. Mom and Nan liked music fine, but neither of them lived and breathed it with the same fire I did. Not everybody fixated on it quite the way I did, memorizing every lyric of every song. Nor did they feel the urgent need to collect and catalogue it the way I did.

The intensity and narrow scope of autistic SPINs is what sets them apart from the realm of mere hobbyism.[54] In many cases our interests veer into the territory of obsession, leaving us unwilling or unable to shift our attention to anything else. The tendency to focus intensely on just one or few subjects rather than less intensely on a broader number of subjects is known as monotropism.[55] Such all-consuming interests were once pathologized and discouraged because they were thought to interfere with daily functioning. Now researchers are beginning to see the good that can come from pursuing our interests. In certain cases, these interests may lead to groundbreaking innovation and social activism. Consider Temple Grandin's contributions to the cattle industry, Greta Thunberg's unwavering commitment to environmental justice, and the work of countless others in countless other specialist fields. Not all SPINs have the power to change the world, but they do play a critical role in reducing stress and improving well-being among neurodivergent populations.[56]

My musical odyssey began in earnest after I saw an ad for a subscription service to Columbia Records. When you signed up, you received 12 cassettes in the mail for a penny! Afterward you committed to buy at least one cassette each month at the full retail price for the rest of the year. And if you forgot to order on time, you were sent the selection of the month, which could be an album you hated. Like countless others, I took the Columbia Records bait hook, line, and sinker. Even though my single mom had a million better things to spend her money on, I hounded her until she acquiesced and signed up.

Every day I checked to see if the latest Columbia Records catalogue had come in the mail. The arrival of that catalogue was rivalled only by the *TV Guide*. After school I sat at the kitchen table studying the open catalogue, circling the albums I wanted, crossing out those I already had. Anguished, I chewed my nails as I deliberated over which cassette to order next. Prince and the Revolution or Culture Club? Hall & Oates or Huey Lewis and the News? Duran Duran or the Police? Billy Joel or Lionel Richie? Michael—or Janet— Jackson? These were impossible decisions. On rare occasions, my mom would choose a tape she wanted from the catalogue (Foreigner or Dan Fogelberg), which only added to my malaise.

If the Columbia Records music club sounded too good to be true, that's because it was. Eventually our subscription lapsed, and my mother refused to sign up again "to that gimmick." But I needed to get my fix somewhere. By the time I turned 13, the writing was on the wall: I had to start saving and buying my own tapes. And even though I'd planned to spend that summer the exact same way I spent every summer (reading, drawing, and listening to music), I needed a job.

One of my aunt's colleagues was looking for someone to watch her kids during the day. Unlike a lot of girls my age, I had never done any babysitting. I had always felt nervous and vaguely uncomfortable around children. They were cute, I guess, but they made so much noise and mess. Plus, I had no idea how to act around them. I didn't even know how to act around other kids when I was a kid myself. But out of sheer desperation, I told my aunt I would do it.

⌒

A boy and a girl. You don't remember how old they were that summer. But you can still see their sweet faces in the Polaroid you took that summer afternoon before things turned sour.

The time feels long and tedious, and you have no clue how to entertain these small children. You could take them to the library or to the playground, but you don't. You could colour in one of the myriad colouring books strewn across the dining room table, or wade in the wading pool in the backyard. You could make something out of papier mâché. You could recreate the pipe-cleaner critters from your own childhood. But you are not nearly as crafty or enterprising as your aunt was with you and Jess. Nothing about looking after kids feels natural or enjoyable to you.

So, you remain in the shady dark of the living room. On your second day there you notice a sleek free-standing tower. You have never seen anything like it, and you can only dream of owning such a machine.

Compact discs have been around for a while, yet to you they are still a novelty. Shiny, mysterious orbs that seem to demand both reverence and babying. Unlike cassette tapes, CDs must be sprayed with a special cleaning fluid and wiped with a special cloth. Like vinyl, a disc can be scratched, yet unlike cassettes they are impossible to wear out. You have lost track of the times your crappy cassette player jammed and with bated breath you wound the tape back in with a pencil, praying it could be salvaged. Those fraught exercises would all be a thing of the past with CDs.

Every day when you are left with the children, you feel yourself pulled to the stereo in the other room. All the time it stands there like a behemoth, you can think of nothing else. As adorable as they are, the little boy and girl are an afterthought in your care. They are safe, yet you find yourself preoccupied. Your mind somewhere else.

One day you can't resist any longer. You pull a CD from its sleeve and slip it into the stereo drawer. You press the button, and the drawer slides back in. What a magnificent machine! What a monolith! Every day while the children are playing, you sit in lotus before this deity. Eyes shut, you listen as the sounds travels through the tall speakers, vibrating through the oatmeal-coloured shag carpet into your body. Sound enters from the soles of your feet and moves through your legs and stomach. It swells inside your chest cavity, spreading all the way down both arms, before rising through your neck into your head until it fills every part of you. Once the sound diffuses through your body, you are no longer there. You are a mere host to its parasitic impulse.

Eventually you might feel the scratch of the carpet fibres against your thighs. You might notice an ache in your joints from sitting cross-legged too long. Eyelids split open. Objects come into focus. The silhouette of the stereo, black and shiny like a skyscraper at night. Then two small shadowy figures beyond . . .

You are fastidious about the ritual. Every day you take such incredible care, carefully gripping the disc from each side as you slide it into the open tray. But one day after you've finished listening to a Supertramp album, you press the Eject button and nothing happens. There is a faint grinding sound. You press the button again. Nothing.

No no no no no. Again and again, you hit Eject, each time growing more frantic when the tray does not slide open. The CD is jammed.

You can't believe this is happening. Inside your head there is a syncopated beat like you would hear in a nightclub. The beat keeps getting faster, louder, as though someone is steadily turning up the volume. You realize the sound is coming from within. Your heart is the bass; your body the nightclub. It is the sound of your own heart.

Immediately your hands start to shake as you pace the shag rug. You can't believe it. You can't believe you broke the stereo. This nice family who entrusted you with their children. This nice family who owns this fancy and probably very expensive stereo. You will have to pay to have it fixed. You will have to pay for it even though you haven't earned any money of your own yet. Mom will kill you.

You're 13, that's old enough to know better. You will have to confess. You will have to fess up and tell them everything. You will have to admit that you were listening to music while you should have been looking after their little boy and girl. You feel sick with shame as you continue to pace. Now in the kitchen, you hunt around the counters full of crumbs and cereal boxes and empty juice boxes, for a scrap of paper and a pen. You know what you must do.

On the back of an old grocery list (milk, animal crackers, TP, toothpaste), you start writing. The rest of the afternoon crawls, slug-like.

By the time the car pulls into the driveway, your hands are still shaking. The front door opens. It's the kids' mom. You press the note into her hands, then stare at a faint stain on the shag carpet. As she reads, you wonder what spilled there and when. The next thing you know your mom is picking you up in the Dodge.

Sometime later you hear back from your aunt. She tells you the dad managed to get the jammed disc out of the fancy stereo. And by some miracle, it still worked. But you didn't. There were no hurt feelings, they said. Yet you never returned to the house with the shag carpet, and you never babysat again.

⌒

By some fluke Carson hears "When I'm Sixty-Four." I'm not responsible. As far as Beatles tracks go, it's one of my least favourites. I've always found it unbearably cheesy. Not Carson, though. When it plays, a light kindles in his hazel eyes. The boy who seldom smiles sports a huge, goofy grin. The boy who until now was utterly unmoved by music, *moves*. When Paul McCartney sings the words "birthday greetings" and "bottle of wine," Carson bends at the hip, then tips his arm in a I'm-a-little-teapot pantomime.

"Look," I whisper into Aidan's ear. "He's *dancing*!" I don't dare say it too loudly, though, lest my nine-year-old become self-conscious and stop moving. The sight of him dancing to the Beatles is overwhelming. I feel fizzy, like the bottle of wine that Paul sings about. And though it probably seems like a minor deal, this performance is cause for a major celebration.

Every night we head downstairs after dinner. Aidan and I take our reserved seats and wait. Every night we go to Vegas without ever leaving the couch. Carson takes centre stage on what he calls the "dance carpet" (an area rug we haven't gotten around to covering with a coffee table). At the sound of clarinets, the show begins. My boy moves fluidly through his choreographed routine to "Sixty-Four." Every verse has a corresponding action. Next up is "Drive My Car" followed by "Yellow Submarine." No matter how many times we watch, the performance never gets old.

Over the coming months, and since I'm something of a Beatles connoisseur, I take it upon myself to expand Carson's repertoire. We start slow and gently, with crowd favourites. My plan is to introduce him to the entire back catalogue, one album at a time. From the deceptive simplicity of *Please Please Me* and *A Hard Day's Night* through the trippy experimental turns of *Magical Mystery Tour* and *Sgt. Pepper* and at last to the masterful turns of *Abbey Road* and the *White Album*. Despite my attempts to broaden my child's horizons, "When I'm Sixty-Four" refuses to loosen its chokehold. The ultimate earworm, the song plays on repeat, as though the needle got stuck on the record. It's the same with Carson's brain, I think—mine too, to a lesser extent. When we like something, we really *really* like something, and find it hard to move on. Even when we want to. There are weeks when I listen exclusively to the same artist (or the same record or even the same song) on loop. Autists tend to do this. We can get stuck on certain topics or phrases. It's called *perseverating*. We want to lift the needle. We want to switch gears, we genuinely do. But we can't. Just once more, we say after repeatedly playing the chorus of a song or the same clip from a favourite TV show or movie. Something about it feels too good to stop. Like an itch you can't stop scratching because scratching feels too damn good.

Fortunately for Carson, he is growing up in the digital age. It is no longer necessary to purchase music in a physical format the way I did with the Columbia Records music club. There is no need to transport crates of vinyl, tapes, and CDs from one home to the next or hoard collections in cobwebby basements as Aidan and I have done for decades. Streaming services allow you instantaneous access to a database containing virtually every song ever recorded. It's mindboggling that in my short life span we have moved from crackly records spinning on turntables—to this.

My Carson has no idea how lucky he is. Never will he experience the abject heartbreak of a chewed-up cassette or a scratched record. As his mom, the downside of this brave new technology is that he is free to play "Sixty-Four" to his heart's content. No sooner has Paul sung the last note, does Carson pipe up and tell the robot DJ (Google Nest) to "repeat song." I'm glad for him, but I'm also human. I have a breaking point. And this song is pushing me to the brink. When I don't think I can take any more, I march over and unplug the speaker. It takes every ounce of resolve in me not to hurl the damn thing against the wall.

⌒

Spurred by our shared interest, I decide to go out on a limb and do something rash. I order three tickets to see a Beatles tribute band at one of the chic downtown theatres. The tickets are eye-wateringly expensive, considering we are not seeing the actual band. The moment I purchase the tickets, panic sets in. What have I done? What possessed me to think this could work? My son is allergic to noise and crowds. Almost every outing we have ever attempted has been a bust. We haven't taken Carson on a plane since he came to Canada as a baby for a reason. Faced with the prospect of public meltdowns, we have all but given up on trying to plan any major outings as a family. It's simply too risky, not to mention costly. Our road trip to the most picturesque beach in the province was an epic failure . . . That's not to say this will always be the case, but right now our track record leaves a lot to be desired.

Now I expect my autistic child to sit through a two-hour musical matinee. Clearly I have lost my mind, not to mention all common sense. When I tell Aidan my plan, he just shrugs in a way that says, "Don't get your hopes up." The reminder isn't necessary. My hopes stay firmly planted, where they always are.

When the day of the performance rolls around, I brace myself for impending disaster. We take the subway downtown. If nothing else, the subway ride will be a treat for my son who like many other autists has a sweet spot for trains. From the time he could talk, he had memorized every stop on every line. Now we pass through the opulent theatre lobby and wait for the usher to show us to our seats (in the back row in case we need to make a quick exit). Carson sinks into a plush red seat, looking small and dazed by his grand surroundings. Anxiously, I root around in my oversized handbag for something to keep his hands busy while we wait for the show to start. Earplugs, granola bars, an arsenal of fidget toys . . . I brought it all, just in case.

It isn't necessary. The second the curtains part to the explosive opening bars of "She Loves You," my son lurches to his feet. The band is from New York, I think, and clearly skillful. On a screen behind them plays a montage from another place and another era: black cabs, red double-decker buses, a black-and-white clip from *The Ed Sullivan Show*. Four dewy-faced boys with mop tops cuts to footage of throngs of girls screaming and crying and fainting, one after another. This makes me laugh. That level of hysteria reminds me of my days with Carrie and NKOTB. Of course, the New Kids had nothing on Beatlemania.

Then the movie changes. Hair grows longer before our eyes. There are flashes of bell bottoms and peace signs and kaleidoscopic swirls of colour. In the glow of the darkened theatre, I shift in my plush seat and steal a sidelong glance at Carson. Wide-eyed, his mouth slung open, he takes it all in. He looks the way I imagine I must have all those years ago, seeing Cyndi Lauper descend from the rafters in a garbage can. I hope it's not too much. I worry that it will be too much for him. I tell myself to relax and enjoy the show, but relaxing feels hard. There is too much at stake.

Somehow we make it to intermission. It's going well, better than I had any right to expect. I hear Aidan's voice telling me not to get ahead of myself. And I foresee trouble ahead. The band hasn't played "When I'm Sixty-Four" yet. Given it wasn't one of their bigger hits, there is a good chance this cover band won't play it. What then? Carson will surely lose his mind. My palms start to sweat, imagining him kicking and screaming in this beautiful theatre. I nudge Aidan and suggest he take Carson to the washroom. My husband and I exchange glances. Is he thinking what I'm thinking? Of course he is. *What if they don't play the song? What if Carson has a huge meltdown here in the plush red seats, in front of all these people who have also paid a lot of money to sit in their plush red seats?* While I wait for the boys to return from the toilets, I send a silent prayer to the ghost of George Harrison and to John Lennon himself. *Please, please me. Just this once. For this boy.*

The curtains open. At the all-too-familiar sound of clarinets, my nine-year-old leaps to his feet. In the glow of the stage lights, his expression transforms. Is it rapture, or ecstasy? It's like he's seeing the face of God. There is no other way to describe it. Something divine or sublime is happening right here in this theatre. While Carson watches the band play his favourite song, I watch Carson. I have never seen him quite like this. I recognize the look on his face, though. I know where he has gone in his mind because it's a place I've been once before, in a room with a shag carpet. As he mouths the words and moves through his meticulous choreography, hot tears streak my cheeks. The auditorium is dark, I don't even bother to wipe them. Who cares if anyone sees me cry? I am past that. I am past so many things.

Sinking deeper into the plush seat, I let my eyes close. Just for a moment, I let the music wash over me. Wave after wave, it washes away the years, stripping the layers of time and space, until I'm back on the sticky-hot seats of the Dodge. Back and forth, the waves of nostalgia push and pull me in their undertow. Somehow I had forgotten that music could have this effect on a person. That it could have this effect on me.

My eyes open just as the song finishes, leaving me disoriented in the darkened theatre. There is an insistent tugging on my sleeve. "Mommy, Mommy," Carson is saying. Yes, yes. My boy has seen what he has come to see and now he is ready to leave. I tap Aidan on the shoulder. Quickly and quietly, I help my son into his coat. As we duck out of the back row of the theatre, I voice a thousand thanks in my head. *Thank you, John. Thank you, Paul. Thank you, George. Thank you, Ringo and all the saints.* (Wait, is there a saint called Ringo? If there isn't, then there probably should be.)

⌒

That day in the theatre does not spell the end of Carson's Beatlemania by any stretch. At the local library, we borrow DVDs and every book we can find about the Fab Four. At home, my son confiscates every Beatles CD we own and pours over the inserts until they are creased and dog-eared. He is not as delicate and precious about these things as I am. Usually this would set my teeth on edge, but I figure it's a small price to pay to see him so happy.

Our car lease comes equipped with satellite radio and (who knew?) a dedicated Beatles channel. A channel that plays the Beatles and nothing but the Beatles all day long, every day. For Carson, who has by now memorized every song duration down to the minute and second, this development is a dream come true. For me, not so much. While listening to the Beatles channel on the drive to and from school, he regales me with trivia.

"Did you know 'Come Together' is four minutes, 20 seconds long, which is exactly double 'All Together Now,' which is two minutes, 10 seconds long?"

"Mommy," he says, "who sings 'Within You Without You'?"

"I think it's George, honey."

Not five minutes pass before my boy asks the exact same question. Not because he's forgotten or doesn't know the answer, but because he likes to hear me say it. The repetition of facts is somehow soothing to him much in the way that systematizing and alphabetizing my CD collection is soothing to me.

As a girl I collected many things: cards, pins, alleys, records, cassettes and later CDs; while my nine-year-old collects trivia. I think back to all those times he tried to teach me an alphabet in Mandarin, Hebrew, or Cyrillic. I never could pick it up. Now finally Carson is speaking a language I can understand. A language I love. Music has been and always will be my first language, my love language. For the first time my little boy wants to speak it with me. For the first time in our relationship, it feels like we are really communicating in a way that is pure and true.

In the car these days, Carson listens to the Beatles, and I listen to Carson. My son has never been so chatty. These past months feel like a turning point, what his former therapists would no doubt have called a "breakthrough." I imagine them furiously scribbling notes in his chart. Keeping track of his progress as though they had anything to do with it. I feel proud and secretly smug of his growth, but I know I really didn't have much to do with it, either.

Meanwhile, Carson's questions come thick and fast, and I do my best to answer them.

"What are the black holes in 'A Day in the Life'?"

"Did Yoko Ono really break up the band?"

"Mom, who sings 'Blackbird'?"

"Honey, you *know* it's Paul."

"Did you know 'Something' is three minutes, two seconds long, which is exactly double 'Golden Slumbers,' which is one minute, 31 seconds long?"

Right. Sometimes I don't even bother answering. Carson doesn't seem to notice my waning attention. My eyes glaze over as I stare at the car ahead of us. If "I Want to Hold Your Hand" plays one more time, I swear to god I will swerve into the oncoming traffic.

I should be grateful. And I am. After all these years, my son is finally passionate about music and not just any music but the Beatles, a band I adore. Or used to adore, past tense—*tense* being the operative word. Tense is what I feel anytime I hear their music now. It almost doesn't matter which song. Beatlemania has left me raw and irritable most days. I want its spirit to leave my house once and for all. I want it cast out, exorcized. Please, I beg Carson, choose a different song. He tells the robot DJ to play "It's All Too Much," and I can't help but laugh.

Why the Beatles, anyway? What is it about their music that is so infectious, I wonder. I try to explain to my boy that too much of something, even something you love deeply, can make you sick. This has never happened to me before, not with the Beatles. Not with music. I have had jags where I listened to nothing but the same song on loop for weeks at a time. But it's never been like this. Never anything quite like this.

One day "Penny Lane" comes on while I'm on my way to pick up Carson from school, and I race to switch it off. I think about tuning the radio to another station, then I don't bother. Silence fills the car, like it did when my boy was younger. At first the absence of sound feels eerie and uncomfortable. The way its languorous shape fills the car.

One day I may be able to listen to the Beatles again without feeling homicidal. One day I am sure I will look back fondly on what those four boys from Liverpool gave my son the year he turned nine. That day hasn't come yet, but I feel that it will. Maybe when I'm 64.

#1 crush

When Carson falls in love for the first time, he falls hard. By now he's in the fifth grade in a special education program at a public school. Ella is a sweet-faced girl with the softest brown eyes I've seen. A guileless Bambi of a girl. Her name means "fairy," and that is how I come to think of her. She's sweetness personified; at least that's how I've painted her in my mind. In truth, I've only glimpsed the girl in the hallway.

Although she herself is not autistic, Ella takes Carson under her wing. Not out of pity or obligation—she does so simply because she is Ella. "Yeah, she is like that with all the kids," her teacher tells me. No wonder Carson falls under her spell. At recess he makes a beeline for her, and she welcomes him into the fold of fifth graders. Is this the reason he falls for her, I wonder. The fact that she does not turn him away as so many before her have . . . Not that it matters. At this stage in my parenting career, I've learned not to look a gift horse in the mouth (whatever that means). A blessing is a blessing is a blessing.

⌒

The first time I fell in love, I was a lot older than Carson. And I didn't have much choice in the matter. I had just turned 18 and was living on campus for my first year of university. Rez, we called the scabby residential dorms on the west campus. I may have won a scholarship, yet my academic prowess did not translate to life. The extent of my cooking repertoire was peanut butter toast and frozen fish sticks. Up until that point I had never used a washing machine; the different dials and settings were an anathema to me. Worried I would not survive my first year away from home, Mom and Mitch purchased the full meal plan option from the campus cafeteria. On a diet of chicken burgers and pizza, I packed on 10 pounds in my first semester and developed high cholesterol, but at least I didn't starve to death.

My lacklustre culinary skills aside, I sensed the main reason my parents wanted me to live on campus was because they feared I would be lonely. I think they hoped I would find my fellow quirky people in Montreal. My best friend at the time had opted to take a year out to work and save money while she decided what to do with her life. Smart. I might have followed her lead, except I was hell-bent on escaping my small town ASAP. My parents' worries were warranted. While all the other undergrads partied, I spent the hours between lectures holed up in my dorm room, listening to music and reading.

I always heard Tom before I saw him. He lived next door and was one of these perpetually good-humoured people, always singing or whistling in the hallway. Normally I can't stand those people. He would knock or, if my door happened to be slightly ajar, poke his head in asking to borrow some random thing: a can opener, a pen, a Band-Aid. He never seemed to have whatever he needed in any given moment. I wondered how it was possible to live this way because it ran so contrary to the way I lived, anticipating every possible scenario far in advance. It didn't occur on me that his absent-mindedness was symptomatic of his ADHD. Or that it might simply have been a ruse so he could talk to the cute, reclusive girl next door. Either way, it worked. One look at those puppy eyes and that lopsided grin, and I couldn't say no. Of course, I always had on hand whatever he needed. He'd come inside while I got it, plunking himself down in the vinyl chair that furnished every room. He'd ask what I was reading and what I was listening to, and before I knew it we were chatting. Even though I found his sudden presence in my room discombobulating, I started to look forward to his interruptions.

Tom was intimidating to look at. At over six feet tall, he had eyes the colour of cocoa powder and hair to match. One side of his head was shaved, while the hair on the other side fell to his shoulders. A red ribbon ran from the back of his skull all the way around his ear—a souvenir from a benign brain tumour that was removed not long before I met him. They had to shave part of his head for the surgery, and he'd kept his hair like that. It made him look like a badass—not that I had the nerve to tell him that. He reminded me of the punks I'd met at the mall when I wrote for the local paper. I had no idea why he kept coming to my room, but I was glad he did. I worried he might suddenly stop coming. There were only so many things he could borrow.

In high school, I had a couple of boyfriends but no one serious. A guy asked me out after we'd passed notes in class. Mom let me go to his place once because his parents were home. I remember sitting in his living room after school, listening to *Double Fantasy*. His parents' record. They had a scruffy terrier who sat between us. We both started petting the guy's dog. At one point, our fingers touched in the dog's fur, and electricity shot up from my fingers through my entire body. While the guy's parents were in the next room, he leaned forward and kissed me. It was the first time anyone had kissed me. John Lennon was singing "Woman" at the time, which made the kiss seem more tender and passionate than it was. This boy and I held hands at school for a few weeks before that romance fizzled out. Then there was the boy who invited me to the movies. I was under the impression that a bunch of kids were going, until he showed up at my house, dressed in a silky shirt and reeking of Polo cologne, to pick me up. No one else met us at the cinema.

I was always getting my romantic wires crossed like that. Since the days of NKOTB, I'd had plenty of unrequited loves and no clue how to "requite" them. I remember liking a boy who sat across from me in math class just because he happened to be into Nirvana before the *whole world* was into Nirvana. I had no inkling that anyone was interested in me unless it was spelled out—like Lloyd Dobler holding a boom box over his head and serenading his true love in *Say Anything*. And I had no idea how to make my feelings known, either. Because autists struggle to read social cues, it follows that we also tend to miss romantic cues.[57] We find it hard to tell, for instance, when someone is flirting or making a pass at us. Needless to say, I missed a lot of signals in those days, from boys and girls alike. Because I was intensely shy and aloof around boys, some kids assumed I must be into girls instead. A high school friend invited me for a sleepover at her place. At one point, she offered me a massage. *That's so nice of her*, I thought. My muscles were tense, and I loved having my back rubbed, so I graciously accepted. I wasn't trying to lead her on; I genuinely had no idea that she was coming onto me. Ditto to the undergrad I met in a Women's Studies class. She had long dark hair and hooded eyes. She invited me to her apartment for dinner. The fact that she made spaghetti from scratch wasn't enough of a clue. Nor were the candles, or the Paula Cole album playing in the background. I sat back soaking in the ambiance, thinking, *How nice of her to go to all this trouble.*

I wasn't exactly a serial heartbreaker, yet I am sorry for the hearts I inadvertently broke. In my second year in Montreal, I reconnected with a guy from high school, a prodigious pianist with wiry, Einstein-like hair. We'd met through the gifted program. He invited me to his place on the Plateau, where he lived with his long-time girlfriend. She had dyed black hair and pale French-Canadian skin. The way she dressed . . . She looked a lot like me, actually. At the time I was still riding out the dredges of my goth phase. When I went out, I wore black eyeliner and matching black lipstick. In the mid '90s, I listened to a trifecta of angry young women—Alanis Morissette, Tori Amos, and Courtney Love—singers whom my mom dubbed "screech owls."

"So, I finally get to meet you," said Einstein's girlfriend in a tone that was decidedly unfriendly. Uncomfortable, I must have made some kind of quip, and there was a long, drawn-out silence. While he scrambled to get me a drink in the kitchen, she turned to me and narrowed her black-rimmed eyes. "You know he's been in love with you for years, right?"

As a matter of fact, I didn't. There hadn't been the slightest intimation that our relationship had ever been anything but platonic. Or if there had been interest on his side, that news had entirely bypassed me. Right then he came back into the room and handed me a glass. I gulped down my mortification. No one said anything. The rest of the visit was protracted and painful as a dental procedure. As soon as I could, I made my excuses, grabbed my coat, and left their place on the Plateau. I never saw either of them again.

Like many autistic girls, I was naive, innocent, and overly trusting. I was also grossly inexperienced. My first kiss came much later than that of my friends. I lost my virginity much later, too. Research suggests that we are two to three times more likely to be affected by sexual violence than neurotypical women. As many as nine out of 10 autistic women have been victims of sexual violence, with many first assaulted as children or teens.[58] Compared to other girls, I was lucky. I was sheltered from situations where I might have been taken advantage of—until I left that shelter behind.

The first year of university, a bunch of people from Rez went to a pub downtown. In the wee hours, we all climbed into a taxi to head back to the west campus. There was no way the cab could fit all of us. Still, we laughed and laughed as we piled in. The more bodies, the cheaper the fare would be when we divvied it up. The driver turned a blind eye as we clambered in. I hesitated, but my friend coaxed me after her into the back seat. I contorted myself into the cab and onto someone's lap. In the dark I couldn't see, though. I thought I recognized the reddish goatee of a football player, an undergrad like me. I'd seen him around campus during frosh week but didn't know his name. As the taxi sped off, we jostled around in the back seat, slamming into each other.

When the driver braked suddenly, I felt a hand graze my left breast. The lights changed, and the cab kept moving. The hand fell away. *Oh, that was an accident*, I told myself. *A reflex*. Then the hand shot up again, this time greedily cupping my breast. Stunned, I swallowed and elbowed the hand away—there was no accident. Again and again, in the dark backseat of the cab this stranger groped me. Should I scream? Fight him off somehow? I couldn't move a muscle. The ride back to campus felt never-ending. I fought back tears as his hand did what it wanted.

The next day when I finally mustered the courage to tell my friend what had happened, she was incredulous. She knew who he was, the guy with the reddish goatee. "But he's such a *nice* guy," she said. He was probably drunk. I'm sure he didn't mean any harm, she said. If my best friend reacted this way, there was no point in telling anyone else. Was I overreacting? Maybe she was right. Maybe it wasn't a big deal.

At my first campus party, I drank a bit too much and like Billy Idol ended up dancing with myself. When the music entered my body, I closed my eyes and fell into a kind of trance. Music always affected me this way. After a while I could feel someone dancing near me. I could feel the heat coming off his body; I could smell him. He didn't smell strongly of sweat or cologne, but just of himself. Not wanting to break the spell, I still hadn't opened my eyes when I felt him edge closer until our bodies were just touching. I could feel the taut muscles of his chest under his shirt, his warm breath on my neck. I finally opened my eyes, and we stared directly at each other. He had dark wavy hair and deep, mysterious-looking eyes, a lithe body that knew how to move in time with mine. His hands settled on my lower back as he drew me closer. My god he was sexy. He leaned in my ear and asked in broken English if I wanted to leave with him. He was going to a party with his friends. Did I? Every nerve ending in my body was pulsing, saying *go go go*.

The song ended, and it was as though the lights suddenly switched on in my mind. I shook my head and told him I was sorry. Then I hurried and found a girl from my dorm and headed back to Rez with her. Something told me if I stayed a minute longer, I would lose my resolve. Something told me that if I went with this sexy stranger and his friends, I might never come home. Or I might come home but never be the same. As naïve as I was, I knew enough to know there are some situations from which you can never recover. Not all autistic girls are so lucky.

Everything was different with Tom. The first time he invited me out it was with a bunch of people from Rez, so maybe it wasn't a date, after all. My heart sank a little. He arrived all gallant at my door wearing a grey tweed overcoat like Bender in *The Breakfast Club*. I'm not sure why it took me so long to realize I was attracted to him. Sometimes I was the last person to know what I was feeling. That night, like every night, he was the centre of attention. But I was the centre of his. His scattered focus could have landed anywhere, yet for some reason it landed on me. The sidelong glances, the private jokes, the whispers in my ear, the hand on my arm. All of it was strangely reserved for me.

From that night on, we were inseparable. I stayed in his room or else he stayed in mine, depending on whose roommate happened to be away. His was a pigsty: all grease-sodden pizza boxes, deformed candle stumps, upturned beer caps, dirty boxers. The kind of detritus that made my skin crawl. I perched on the edge of his bed while he worked through a tricky chord change on "Breaking the Girl" by the Red Hot Chili Peppers. I could have listened to him play guitar all day long. Tom wasn't studying music, though. He was an English major like me, apparently. I say *apparently* because I never once saw him study or write a paper. From what I could tell that first year, the only thing he majored in was drinking copious amounts of beer. So not very different to most undergrads. But Tom drank until his words slurred, until he eventually passed out. After last call (3 a.m. in *la belle province*), we returned to his room and listened to Miles Davis or *The Mission* soundtrack. Music was the only thing that seemed to calm him. We had that in common at least. He begrudged having to take medication following his brain surgery. Sometimes he took it. Most of the time he did not. I had no idea what the drugs were for, though I doubted the drinking helped their efficacy. His cavalier attitude toward his meds worried me. I couldn't understand why anyone would resent a procedure that had saved their life.

Over the reading week, a few months after we started dating, Tom invited me to Toronto to meet his family and friends. The invitation marked a significant point in our relationship, a sign that things were getting more serious. But as usual, I missed the memo. The weekend got off to a good start. His mom was a sweetheart. We had fun perusing his local Salvation Army for second-hand clothes. That night his best friend threw a house party. Once we got there, I immediately reverted to form: shy, awkward, and deeply uncomfortable. I became Mute Girl. If this party was supposed to be some kind of girlfriend test, then I failed abysmally. Maybe he had misjudged my potential from the start.

When we returned to campus, Tom seemed different. He became unusually morose and aloof. Utterly not Tom-like. Everyone is entitled to a bad day, I thought. But this was more than that. In my room, he slumped in the olive-coloured vinyl chair. When I asked what was wrong, I fully expected to hear him complain about how weird and stuck-up I had seemed in front of his friends. Instead, he told me he was in love with me. I was thrown. This was the last thing I was expecting to hear. But even I knew that such a declaration should have been a happy moment. Instead, he sounded sad, almost resigned, as though he was being held hostage by his emotions. And although I could not have been more confused, I was elated. I told him I loved him too because at that exact moment I realized that I did.

Tom loves me. I kept pinching myself. *He loves me.*

The next day, when he came into my room and sat in the same lumpy vinyl chair, he was no longer sullen. But something was still off. Something had changed. Everything had changed. He told me it was over, and his words had the effect of emotional whiplash. "What do you mean *over?*" I asked him, flabbergasted. "You literally told me that you love me."

Tom ran a finger over the scar by his ear. "I don't know," he mumbled.

None of it made sense. My confusion swiftly turned to indignation. "What do you mean you don't know? You're the one ending it. The least you can do is tell me why."

Tom said nothing. For all I knew he might have been as confused as I was, yet his silence came off as cruel. Indignation soon gave way to pleading. "You don't have to do this." I slumped on my mattress and cried hot, ugly tears. I asked him what I had done wrong because I knew I must have done something to make him break up with me. It never occurred to me that it might not be my fault. Had something unexpected happened in Toronto, or had something expected not happened in Toronto? I didn't have a clue. Was I enough for him? We were having sex, sure. But I wasn't experienced enough to know if it was *good* sex. Other girls on campus knew what they were doing in bed, and they made no secret of it. Tom needed to be with a girl like that.

In the weeks that followed, I waited for him to change his mind and come to his senses. When that didn't work, I tried being cool and casual. All I had to do was be the girl he fell for and he would want me back. The trouble was, I wasn't sure who that girl was, exactly. Which version of me had attracted him in the first place? *Just say the word*, I thought, *and I will be that girl. I will be her, whoever she is.*

Autistic women and girls are notorious for camouflaging or masking.[59] We mimic others and wear metaphorical "masks" to fit in with peers and even to please romantic partners. In doing so, we lose sight of our identity and risk burning out or shutting down. By university, I was a master masker. I had been doing it for as long as I could remember. First, by copying my cousin Jess, then my best friend, Carrie. I was a shapeshifter, perpetually moulding myself into whatever I thought other people expected or wanted me to be. And here I had done it again with Tom.

He could smell my desperation. I was sure he could smell it on me the way bears smell fear. Suddenly there was nothing he wanted to borrow. Nothing he was missing—or nothing he needed from me, at least. For once I was the one missing everything. His head poking into my room. His brown eyes focused on me. His soft lips. His corny jokes. His sexy overcoat. His gentle guitar strumming late into the night. I wasn't above pressing my ear to the wall so I could hear him playing. I liked to pretend he was playing just for me.

While he was busy partying with friends, I made myself elusive. I stayed at the campus library for hours on end. I ate far too many chicken burgers alone in the cafeteria.

A few more weeks went by. I listened to *The Misson* soundtrack on repeat. Tom had introduced me to it. Morricone's score was so beautiful, I cried every time I heard it. Quiet enough that he wouldn't hear. I needn't have worried. By the time he finally stumbled back to his room, I could hear him clumsily stripping down and crashing, alone at least. That was one consolation.

⌣

When Ella's light shines on Carson, he can't help but bask in its buttery glow. But it's not enough for him. He soon turns possessive, demanding that she play only with him. He wants her all to himself at recess, yet that's not who Ella is—exclusivity is antithetical to the very nature of Ella. After all, a fairy cannot be captured and bottled. Or should not be, at any rate.

One day after school, the teacher pulls me aside. It seems Ella is "uncomfortable" with my son's attention. He is suffocating her. She wants to play freely with other kids, which is her right. The teacher tells me Carson needs to stay away from Ella at recess. From now on, he is forbidden from entering a certain area of the playground designated for her and some of the other fifth graders. It's the elementary school equivalent of a restraining order.

On the drive home, I attempt to explain the new rules to my son. Namely, that he can no longer play with his best friend at recess. Not only does this decision feel excessive, it seems patently unfair. Nothing makes an autistic person angrier than an injustice, real or perceived. Carson may be clingy, but he's no stalker. Surely he just needs to be taught clearer boundaries. Nonetheless, I back up the teachers because the last thing I want is Ella complaining to her parents about the boy in the special class who's making her "uncomfortable."

When I drop him off at school the next morning, he is quiet. He doesn't seem sad, but I know he will be once it sinks in that he can no longer play with Ella. Right now he hasn't processed the news. Long after the bell sounds, I linger in the parking lot. I wait until the playground slowly empties of children. There are few sights sadder than an empty playground, I think. I stare through the chain-link fence, imagining Ella laughing and running around with a posse of adoring children following her. Then I imagine a boy at the other end of the yard wandering alone, talking to himself as he kicks a pinecone.

That image breaks me. I weep while sitting in the car with the engine off. Just when I think my heart can't break any more, new fissures appear in this old stone. I'm not yet forty, yet I feel ancient. Like other parents, I wear my child's suffering as though it's my own. Something about this sorrow feels worse than all the other times, all the other sorrows. It's worse because Carson knows. He knows how it feels to be wanted by someone, to be accepted. This time he knows exactly what he is missing.

At some point during that interminable winter, circa 1996, your best friend talks you into going out. You only agree because it is someplace you've been with Tom. He has a thing for dive bars, and clearly you must have a thing for torturing yourself. After all, you've been listening to *Disintegration* for weeks on end. No one does melancholy quite like the Cure. You listen on your Walkman as you cut through a deserted park. If it's raining, and the sky turns the colour of a used tea bag, all the better. In literature when the weather reflects the protagonist's mood it's called "pathetic fallacy." And you think that's an apt descriptor for your current state. Pathetic.

Once at the bar, you nurse a rum and coke while your friend rambles about one of her profs. You can't focus on her words. You sip your drink, distracted. Going out tonight was a mistake. It's too soon. You aren't ready. You aren't in the right frame of mind—if ever there was a right frame for your mind. You think you are hallucinating when you see him at a nearby table. That's how far gone you are. It's so uncanny, and pathetic. But no, you double-take. You can't believe he's here. It really is Tom. Your Tom except he's no longer yours. Of course there is a girl at his table, drinking beer and hanging off him. Practically throwing herself at him. *Slut.*

Your friend stops mid-sentence and turns to see where you are looking, why you are not paying attention to her. She rolls her eyes when she sees Tom.

You tell her you feel like dancing. And you slip out of your seat before she can say anything. She knocks back her drink. You can tell she's pissed. You'll have to make it up to her later. If she's any kind of friend, she will understand. Right now, you have only one thing in mind. As Tom makes his way back from the bar with a pitcher, you dance directly into his path. Accidentally on purpose. When he sees you, his face lights up. You haven't seen each other in a long time. He looks good. His hair is growing out. He glances from your eyes to your lips, which are painted the same deep plum shade as your your fitted top. You are glad your friend persuaded you to go out, after all.

In a matter of minutes, his mouth is on yours, and his hands are all over you. Muscle memory. The body cannot forget what the mind seems determined to remember. When you pull away, you shout over the bass that you missed him. Soon you are kissing again like you never stopped. As though all these dark weeks without him never happened. You picked up where you left off. Even though the dive bar is dingy and dark, the ceiling seems to crack open. Light from a thousand stars pours in, swirling around you.

In the wee hours you travel back to campus together and you wake in his room, in his arms. For a long time, you do not dare move. You don't want to jinx the perfection of the moment. And anyway, you can't move even if you wanted to because his arm is slung across your stomach, pinning you in place like a butterfly. In the grey Sunday light, his room is as disgusting as ever—there are broken CD cases, dirty dishes, clothes, books, and papers littered all over the floor and desk. His guitar slumps like an old man in the corner. But you are smiling. You have never felt so peaceful.

You watch him sleep. When his eyes open, Tom looks at you with a quizzical expression.

"Hey," you whisper.

"Hey," he mumbles back, his mouth chapped with sleep.

You smile and burrow into his chest. The hair is dark and wispy but not too thick.

"Last night . . ." he starts to say. And you smile, remembering. You nuzzle into his warm-milky skin. You want to stay here all day.

You want to be like John and Yoko. You want to trace the contour of his lips and his strong nose. You want to trace the path of his scar as it winds around his skull. He is imperfect and so beautiful.

"I don't remember," he says, his hair hanging flaccid in his eyes.

"What?" You draw back, struggling to extricate yourself from under his arm.

He tells you he blacked out and doesn't remember anything from last night. Not the kissing. Certainly not the coming back here with you.

You slide out of the bed as fast as you can. You fumble along the floor for your clothes, not wanting to touch anything in the squalid room. "Hey," he says, but you can't look at him. You hurry next door, which is not nearly far enough. And you lock the door, even though something tells you he won't come after you. Then you lie with your face buried in the pillow, so he won't hear the sounds that come from your body.

⁓

Throughout the summer and into the fall, I pined for Tom. Neither one of us moved back into Rez the following year. My heart had been bruised, and every day the reminder of how he ended things poked a sharp finger in my tender places. Blacks and blues. Blues and blacks. Where the first year without Tom was mainly black, the colour of nebula, the second was blue: a deep, drowning blue. Joni Mitchell blue. The only thing worse than rejection, I decided, was rejection without explanation. Tom told me he loved me, then almost immediately redacted it. Those words were on record; you couldn't just take them back.

We hadn't been together long enough to justify my reaction to the breakup. My friend never said so, but I could tell she wondered why I couldn't move on. Tom and I hadn't even been together long enough to know each other well. And yet I knew he'd seen me. He'd seen something in me that I hadn't seen in myself.

Maybe Tom wasn't being obtuse when he sat in that olive chair nearly 30 years ago. Maybe he genuinely didn't know what he was doing or why he was doing it any more than anyone else on the planet. People are messy and chaotic beings, after all. We behave in ways that sometimes defy logic. We hurt people, often without meaning to.

Many autists struggle with rejection in a way that goes beyond simple hurt feelings. As children, we may experience more frequent rejection and criticism because we are different. These formative experiences can lead us to develop a hypersensitivity to rejection known as rejection sensitive dysphoria (RSD).[60] At times, the fear of rejection is so potent, it can make us paranoid and prone to cognitive distortions. If a friend hasn't texted me back right away, instead of assuming she is busy or wrapped up in her own life, I will automatically conclude that I've said something or done something to offend her and that she no longer wants to be friends with me rather than consider other, more likely scenarios. Such heightened sensitivity around rejection can drive autists to avoid people or situations with any potential for criticism or rejection, thus further isolating us.

To me, RSD is a lot like a layer cake, with each new rejection piled on top of a past rejection and another before it, dating back as far as I can remember. Tom turned out to be the icing on a pretty, tiered cake.

⌒

Tom and I never shared a class, which is crazy given we were both English majors. However, one afternoon we both showed up at an open meeting for the school paper. I had fond memories of my time writing for my local newspaper in high school. By then I had finally stopped listening to the Cure, but only just. I thought joining the paper might help bust me out of my rut, not to mention my comfort zone, which had become increasingly claustrophobic.

Tom smiled at me across the table, and my heart tripped as though no time had passed. A year later, the electrical wire that ran between us was still live, still lethal. I said nothing at the meeting and cut my losses. I might not have been pining for him with quite the same intensity, yet that didn't mean I was ready to be in the same room as him every week.

Following that botched school paper meeting, I only saw him once. He was walking downtown, on the other side of the road. I couldn't help but notice he was wearing the overcoat I loved. When he saw me, he called out my name, and his face lit up the way it always had. And I felt that familiar pull, the way I always had. The way Carson had, when Ella smiled or waved at him. Nothing in the world compared to that feeling.

In that split second, it took everything I had not to cross the road, not to go to him. There are some things you never get used to. I nodded and carried on walking.

The wanderer

At exactly 12:34 your phone rings. You remember the time—1, 2, 3, 4—because you remember thinking your 10-year-old would find it cool. The school number flashes on your screen. You answer and hear the words that no parent wants to hear. "Mrs. Green? Your son is missing . . ." The woman speaking is the interim principal, but all you hear is the squawk-squawking of Charlie Brown's teacher. "He wandered from the playground during recess. Staff are out looking for him. The police have been called—"

"On my way," you say, hanging up before she can finish. Keys. Door. Car. Foot on the brake. Start the engine. Not for the first time, you observe yourself with a strange detachment, as though you are watching a scene in a movie. A taut thriller with a strong female lead, Emily Blunt or Jennifer Lawrence, maybe. But this is no movie. It's your life. It's your fucking life.

Hands shaking, you reverse too fast out of the driveway. Or rather Emily or Jennifer does. You're not the one driving here. It is not your white knuckles gripping the wheel. Not your foot flexed on the gas pedal.

As the car pulls onto a busy overpass, your mind hurtles ahead. Is Carson okay? Is he hurt? Is he——? You see it clearly, then. Blood pooling from the side of his small skull. Cars swerving to avoid his limp body.

You shiver. Would you know? *Would I be able to sense it if he was . . . gone*, you wonder. Is that what is meant by a mother's intuition?

This habit of yours is sick. You know that. If your husband is so much as 10 minutes late home from work, you start pacing the room and picking at your cuticles. Various gruesome scenarios playing out in your mind.

Bad things don't happen just because someone is a bit late. The rational part of your brain knows that. And yet, sometimes your instincts are spot-on. Sometimes bad things do happen. Bad things happen to people all the time. Like when you still lived in London, a year or two before Carson was born. Aidan left for work before you, but he was back already, limping into the master bedroom with blood dripping down his leg. It had rained and the roads were slick. He slipped on a manhole cover and was thrown from his bicycle. A car or bus could easily have hit him. No one stopped to help or to see if he was okay. It was London, after all. But he was okay. Aside from a gash that was minor enough not to require stitches, he was okay. He was only a little shaken. But you were not.

This habit of imagining the worst is known as catastrophizing, and though it's not exclusive to autism, it is common among our population.[61] Catastrophizing doesn't care about the laws of logic or probability. Our anxiety amplifies the idea that the worst can and will happen, and all-or-nothing thinking leaves no room for considering a more probable or realistic outcome.

Catastrophizing can have a catastrophic impact, leading people to avoid situations that would otherwise be beneficial or enjoyable because they have already visualized the potential grave danger lurking. The subsequent avoidance and isolation in turn contributes to symptoms of depression and anxiety, thus creating a cycle so vicious it can prove difficult to break.

Why does your mind automatically go to the darkest places imaginable? You don't know. It's as though by rehearsing the worst possible fate, you are somehow steeling yourself against it. And when the worst doesn't happen, well, then you can breathe a sigh of relief because you somehow got escaped unscathed. Until now, that is. Now, your only child has gone missing. Carson is alone and probably scared. You imagine him clutching the big blue ball he insisted on taking with him to school that morning, even though you tried to talk him out of it. (You worried he might lose it or have it stolen by some kid.)

The light turns red suddenly, and Emily/Jennifer brakes so hard your body slams against the seat belt. *Please let him be okay. Please please please.* You aren't the praying type, having lost any vestige of faith many years ago. Still, you beg. You plead shamelessly to some higher power you aren't sure you believe in anymore. Yet you are willing to hedge your bets, just this once. Just in case.

Your boy is 10 years old. Ten seems old enough to walk alone—except this 10-year-old lives three miles from school and is on the autism spectrum. He may or may not remember to look both ways before crossing the road. He may or may not talk to strangers. He may or may not say things he shouldn't and forget to say things that he should. In other words, he's vulnerable. You wouldn't know it to look at him. In track bottoms and running shoes (Velcro because he can't tie his shoelaces), he looks like any other 10-year-old. That's the problem.

His difference is invisible. That invisibility is what keeps you up at night. It's the reason the dark circles under your eyes never disappear. His difference is not exactly a blessing, nor is it a curse. Not a tragedy, or a superpower . . . It is complicated. You want Carson to be happy. You want him to grow into a capable adult who will take pride in himself and his accomplishments, whether that's going to college or to the corner store to buy milk. You want the same things any parent wants for their child. Yet you have learned to temper those dreams in case they don't pan out. Over the years, you have balled up those dreams and stuffed them deep into your pockets like so many tissues. You don't allow yourself to hope too much because hope is a minefield. The truth is, no one knows what the future holds for their kids.

The light turns green.

⌒

Wandering, or elopement, is many parents' greatest fear. And it is not the mainstay of the helicopter generation, either. The danger is clear and present: around half of all autistic children and adults are at risk of wandering.[62] They might bolt when triggered by a social situation or overwhelming sensory stimuli, such as flashing lights or blaring noises, or be lured away by something that piques their interest. They may not understand the hazards of traffic or open water. They may get lost or badly injured. They may not recognize dangerous people or situations. In an emergency, an estimated third of autistic children would be unable to communicate their name, address, or phone number.[63] Altercations with police or first responders may result in trauma or worse.

Caregivers can invest in locks and GPS tracking devices and security cameras and cutting-edge alarm systems. But even the most secure set-up is not foolproof. Those who wander often require medical attention or end up dead. That's not paranoia; that's a public health crisis.

⌒

Last year I had travelled with my son to visit my parents: a five-hour journey by train. At one point, he needed the bathroom. "I can go by myself, Mommy," he said. "I'm a big boy."

"Okay," I said, biting my lip, "go and come right back." Carson was at a tricky age—too old to be accompanied to a public washroom, yet too vulnerable to go it alone.

As soon as he stood and walked down the aisle, I felt nauseous. There was a metal taste in my mouth. I picked up the menu in the seat pocket in front of me and stared at it blankly before putting it back. I twisted in my seat, looking down the barrel of the train carriage, where the washroom was located. Should I have gone with him and waited outside? What if he needs my help? Will he remember to wipe properly? Will he wash his hands? What if he gets stuck and can't unlock the door?

The onslaught of what ifs wouldn't leave me alone. I gripped the arm rests and told myself to breathe. He's fine. Nothing is wrong. *But what if he's not fine? He's taking too long. Something must be wrong.*

Still Carson didn't return to his seat.

When I left home for the first time, I was grossly unprepared. Montreal may have only been an hour's drive away, yet my parents picked me up most weekends. I hauled textbooks and dirty laundry behind me as though dragging my own corpse. I may have left home, but I hadn't exactly launched.

After graduating from university and working one summer in Montreal, I decided to take a year off. My friend Trish and I got visas to the U.K. I had grand plans. First, I'd land a dream job as an editorial assistant at one of the big publishing houses in London. Trish and I would save up, then backpack through Europe. We'd visit famous galleries in Paris, eat amazing food in Italy, check out gorgeous architecture in Spain, and soak up the sun in Portugal . . . The reality was a lot less glamorous than my vision board would have it. Trish and I found a hostel when we arrived in London. We shared a room with an Australian couple. The room had one mattress, so the four of us took turns sleeping on the floor. There, I learned two important lessons: always wear flip-flops in the shower and never put anything in the communal fridge if you want to see it again. Even English mustard had a habit of mysteriously disappearing. The hostel was obscenely expensive—an obscenely expensive dump.

The exchange rate of Canadian dollars to pounds sterling was brutal that year. Within a matter of weeks, the money I had saved up over several years had evaporated. I was so broke I ate one meal a day—usually an egg salad sandwich from a petrol station. I registered with an agency and, thanks to my typing skills, got a job temping. No call backs from the publishing houses, though. When I could afford to, I called home from a quaint red phone booth across the road from the hostel. My prepaid calling card lasted exactly five minutes, during which I lied through my teeth to my mom that everything was going great. I was a terrible liar, but I didn't want her to worry. I thought maybe she'd see through my lies and tell me to come home. But she didn't. So maybe my acting wasn't as bad as I thought.

I couldn't endure another week in the "hostile" as I called it. So, Trish found us a house share in West Kensington that was full of expats, most of them American. Our room was a shoebox, but at least it was clean. Rent was not cheap, but I didn't care. I was just grateful to be out of the hostel and working. Without Trish, I would not have survived in London.

Before long, Trish got a job at a store in Covent Garden, and I landed a full-time admin job for a company that sold postal franking machines. It was a far cry from my dream job in publishing, but it paid the rent. Over the following months, thousands of miles from home, I learned to: wash my clothes, shop for food, and cook a basic meal (pasta with store-bought pesto). Without my mom putting the "smother" in "mother" and pandering to me, I finally grew up. I had no choice.

It's different with Carson. At least that's what I told myself that day on the train when he eventually made his way through the carriage and sat down in the seat next to me. As if nothing the least bit remarkable had just happened.

⁓

By some miracle, my car pulls into the school parking lot. I have no idea how I got here. Thanks to Emily, thanks to Jennifer, I am still in one piece, intact at least physically. How much time has elapsed since the phone call from the school? I have no idea about that, either.

If Carson is hurt, I will not survive this, I think as I break into a run down the empty corridor toward the principal's office.

When he sees me, my boy leaps out of the chair and rushes into my arms. As I squeeze him, I feel his skinny body relax.

I wandered once as a child. Something caught my eye in the toy aisle of Kmart. My mom had said something I didn't hear, and when I finally thought to look up, she was gone. I walked up and down the aisles, growing more terrified with each passing minute. Eventually I left the toy section and headed into the women's clothing department. My breath quickened as I scanned the backs of every woman I saw—none of them her. Soon I could not see for the tears streaking my face. My nose dripped with snot. A man crouched before me and asked my mom's name. *Mommy*, I said, sobbing so violently he couldn't understand me. *Mommy*, I said again before realizing that he meant her actual name. Dazed, I followed him to the cash. The man spoke to the woman at the register, and a moment later my mom's name rang out through the store. Within seconds, she came running breathlessly toward me. It was the longest 10 minutes of my life. Until now.

"Mommy," Carson says. At 10, he still calls me "Mommy," and it might just be my favourite word in the English language. I swear I will never tire of hearing it.

"I decided to walk home." His smile is wide and bright as an LED. "Aren't you proud of me?"

What I feel in that moment is not pride exactly but an entirely different emotion. Luck mingled with relief. Every year, countless autistic children wander. They vanish from their neighbourhoods, never to be seen again. Some are struck by cars; many more drown. Others are shot dead by police. In the blink of an eye, they are gone. It can happen. It happens. Never again will those mothers get to hold their children as I am holding Carson right now.

Only when we pull apart do I notice the blue ball resting at his feet. Only then do I notice the interim principal with her string pearls and greying bob. Words fly like so many moths from her mouth. I cannot tell whether she is offering an explanation, an apology, or a defence. No one saw my son leave the playground, even though he was supposed to be supervised. The school secretary, who happened to be driving back from her lunch break, noticed him walking alone toward the overpass. If she hadn't pulled over at that moment and managed to coax Carson into her car, this story might have had an entirely different arc. One with an ending I don't want to contemplate.

The thought alone compels me to draw my boy back into my arms. For once, he doesn't squirm or protest. So I bury my face in his soft curls that smell of our shampoo, of our home. Then I cup his face in my hands, and he lets me do that, too. He may be 10, yet his cheeks still have all the plumpness of babyhood. For now. For now, I breathe in the smell of him. I want to fill my lungs with him. I close my eyes and concentrate on the feel of his small frame in my arms. I hold him close, knowing everything is about to change.

Funny guy

My son has a funny bone. A tibia. A fibula. In the Bible, Eve was created from Adam's rib. Did he have a spare one? All I know is that Carson didn't get the funny gene from me. I mean, sure, I have my moments, but by and large my kid's sense of humour comes from his father's side of the family. Aidan is a funny guy, too—as is his brother, who did a spate of stand-up shows in south London a few years back.

Carson's particular brand of comedy is improv. It's spontaneous, unscripted, and often near to the bone. The borderline offensiveness of his humour is arguably what makes it funny. There's a whole school of comics who get their laughs from an audience's discomfort, who exist in the liminal space between outrageous and hilarious. Aidan and I once went to a comedy night at Yuk Yuk's, where one of the comics had material about pedophilia. There are some lines you just don't cross, ever. The guy persisted, until he was "gonged" and forcibly removed from the stage.

Young Carson's routine does not happen onstage. It happens in the drugstore checkout line when he announces to everyone within earshot, "Hey, Mom, don't you need this cream for your *freaky lip?*" It happens at the hardware store when he drops his pants and attempts to use the display toilet. It happens at home when I host my monthly book club meeting. Fresh out of the tub, before Aidan can wrangle him into a towel, my seven-year-old comes downstairs wearing nothing but a smile. *Adam was naked but felt no shame.* "Welcome, *ladies*," he says, inviting them in. One by one, he shakes each of their hands with the formality of a maître d' in some posh restaurant. I want to die. Luckily he's still of an age where nudity is considered more cute than creepy. But that day will come soon enough.

Part of the reason my son is so funny is because he isn't trying to be funny. Like my nan before him, he simply tells it like it is. Because he doesn't intrinsically know the secret social code that others adhere to, Carson enjoys a rare freedom from censorship. When you don't know what you should and should not say to a person's face, anything is fair game. That's why I've learned never to ask an autist what they think of your new haircut unless you really want to know. Recently I taught my boy the adage "If you can't say something nice, say nothing at all." Instead of saying nothing, Carson now informs me when he's *thinking* something unkind so there is no doubt in my mind that the haircut looks shit.

His lack of social filter and impulsivity compel him to blurt what he's thinking without considering the fallout.[64] In other words: he doesn't read the room. Being blunt and socially awkward may not be virtues out there in the wild, yet they are gold on the comedy circuit. In recent years there has been a surge in autistic comics openly mining their neurotype for punchlines. Fern Brady and Hannah Gadsby are among a wave of comedians who are "out" about their diagnoses. Even Jerry Seinfeld famously self-identified. In fact, autists have probably always been overrepresented in comedy. As Brady claims, everything that made her "a problem" at school and at work is paradoxically what made her successful at standup.[65] That tracks. Autistic people have a unique and often unusual perspective, and our tendency to deep dive makes for solid observational humour. Performing is repetitive and highly scripted, which holds great appeal to the autist. There is no need to interpret an audience's reaction; laughter signals approval. It beats a day job in an office, where you are expected to fawn and mask all day.

Comedy allows us to be honest in a way that costs us out in the world. The autistic tendency toward moral absolutism and truth-telling over tactfulness often loses us friends and wins us enemies. Billy Joel had it right. Honesty truly is a "lonely word." As children, we are taught in terms of binaries—lying is wrong, telling the truth is right—but the reality is far more complicated. People lie all the time. So-called white lies are not only considered harmless, they also fulfill a social expectation. The autist does not make such distinctions. As far as we're concerned, lies are lies.

Honesty is the best policy, until it's not. I've learned the hard way that people do not want or expect complete honesty. They say they do, but that itself is a lie. Most people, for instance, do not care to hear an honest answer when they ask, "How are you?" They do not want to hear, for example, that you are feeling depressed, pissed off, awesome, even. A transactional "fine" will suffice. Anything else, and you have broken the social contract. To the autistic person, this exchange makes no sense. Why ask someone how they are if you don't expect an honest answer? It took me years to understand this pointless convention, and I still struggle with it at times.

Given that lying is wrong, people do it an awful lot. Far from being perceived as a virtue, my honesty is something of a fatal flaw. Ditto for Carson, who often prefaces statements with "I probably shouldn't tell you this but . . ." and then proceeds with a wholly unnecessary confession. As though withholding a truth (even a minor one, even one that is guaranteed to get him into trouble) weighs so heavy a burden, he needs to get it off his chest immediately. Perhaps Catholic guilt runs deep in his DNA.

The truth is, lying is hard. It is stressful. Having to bend the narrative and then remember the various strands of that fabrication is simply too complicated for us to keep in our heads. Since many autists struggle to know when to lie and when to tell the truth, our de facto response becomes the truth, every time. Imagine our confusion, then, when we are punished for it.

⌁

A lie from childhood haunts you to this day. In the summers before computers and smartphones, you and your cousin Jess must manufacture your own fun. The days are long, and no one will fill them for you. Camp is too expensive. Your parents work. So, you set about exploring the local wildlife in your neighbourhood. You nurse wounded birds. You capture as many grasshoppers as you can in an empty margarine container, then you release them on the driveway. Watching their mad, mass hopping is thrilling, but it also reveals the extent of your boredom. One day, Jess asks if you want to go to the creek near her place to catch tadpoles. The idea is that you will keep them in her old fishtank and chart their development into frogs. No one knows or seems to care what you get up to as long as you and Jess stick together.

The plan is going to plan until one of you (probably you) leans too far forward and slips. The other (probably Jess) tries to help, and soon both of you are submerged to the ankles in pond scum and mud. On the bank of the creek, you sit peeling off your soaked socks and running shoes. Eventually you give up and head home carrying your muddy shoes and socks in your hands. You want to cry. Not only was the expedition a failure, now you must walk the couple blocks back to Jess's place barefoot, carefully avoiding small stones and cigarette butts on the hot pavement. As you near her house, there is a heavy feeling in your chest. Dread. You stink of the creek you probably weren't allowed to play in. Also, your uncle, Jess's dad—a bear of a man who works nights and sleeps during the day—is currently hibernating after a shift. You do not want to wake him up. Your aunt is home. She can be sweet, but you know she also has a mean streak and a witchy cackle straight out of *The Wizard of Oz*. You do not want to cross either of them.

Mostly, though, you worry about what your mom will say when she finds out. Your greatest fear is disappointing her. Will you get spanked? It doesn't happen often, and the sting to your pride is always worse than any residual mark left on your backside. And anyway, it's better when she does it. When her boyfriend hits you, it hurts twice as much because his hands are twice the size of hers. They leave an imprint, as though someone has traced the outline of his hand the way you would a leaf in autumn. After he hits you, his phantom hand throbs for hours. Other times he uses the brush—the big round one with the yellow handle that you and Jess hold when lip-syncing to your favourite songs. You remember how red his face gets when he's angry, which happens a lot. His anger is hot like a stove burner you shouldn't touch. One day he punches one of the doors in the apartment, and his fist leaves a crater in the wood. After that he stops coming to the duplex. You are glad when it is just the two of you again, you and your mom. When she meets Mitch a few years later, you remember the crater. Mitch is mean in so many ways, but he never lays a hand on you. Not once.

When you get to Jess's house, you step gingerly onto the back porch. But your aunt hears you and opens the screen door. She takes one look at the muddy shoes and scummy socks, and you brace yourself. Jess is ready, though, immediately spinning a fantastical tale about some guy who showed up and asked if you knew where his girlfriend was. When you said you didn't know, he pushed you in the creek. To your amazement, Jess starts crying. Her crocodile tears are impressive, even if her storytelling skills leave a lot to be desired. Your aunt says to Jess, "Wait till your father finds out." After insisting you wash off your feet with the garden hose, she lets you come inside to watch TV, and you think maybe you got away with it.

No more is said about what happened at the creek that day, even when your mom picks you up. You wait for punishment. At the very least you wait for a lecture when she sees the state of your socks and shoes. But it is not necessary. You have never lied to your mom before. The guilt and shame you feel are more than enough punishment.

You and Jess never speak of the expedition gone wrong. You don't know about Jess, but you never set foot near a creek again.

It's hard to believe that being honest can get you into so much trouble. And it goes beyond telling someone what you really think of their new hairstyle or outfit. Sometimes it's giving advice to a relative who asks your opinion and then doesn't like said opinion. It's telling your boss why it makes *no sense* to perform a task the way they want you to and then doing them a favour by suggesting a far more logical approach. It's playing devil's advocate when your friend complains about her spouse instead of automatically taking her side.

We offer such truth-telling as a service, a kindness, but alas it is rarely taken as such. This dogged need for honesty comes with a price; we are reprimanded, shunned, accused, and we are often shocked by the rebuke because we were led to believe being honest was a good thing. A virtue, even. It took a long time for us to reach the moral high ground. Now we have arrived, only to find the air up here is super thin, it's hard to breathe, and the place is practically deserted.

This is compounded by the fact that you are a woman. The patriarchy is still not comfortable with women who are opinionated and direct rather than meek and submissive. And yet—you wish people would tell the truth more often. When faced with personal and professional rejection, you wish someone would point out where you went wrong rather than beat around the proverbial bush. Then and only then would you be in a position to improve. All this pussyfooting around the truth only leaves you second-guessing yourself and chasing your tail in perpetuity.

⤳

Taking people at face value has made a fool of me; trust has made me hopelessly, painfully gullible. One of the worst betrayals came one Easter when I was in my tweens. Naturally I preferred receiving books and magazines over chocolate. Keen to win me over, one of Mom's boyfriends once bought me a three-foot chocolate bunny, which sat untouched for a year in the freezer. (As an adult, I have more than compensated for my childhood aversion to chocolate.) My lack of enthusiasm did not extend to the Bunny, however. I looked forward to Easter as much as I looked forward to Christmas. In the lead-up to the holiday one year, Jess and I wrote and recorded an original song. We even cued the tape recorder so that the oversized rabbit just had to hit Play. It went something like, "Easter, Easter, it is here / Think of all the fun we had this year." We were no Lennon/ McCartney, but we didn't let mediocrity tamp our spirits.

Being the more worldly of us, Jess clearly knew what was up. She knew the deal with Santa Claus and the Easter Bunny long before I did, but she played along, committed as she was to safeguarding my innocence. The enormous bubble of my naïveté would not be burst on her watch. While rooting around in my mom's drawer one day, I came across a little stuffed yellow chick nestled in a pink half shell. When you shook it, the chick squeaked. Sensing it must be an Easter present, I hid the chick back in my mother's drawer. Days later, the squeaky chick resurfaced—a supposed gift from the Bunny. As soon as I saw it, I burst into tears. I cried so hard I gave myself hiccups. My mom was flummoxed. The game was up. At around 12, I was far too old to believe. And yet I believed, fervently.

The betrayal extended so much further than the Easter Bunny. It was as though I had singlehandedly uncovered the world's biggest conspiracy. Everyone I loved and trusted, including my own mother, had banded together to deceive me. In a world where nothing was as it seemed, how could anybody be believed or trusted?

⌣

There is something admirable about my son's brutal honesty, even if I frequently find myself its casualty. In his presence, I have no hope of maintaining a shred of decorum or dignity. In his presence, I will not be spared. If I wake up with a monster zit on my chin, I can almost guarantee he will home in on it. It will become *material*.

Being Carson's mom is like walking around in a state of permanent undress. There is no option but to shed any lingering hang-ups. The alternative is to shrivel and die of embarrassment. In order to survive, I have grown rhinoceros-thick skin. I don't know Jim

Carrey's mother personally, but I feel a certain kinship toward her and the moms of other famous comedians. I know how it feels to live on that razor's edge, never knowing what will come out of your son's mouth at any given moment. When everything is a potential punch-line, we moms are often the ones who get punched. And since the show must go on, better to be in on the act. Better to laugh alongside Carson like a willing sidekick rather than the butt of the joke. Butt, get it? Still, keeping up with his one-liners and outrageous repartee can be exhausting. Sometimes I imagine what life would be like if my child wasn't a funny guy. If he was just a regular, run-of-the-mill guy. I've been around other people's kids, and I am sometimes secretly relieved these dull and tedious creatures aren't mine.

⌒

People on the spectrum are literal thinkers. We supposedly struggle with things like sarcasm, puns, and idioms. With this in mind, I draw up a list of figures of speech. Carson designs a Go Fish–style card game in which you match the illustration to the idiom, e.g. "It's raining cats and dogs" and "A bird in the hand is worth two in the bush." (That last one I will never pretend to understand.) We start jotting down some of his jokes in a notebook, so we can share them with his grandparents.

> *What kind of coffee do owls like to drink?*
> *Tim Hoot-ons*

> *What do you call a teacher with gas?*
> *A toot-or*

> *Knock-knock*
> *Who's there?*

iPad

iPad who?

iPad enough of your attitude!

Who's a chicken's favourite composer?

Bach

If bread wears loafers, what do nuts wear?

Ca-shoes

By the sixth grade, the principal takes notice of Carson's burgeoning sense of humour and invites him to his first gig. Every week after the morning announcements, my son takes to the airwaves and recites an original joke over the school PA system. It's a risqué move on the principal's part, given he doesn't screen the jokes ahead of time. But I love the man for seeing my boy and for shining a light on his strengths rather than simply dwelling on his shortcomings the way other school admins have. *This is the power of real inclusion,* I think, *not some performative brand of allyship.*

Carson doesn't crash and burn in the limelight. While not every joke lands, his material remains mostly clean and above the belt. (At least until he hits puberty, when the punchlines he throws down would make Ali Wong blush.) To my surprise and utter delight, the "Friday Funny" segment is a hit. Overnight, Carson becomes something of a celebrity at his elementary school. In the halls, kids call out to him. This is new territory. I marvel at the effect popularity has on him, the way it transforms his physical body. I swear he walks with longer strides, his head held higher, his posture straighter. It's the first time that kids see Carson ahead of his disability. The first time they see him the way I see him: smart, charismatic, and funny as hell.

Rx

The worst days rarely announce themselves as such. They don't come with brash bells and warning whistles. Most of the time the worst days start out like any other day, innocuous and perfectly ordinary.

After school, you unload the dishwasher, plate by plate, cup by cup, while Carson unwinds on the couch with the iPad. You can hear the soundtrack of the game he's been playing for weeks: a quasi-obstacle course in which the player must deke panes of glass to avoid shattering them. The strangely melodic music belies the intensity of the game, which is hard, bordering on impossible. You tried once and couldn't make it past the first level. Carson, though, is a master. But even a master cannot beat a game that is rigged, that is designed to be unbeatable. You try to tell him as much, to caution him against the inevitability of defeat. But he's not having it. At best, his tenacity and single-mindedness are a gift that will serve him well in adulthood. At worst, you think this rigidity will be his undoing.

When the time comes to switch off the game, you issue the usual countdowns and warnings: 10 minutes, five minutes, two minutes. You've read all the parenting books. You know firsthand how hard transitions can be for autistic folks. You struggle with them yourself. When you are in the zone, it's often hard to change gears without warning.

If Carson has heard you, he doesn't let on. He stares, hardly blinking, at the touch screen.

"Hey," you say gently, moving toward the couch. "Time's up."

It is only when you reach for the iPad that your son seems to register your existence. He looks up with narrowed eyes and swears at you. Then he starts to scream. The sound slices through you. He leaps off the couch and lunges for the iPad. But you hold it aloft. He lunges again, and the movement is so deft, so agile. Caught off guard, you stumble backward. There is a bright flash of pain. It radiates like a bull's eye, spreading outward in concentric rings from your left breast, where, you realize, he has bitten through your shirt. Later that night, when you are undressing in your room, after everything that has happened, you will come face to face with the abrasion in the mirror. Faint red teeth marks just below the nipple. From his baby teeth.

Instinctively you wince as you clutch your wounded breast.

Taking advantage of your distracted state, Carson to tries to swipe the iPad out of your hands. You swerve in time and hide the device behind your back. There follows a sequence of movements. He swings while you dodge. Swing, dodge. It's as though the two of you are performing a mother-son dance no one wants to watch.

He steps back and looks you straight in the eye, something he rarely does. His pupils shrunken to black pinpricks. "I will get you," he says, and your blood runs cold. A few weeks ago, he turned 10. You sang to him. You had cake and balloons and presents, the works.

Now you take two stairs at a time, clutching the iPad to your chest. Heart thumping, you hurry into your bedroom and then into the ensuite bathroom. You lock the door behind you and slink on the tiled floor, panting. You set down the iPad and bring your knees to your chest.

Seconds later, you hear his footsteps in the bedroom, then his small fist pounds at the door. *Come out come out wherever you are.* You wish this was a game of hide and seek. You would come out with your hands up. You would come out laughing.

Instead, you stare at the locked door in disbelief. You are hiding from your child. Today's trigger is the iPad. Tomorrow it could be the wrong-coloured mug you hand him. Or it could be telling him to wear a raincoat because it's raining outside.

He bangs on the door again, and you hold your breath. You say nothing. You wait until the sound of his footsteps grows fainter. Your phone is downstairs, so you pick up the tablet and type a message to Aidan telling him to come home right away. Then you type another to your mom and Mitch. There's no reply from Aidan, who's probably in a meeting. And your mom? You're not sure where she is at. But Mitch responds saying he'll come right away. Right away is, in fact, *five hours* by car. So, you stay put. You stay sitting on the bathroom floor until your legs and butt go numb. You wait until the coast is clear. Until you are home-free.

⌣

By the time I hear Aidan's key in the front door, I already know what needs to happen next. We pile into the car and head straight to the Hospital for Sick Children. *Is that what Carson is—a sick child?* I wonder as we crawl through rush-hour traffic. You wouldn't know it to look at him. But then, not all sicknesses are visible. And right now that's how I choose to view his aggression, as a sickness. It's the only way I can think of it at all.

Once we arrive at triage, Aidan sits in the waiting room with Carson while I tell the nurse what happened. When I explain that Carson is autistic and volatile, she moves us to a private room down the hall. By now my boy has simmered down, although occasionally he swears and growls at us from where he sits on the gurney. His feet don't even touch the floor.

In this windowless room, time grinds to a halt. Eventually Mitch arrives at the hospital and finds us. Relieved to see him, I go over and give him a big hug. The affection that has run between us ever since Carson was born still feels strange. So much of my life was spent despising, or at best tolerating, this man. Now I'm hopeful that his presence will have a calming effect on my son. They've had this inexplicable bond since Carson was a baby.

But instead of saying hello, he eyes Mitch with cold indifference. After hours cooped up in a small room, my child starts to pace. Worried that he may escalate again, I step into the hall and flag a nurse to find out how much longer we must wait.

Not all kids on the spectrum are aggressive. Not all kids on the spectrum are . . . anything. They are each as unique as their own fingerprints. Behaviour is a form of communication, after all. And aggression is merely a symptom, a sign of a breakdown in transmission. A lagging skill. A cry for help. Research suggests that aggression rates may be higher in autistic individuals than in typically developing individuals and those with other developmental disabilities.[66] For children and their caregivers, aggression has negative outcomes. For kids, there is a risk of physical intervention and victimization, difficulty with relationships, and restrictive residential or school placements. For caregivers, there is an incumbent lack of support and increased financial and emotional stress, all of which impact well-being and family life.[67]

Nonspeaking autists may bang their heads or bite their hands out of frustration, because they cannot communicate any other way. Others, like my son, lash out. They may hit and kick and spit and throw things. Such behaviour is not a tantrum, though it may look that way to an outsider. Whereas a tantrum is a wilful reaction to a situation (say, a child not getting something they want), a meltdown is an involuntary response to autistic overwhelm. The operative word here being *involuntary*. A meltdown is the tornado that no one saw coming. By the time the twister appears on the horizon, it is usually too late to intervene. Once it gains momentum and velocity, it will destroy whatever is in its path. In a matter of seconds, papers and toys are scattered everywhere, books flung across the room, glass shattered, furniture upturned. Entire rooms trashed. There is nothing to be done except evacuate and make sure that everyone is safe. Nothing to be done but hunker down and wait for the calm of the aftermath. Being in the path of a tornado is terrifying, no denying it. But being the boy inside the tornado must be equally terrifying.

Eventually the doctor on call arrives, and we debrief. She refers us to a developmental pediatrician and a behavioural therapist. By the time we finally get seen, Carson is tired and ready to go home.

The storm has passed, for now.

⌐

There is no cure for autism because autism is not a disease, nor is it an illness. Even so, many of us take medications to treat co-morbid, or co-occurring, conditions. Rates of depression and anxiety, for instance, are significantly higher in autists compared to the general population.[68] I have taken an SSRI antidepressant off and on for most of my life. I have also taken prescription drugs for the debilitating headaches I've experienced since I was a child. When I was Carson's age, I frequently became overwhelmed and fell ill. My vision scrambled, and one hemisphere of my skull throbbed. Nauseous, I often threw up several times. No one had any idea why this was happening. Doctors glued electrodes to my scalp to find out what was wrong. Tests came back normal. My mom must have felt helpless seeing her little girl suffer. The doctor prescribed a strong painkiller known as a barbiturate to treat the pain.

Research has found that migraine is more common in autistic people and more common in women than in men.[69] The reasons for this connection remain unclear. Often what triggers my migraines can be traced back to autistic triggers, such as stress and anxiety, insomnia, and hypersensitivity to sensory stimuli from loud noise, bright light, and crowds.

Autistic aggression is also treated with medication. But medication alone is not a silver bullet. Doctors play around with different medications and doses, striving to balance side effects against efficacity in a perpetual cost-benefit analysis. The workings of the autistic brain are still scarcely understood. No wonder practitioners take a haphazard approach to treatment, then. Like maverick chefs, they throw in a pinch of this and a dash of that and hope for the best. Most are doing what they can, armed with only a prescription pad and paltry knowledge of our neurology. Professionals routinely fall short of being able to adequately meet our needs and improve our well-being. As a society, we have a long way to go in providing holistic and informed care for people on the spectrum. As Carson's parent, all I want is for him to lead a healthy, happy life, but by whose standards? The road to hell is certainly paved with good intentions.

Like many autistic kids, I fear that my boy has become a guinea pig in a vast experiment.

Years from now, I will sit in another hospital across from another psychiatrist who will add new labels to go along with Carson's existing ones: autism spectrum disorder and attention deficit hyperactivity disorder. All these labels are as important as they are meaningless. Labels exist because of our constant need to place people into neat boxes. When we label, we reduce complex individuals to a checklist of "symptoms," thereby pathologizing different ways of being. Nowadays most people tend to think about neurodiversity much in the way they think about biodiversity. Namely, that there are natural variations in human neurology. Every year autism rates continue to rise. Contrary to popular belief, there is not a sudden influx of autistic people on the planet. Rather, there are more of us being *identified* owing to better, earlier, and wider, diagnostic practices. By 2020, the prevalence of autism in the U.S. was approximately one in 36 (2.8%) children, with noted increases in the diagnostic rate of "girls and non-White boys."[70] In Canada, as of 2019, the highest estimate was one in 40 (2.5%) children, with boys four times more likely to be diagnosed than girls.[71] When we further take into account other forms of neurodivergence (including ADHD and specific learning disorders, such as dyslexia, dyspraxia, and dyscalculia), those percentages climb significantly and are thought to affect as many as 15% to 20% of people worldwide.[72]

Since Carson was diagnosed, there has been a marked paradigm shift, with autism being reframed as a difference rather than a deficit. Neurotypicals may form the majority, and as such determine the basis of our societal structures. However, being in the neurominority does not necessarily mean our way of being is inferior. We are steadily moving away from a medical model of disability toward a prosocial one, and that's got to be a good thing. If we want to create a more inclusive society, we need to support neurodivergent people where they are at without trying to make them more "neurotypical."[73] I only wish the shift had come sooner. After all this time—and in spite of all these labels—my boy remains an enigma, a beautiful enigma.

Before I became a mother, raising a child seemed straightforward enough. Bedtime routines. Nutritious meals. Screen time limits. I had it all figured out. All the things parents were doing wrong seemed glaringly obvious to me. My judgment of other parents was swift and exacting. (Typical black-and-white autistic thinking on my part.) I regularly tutted under my breath at what I saw go down at the park, the restaurant, the grocery store . . . *Never will I ever do* that *with my child*, I thought. Never ever say never. Before I became a mom, the idea of medicating a child topped that list. Drugging your child seemed unfathomable, even immoral, to me. A cop-out of the worst kind. It was lazy, borderline abusive parenting. It was pandering to Big Pharma. It was reaching for an easy solution to a complicated problem.

That was before. Before the kicking and screaming. Before the broken glass, the smashed plate. Before the upturned chair and the shattered vase. Before the crying and the wishing to die. That was before my child fell apart before my eyes.

Before I became a mom, I used to wonder, who would do that? What kind of parent would medicate her child? Now I know the answer. I am. I am that kind of parent. Maybe my mother was, too. The kind who has grown tired of watching her baby suffer. The kind who will do whatever it takes to help her child feel better, even if that means doing the exact thing she swore she would never do.

⌒

Before I had Carson, I remember watching other moms and thinking I could do better, I would do so much better when my turn came.

You may be thinking that very thought as you read these pages. In my situation, you would do any number of things differently. And who knows, maybe it would make a world of difference. Then again, maybe it wouldn't.

If I could do it all over again, what would I change? Everything... and nothing. Each day we inhabit these moments and make split-second decisions based on the information we have in front of us. We cross our fingers and hope for the best. Sometimes you can do all the right things as a parent and still end up failing your child. Sometimes you can do all the wrong things as a parent, and your kid still turns out okay. This is not what society would have us believe. We are told that good things come to good people (not necessarily true); and that bad people will get what is coming to them (also patently untrue).

Mothers of autistic children fall into the damned-if-we-do, damned-if-we-don't camp. Maligned in the autism community, these mothers love their children with a frightening ferocity. Some even refer to themselves as "warrior moms," though it's unclear who or what they are battling exactly. Are they fighting for increased inclusion and awareness, or is the war they wage against the ultimate enemy—autism itself? These mothers have sacrificed careers and marriages, devoted themselves to being full-time carers, administrators, teachers, and therapists. They have given over so much of themselves in service to their children; they have scraped the barrel until there is nothing of their *selves* left. Their exhaustion is not merely physical; it is emotional. It is psychogenic. Advocating for your child year in, year out has a hollowing effect. These moms are accused of being martyrs.

But I defy anyone to judge families with our lived experience. Such ignorance must surely be blissful. When Carson was first diagnosed, before I knew better, I drank the Kool-Aid. I believed the experts who pushed their agenda. I subjected Carson to various therapies, many of which left him with lasting trauma. At every turn he was reprimanded and corrected, fed the message that he was not okay, not enough as he was. He had to be, if not "cured" then "fixed" or "improved."

Now I understand the ableist frameworks that often guided—and misguided—me. These days, the only "interventions" Carson needs relate to his mental health, to repair the harm inflicted from living in a world that fundamentally rejects his way of being. These days, my only job as his mother is to love and accept him for who he is, and to love and accept myself as I am.

We are the proverbial square pegs in a world of round holes, Carson and me. If we don't stop trying to whittle and carve ourselves into a shape that is unnatural, we will be damaged beyond recognition.

I no longer strive to be the perfect parent because the perfect parent does not exist. She is a figment of our collective imagination. The perfect parent is a fabrication, a bald-faced lie. I try not to judge others that way. I try not to judge myself that way. I am far from perfect. I have done things that I regret and said things that have left my face hot with shame. But I have also done many good things, many true and right things. I may not always have been the best mother, but most of the time I have been exactly the mother Carson needed.

⌒

When I tell the developmental pediatrician the story of how we ended up in the E.R., he listens quietly, then scribbles something on his notepad. A new prescription for an antipsychotic drug. He tells me the medication is typically used to treat schizophrenia but is also approved to treat "irritability" or aggression in autistic individuals.[74]

Just hearing the word *antipsychotic* makes me feel sick. The way it conjures visions of Jack Nicholson's sweaty, demented face in *The Shining*. Now I watch as the doctor tears the slip of paper from his notepad and slides it across the desk. I stare at the script for a while, not wanting to touch it. I don't know what else to do. All I know is that I cannot live in fear anymore. All I know is that I want my son back. I slip the paper in my purse.

These are the things that no one writes about. And because no one writes about them, no one reads about them. And because no one reads about them, no one talks about them. And that's a problem.

That night, and on the nights that follow, sleep eludes me. It's the first time I have felt truly afraid. It's a perverse combination, this commingling of intense fear and intense love. These flavours that should not, by rights, go together. The sweet and the sour. The ugly and the sublime. There will be times in the years to come when I sleep with the door to my bedroom locked, times when I hide the kitchen knives . . . because you never know. Will he hurt me? Will he hurt himself? I can't say for certain. And the not knowing is what keeps me up at night.

Before we landed at the hospital, I did not know what it was like to go to bed afraid and wake up afraid. That kind of fear never leaves you; it simply takes up residence in your body. Before that day, I slept soundly, obliviously, the way I imagine other parents do. Now I toss and turn, a million questions cycling through my addled brain. I worry about this antipsychotic drug—what are the side effects, and how will it affect my son long-term? Will it stunt his growth? Will it turn him into an addict, a dropout? Will it make him suicidal? Or homicidal?

Some of my questions are unanswerable, and others soon become apparent. The medication makes Carson gain weight—a lot of weight—in a short space. After one of his raids, we take to padlocking the pantry. At six in the morning, I come downstairs to find my child making his way through a giant tub of ice cream. So, I clear out the freezer. This drug has made him ravenous. And his hunger has a desperate quality that is gross and pitiful to witness. The fact that we have done this to him, that his own parents have willingly reduced him to this, racks me with guilt and shame.

After a few weeks on the antipsychotic medication, Carson's behaviour (and eating habits) stabilizes long enough for us to catch our breath. The therapist asks us to record and send her videos of his meltdowns, so she can make suggestions. Over time, the red marks on my breast fade, but the memory of that day lingers. I do not tell anybody what happened. Other than my parents, nobody knows what we are going through. Nobody understands how we live. Not friends. Not family. Not even other parents of autistic kids we know.

Some kids bite or hit themselves when their nervous systems are dysregulated. It is easy to sympathize with those kids and their parents. It is less easy to feel compassion for a child who is lashing out—breaking property, spitting, biting, swearing, and hitting others.

Aggression has relegated us to the fringes of a fringe group. We are marooned on this island with no means of escape, like the characters in the show *Lost*. I need to believe that one day we will all be rescued. That one day the three of us will find ourselves in a better place. So far, no amount of therapy or medication have managed to mitigate Carson's meltdowns. I can only hope that with time he will find ways to manage his triggers and ward off the storms.

Until then, every morning I hand my son a pill and watch him swallow. And then I swallow my own. It tastes bitter as hell.

Fat-bottomed girls (and boys)

I'm not sure of the exact moment that Carson's eating becomes an issue. It happens so incrementally I hardly notice at first. One minute, he can't get enough of a certain food; the next, he refuses to touch it *ever again*. At 13, my son is ruthless in his culinary cull. Turkey, cream cheese, raisins, melons, shrimp . . . With every passing month, the list of "banned foods" gets progressively longer, and the list of "safe foods" progressively shorter. Tuna, porridge, hummus, olives, grapes . . . The rules, and exceptions to those rules, are so complex and arbitrary that I struggle to keep track. Cheese on pizza is okay but not on anything else. Tomatoes are okay except in a pasta sauce. Bread is okay but only if it is devoid of seeds. Plain potato chips are fine—but show him a tortilla chip, and he will run a mile in the other direction. Crackers are disgusting because they produce crumbs. Bread also produces crumbs, yet somehow those crumbs aren't problematic.

It's hard to reconcile this current version of Carson with the baby who would eat anything and everything put in front of him. And let's not mince words here: my son was a very fat baby. After I tried (and failed) to breastfeed him, the visiting nurse suggested I switch to formula. So, I did. Then, when Carson cried all the time and wouldn't settle, the nurse concluded that he must still be hungry. She recommended switching to a formula with extra protein for "hungry babies." In no time at all, he went from deliciously plump to downright portly. Before long, my baby's folds had folds, and he had dimples in places where babies weren't supposed to have dimples. By the time we emigrated to Canada and introduced solids, it looked as though Carson had ingested several smaller versions of himself, like one of those Russian dolls.

Anytime I took him to the library or grocery store, people stared. At first, I assumed it was because he was so damn cute. Didn't everybody stare at cute babies? Then one day a pensioner approached us on the sidewalk, walking unsteadily with a cane. As he got close, he peered inside the stroller. I waited for him to compliment me on my unbelievably cute baby. Instead he muttered something about Carson's size and shook his head in disgust. Stunned, I didn't know what to say. So I picked up the pace, eager to get away from this man. After all, hadn't I bought a second-hand jogging stroller—with its thick tires and impressive suspension—for this express purpose? I never did jog with it, but it came in handy in times like these. When I had to escape the wrath of a judgmental octogenarian. As I passed him, blood rushed to my head. *Where the fuck does he get off?*

It wasn't just the old man, though. That year I heard it all: sumo baby, little Buddha. Sometimes people tried to pass their comments off as endearments, but I wasn't an idiot. I knew what they were really thinking. Babies should be pudgy, but not too pudgy. Those Anne Geddes babies and Gerber babies represented the ideal. There was a right side of fat and a wrong side, even for babies. When it came to body shaming, I learned that even babies are fair game. And that people (even complete strangers) feel well within their rights to tell a woman not just what is wrong with her own body but with her baby's body, too.

First I hadn't fed Carson enough; then it seemed I'd fed him too much. I couldn't win for losing. Faced with this egregious assault on my motherhood, how did I retaliate? By signing Carson up to an infant gymnastics class, of course. Located above a grocery store in a poorly ventilated space filled with mats, peek-a-boo tunnels, slides, and ramps, it was the equivalent of CrossFit for babies.

At the first session, I glanced around, dismayed to see many of the other babies already crawling and cruising around the circuit. It wasn't long before the instructor zeroed in on us. She was a thin woman with thick grey hair that hung to her waist like drapes. After she watched Carson for a minute with her hands set on her narrow hips, she suggested I put him on his tummy to "build up his core." I obliged. In this position, Carson was landlocked. Despite my cheer-leading, he did not budge. He could barely hoist his giant head off the mat. He simply lay there, resigned.

The instructor scowled, then went over to the next baby. I picked Carson up and sat him back down on his diapered butt.

At the end of each session, the instructor brought out a rainbow parachute. And all the nannies and stay-at-home moms and token dads formed a circle, each grabbing a handle. Together, we waved the parachute up and down while our babies crawled underneath, transfixed by the billowing movement of the parachute. This was my favourite part of the class, if only because it spelled the end. The end of our collective humiliation, mine and Carson's.

My boy loved that rainbow parachute. What he did not love so much was the circuit. Before long, I came to despise it, too. And I despised the instructor, with her hippie vest that looked like a macramé plant holder. I just knew that she had crocheted it herself. Under her baleful gaze, my cheeks burned. *Please crawl for Mommy*, I urged Carson under my breath. But my baby would not crawl. My baby had no intention of crawling. Hell, he wasn't even shuffling. What was he waiting for? He was almost a year old. Some days it seemed like he would never crawl, let alone walk. He would remain sitting in lotus position for life. Clearly his size was an impediment. That was the visiting nurse's fault. If she hadn't insisted that I put him on the steroid infant formula, we wouldn't be here now.

As the instructor loomed over Carson, I could smell the judgment wafting off her, strong as patchouli. She reeked of it.

⌒

I was a fat baby, too. A Pillsbury Dough-girl. My tummy was squishy and not in a cute way, either. No one poked me there except to point out my "problem area." I was 10, 11 maybe, when I became aware of my body. My mother took me to see the doctor, a tortoise of a man who should have retired long ago. Stripped down to my undershirt and underwear, I stepped on the scale. He slid the bar back and forth, tutting audibly at the numbers he read. Shivering, I then sat on the exam table, which was covered in crinkly paper. The sound made my skin crawl. I hated everything about this room with its hard, cold edges, and I hated this man even more. He placed something metal and freezing on my chest and listened to my heart go *boo-boom boo-boom*.

He pulled the stethoscope out of his ears and wore it like a necklace. He turned toward my mother and started lecturing her about my diet. Because of course it was her fault if I was fat, although he never came out and used that exact word. There were so many others to choose from in the early '80s. *Chunky. Big boned. Stocky. Plump. Stout. Tubby.*

He was right. It was my mother's fault but not for the reasons he might have imagined. For starters, she was too young to be raising me on her own. It was hard enough to make ends meet. And my mom didn't know how to cook. If it came in a box with a powdered sauce, chances are I ate it. Vegetables came from cans—if they came at all. Lima beans were the worst. Soft beetles. I let them grow cold on the plate, then squashed their pale green backs with the back of my fork. Because of all the processed foods I ate, I was often constipated. My mom would buy a litre of prune juice. *Pinch your nose, down the hatch.* So many things made me retch in those days. Slimy egg whites, the gelatinous innards of a tomato. The chalky cream of mushroom soup my babysitter made after school. Soup the colour of rain clouds, the colour of vomit in gutters. The smell of it alone made my eyes water.

The doctor scribbled in his notepad, then tore off a page and handed it to my mom. It was a diet. The old tortoise put me on a diet. I was 10 or 11 years old.

⌣

Not long after his first birthday, Carson started crawling. It was Halloween night. My baby looked adorable in a dinosaur costume so tight it was splitting at the seams. While I was minding my own business, he hoisted himself up on his roly-poly forearms. Then, seemingly against the laws of physics, he propelled his roly-poly body forward. A few months later, he pulled himself up using the coffee table, took a few tentative steps, then let go. I had the sense that I watching a miracle happen in real time. Like I had front row seats to Jesus walking on water. In that momentous moment, nothing else mattered. I saw how ridiculous the past few months had been, all that stress and worry and over what? Over nothing. I saw that I had carted around all those developmental milestones like so many bricks on my back, and it was such a relief to finally set them down. My back was breaking.

My first impulse (because I can be petty and spiteful) was to head straight over to the baby gym. I wanted to grab the instructor by the scruff of her crocheted vest and say, *See, my fat baby is walking! My baby is walking!* But by then the gym had long shuttered, and that infernal space above the supermarket sat vacant.

~

At recess one day, a boy calls you the worst possible name he can think of. *Fatso.* It is the worst possible name you can think of, too. And it hits right where it hurts most: in your soft, squishy paunch. He delivers the slur, then takes off running (to kick a soccer ball or to torment some poor sucker) while you stay rooted to the spot.

On the outside, nothing about you has changed. You look the same as you did a moment ago, but internally there is damage. You have sustained extensive injuries, most notably, to your fragile heart.

In the playground that day, you learn two immutable truths. One: Your mom lied. *Sticks and stones may break my bones, but names will never hurt me.* You believed her, but now you know she was wrong. Words do fucking hurt. Two: What the boy said is factually correct. You are fat. The doctor said as much when he put you on a diet. Your mother is always haranguing you to get on your bike instead of watching TV. When the old British lady across the road offers you a second cookie, you look over at your mom and see her mouth contort into a frown. You watch her watching you, eyeballing everything that crosses the threshold of your lips. *A lifetime on the hips.*

She probably doesn't want to have to answer to the old tortoise. You can't blame her, really.

At recess that day, a boy gives you your first tattoo. The word *fatso*—inscribed in a private, hard-to-reach place where nobody will see it. But you know it is there. And now no amount of scrubbing will make it disappear. Over the years, it will fade, but the faint outline of the word remains visible all through elementary school and it stays with you after you graduate high school and move to another town in another province. You see flashes of it every time you get undressed, in the dark. *Fatso.*

That summer you come home from university and get a job at the local library. Working there, surrounded by books, is your dream job. You would probably do it for free. Every day you wake up and pack the same lunch (a can of Diet Coke and a Golden Delicious apple). You load a mixtape into your Walkman, then walk several miles on an empty stomach to the library's central branch. On your lunch break, you park yourself at the picnic table outside. You eat your apple while reading the Gloria Steinem biography you have borrowed from the library. You see yourself wearing the Playboy Bunny uniform: a satin blue, high cut leotard so tight that your hip bones jut out. After a few weeks your cheekbones and clavicle start to protrude in a way that you find both grotesque and secretly pleasing. But the apple and Diet Coke give you cramps that have you racing to the toilet. Whenever you catch sight of yourself in a mirror over the course of the summer, the changes in your appearance seem shocking and obvious, but no one else notices. Not your best friend, who sometimes snacks on laxatives and honestly has her own disordered eating to contend with. Not your mom. Not even Nan, who never misses an opportunity to call someone out on their shit. Nobody says a word. After a while your gaunt reflection and greenish diarrhea scare you enough to stop your brief affair with anorexia.

Yet over the years that boy's voice stays with you, coming and going like an ex-lover you can never completely get out of your system, no matter how much time has passed or how much you swear you've moved on. *Fatso*. His warm voice is a sweet nothing in your ear. Toxic. Intoxicating. *Fatso. Fatso. Fatso. You're disgusting. You disgust me.*

⁓

Some days, I look over at Carson and I still see his baby self so clearly. I picture him seated in his high chair, stubby fingers forming pincers around a lone blueberry. Back then, eating was an odyssey, a voyage of discovery, and he was a fearless explorer.

When he was old enough, we started taking him to local restaurants. We took him to our favourite Italian where he'd devour an entire bowl of gnocchi. Afterwards he looked so content and satisfied, tomato sauce ringed around his mouth. We were regulars, so the owner made a point of coming over and saying hello. "Someone sure enjoys his food," he'd say with no trace of the sarcasm or judgment I had come to expect from strangers. And I'd nod grateful, a little smug even. At least my kid isn't one of those picky eaters who spurns the choo-choo train or who spits out bites of pulverized peas and broccoli. My kid might have been whiny, but he wasn't a fussy eater. Back then, my Carson ate pretty much anything.

I don't know how we got from there to here. Nowadays I agonize over mealtimes. Sometimes I push too hard, only to capitulate and feed my 13-year-old whatever he will eat. I try reverse psychology. I offer but never coerce. I set the buffet and let Carson choose what he wants. I heed the advice of nutritionists and turn mealtime into a game. I allow him to play with his food—encourage it, even. I become a short-order chef, preparing separate meals for everyone. Then exhausted, I sit down to eat, only to find I've lost my appetite. Resentment brews in my chest like heartburn.

Eat a rainbow, the experts say. These days, like many autistic kids, Carson's diet is best described as beige. His gastronomic world has progressively been stripped of all nutrients and flavour. This devolution saddens me more than I care to admit.

Food is so much more than fuel. It's both ritual and celebration, it's culture, passion, and connection. When my son lifts his fork, I want him to sense the magic and potential I do.

Of course, I didn't always experience food this way. Part of the reason I want to raise my child on fresh fruits and vegetables is because I have the means to do so. An incredible privilege in an age of food scarcity. Buying fresh produce was a luxury my single mom couldn't afford. So, I grew up eating (and loving) all the same ultra-processed foods my son loves, which makes me a hypocrite. Kraft Singles. Macaroni and cheese. Hamburger Helper. Chef Boyardee. Cheez Whiz. Fruit Roll-Ups. Grilled cheese. Peanut butter and jelly on white Betty bread. Hot dogs. And of course, the beloved chicken nugget. These were my staples because we were poor; but I now see they were also my staples because I was autistic. These were the foods I could eat without fear or stress or revulsion. Because of their predictability and consistency, these foods were the emotional equivalent of a comfort blanket.

Like many autists, Carson eats the same foods on rotation until, inevitably, he can no longer stomach them. What looks like picky, fussy, or restrictive eating is often par for the course in autistic populations.[75] Texture, temperature, and spice all play a role in what we will and won't eat, and these preferences vary from one person to the next. Selective eating is not attention-seeking, though it is plenty concerning. Parents like me lose their minds over what our kids will and won't eat. We worry about malnourishment and nutrient deficiencies. Because eating chicken nuggets is one thing, but eating chicken nuggets every single day of the week is another thing altogether.

I was raised at a time when you were expected to clear your plate or die trying. Every mealtime, we were reminded of the "children starving over in Africa" as a means to guilt us into eating whatever was on the menu.

He won't starve. She'll eat when she's hungry. That's what people said when my generation was growing up. Who knows, maybe parents still say it today. But for some kids, that simply isn't true. Many people on the spectrum would sooner starve than eat certain foods. Unlike other eating disorders like anorexia, avoidant/restrictive food intake disorder (ARFID) has nothing to do with body image and everything to do with sensory aversion and food-related trauma. Not everyone with anorexia or ARFID is autistic, but the correlation is high.[76] Some people end up on feeding tubes in the hospital. Carson isn't there, yet. But I wonder when it will come down to that. How few foods does he have to eat before his doctor decides to intervene? Five? Three?

Aidan tells me that his younger brother was a fussy eater when they were growing up. For a period of time he ate nothing but white bread and fries. His doctor wasn't overly concerned. This was 1970s Northern Ireland, after all. They had bigger things to worry about. Now in his middle age, my brother-in-law braves curries hotter than anyone else in the family. This fills me with a strange sense of optimism. Carson will not die. He will survive this, but will I? That's the question. Will my anxiety over his eating habits release its chokehold on me once and for all? And will our family mealtimes ever simply be a time to gather, to break bread together without angst?

I have this recurring dream. A young man enters a restaurant. His hair is dark and slightly unkempt, his jaw slightly stubbled. There is not a trace of baby fat left in his cheeks. I watch him take a seat at a table and tuck his napkin into the collar of his T-shirt in a rehearsed way. An older man comes over. Slightly stooped and silver at the temples, he claps the young man on the back. They obviously know each other.

The younger man doesn't bother consulting the menu. And after a while, the older man returns and sets a dish down on the table. Ribbons of steam rise and swirl from the bowl. Even though I'm dreaming, I swear I can smell the tang of the homemade tomato and basil sauce.

The young man picks up a tablespoon and shovels the hot dumplings into his mouth. He can't seem to get them in there fast enough. Thick red sauce splatters on his stubble and dribbles down his chin. But he keeps eating, oblivious. He keeps eating until the bowl is empty.

Every time I have this dream, I can't help but wake up smiling. I wake up licking my lips.

The perfect curse

It all happens at breakneck speed. A realtor sticks a note in our mailbox saying she has a client interested in buying a house on our private road. I assume it's a scam but reach out to her anyway. Within a matter of days, we accept an offer that is too good to refuse. We are moving—and not just out of our current house but out of the city we've lived in since Carson was a baby. As decisions go, this one is reckless and impulsive, even by my family's standards.

It's the summer of 2020, and our timing couldn't be worse. We are just a few months into a global pandemic, and we have no idea what lies ahead—the sheer scope and magnitude of COVID's devastation. Not knowing is a blessing. It allows us to treat the move as an impromptu adventure, a chance to take stock and reevaluate what's best for our family. We settle on a midsized city nearer to my parents. We visit just once and buy the first property we view: a place on the outskirts of town, with big windows that look out onto the lake.

I have to pinch myself. Everything falls into place so easily, I figure it must be fate. Blinded by possibility, all I see are the pros of this move.

One such advantage is that, for the first time since kindergarten, Carson will attend a regular class at a public school. My baby is going into grade seven, officially a middle schooler. Another pinch-me moment. Also for the first time, he has been allocated a dedicated educational assistant. In all the years we lived in Toronto, despite my pleading, he never received this level of support, which I take as an omen. Following several virtual meetings with staff at the new school, I'm apprehensive yet hopeful—always hopeful. And as usual, I am grossly overprepared, handing over reams of notes and reports. I still believe that information is power, and despite how many times we've been burned at the hands of educators and administrators, I cling to the romantic notion that this new school could be "the One," the educational setting that fits Carson rather than the other way around.

What we cannot possibly foresee is that the entire country will soon dip in and out of mandated lockdowns. Over the next several months, my son's learning environment will shift from the classroom to the dining room table, where he will listen to his teacher pontificate through a computer screen. Flashbacks of my brief stint home-schooling Carson in grade three come flooding back. "School of Mom," we called our voluntary exodus from the educational system. Except this time everyone is doing it; no one has a choice in the matter. Unlike many other parents, though, I am in the fortuitous position of being self-employed and thus not scrambling to find childcare. Aidan sets up an office in the spare room of our new home. Over the past few months my own work has slowed down considerably. Many of my corporate clients are small business owners who've been hit hard by the pandemic and can no longer justify employing a professional copywriter. And anyway, what with planning a major move and organizing Carson's school transition, I don't have the bandwidth to write more than the occasional article for newspapers and magazines.

Ever since I left my position as a staff writer, supporting my son has become my full-time job—a fact that sometimes leaves me feeling resentful and frustrated but mostly leaves me feeling intensely fortunate that we are able to survive on a single income. For the time being, at least. Research has indicated that women with autistic children are more likely to give up work in the first five years after birth.[77] It's patently unfair that so many parents, particularly moms, quit their jobs and abandon careers they've built up over many years to care for their autistic kids. Moms who do work earn substantially less than those with typically developing children.[78] Given the added health care expenses associated with ASD, having a single or reduced income places a significant economic burden on many families.

So, I am a statistic, it seems. Although I was able to work part-time when Carson was a toddler, I ultimately had to give up my job. His frequent meltdowns (and the school's inability to support him) meant I had to be on call every day, available at the drop of a hat to pick him up. And it was understood that I would keep him home when there were assemblies or field trips. My story is all too common. Even the most flexible and understanding employer is unlikely to remain so indefinitely, as I discovered. My parents do what they can to provide us with respite, but they live hours away and have their own commitments. They say it takes a village to support a child, yet many of us with autistic children aren't lucky enough to have a trusted neighbour, let alone a village, at our disposal.

We move in early November. Although it is unseasonably warm, we see few people. Everyone stays tucked away, hibernating and riding out the long winter. The entire world waits with bated breath for an end to this plague, or at least a vaccine. Six months in, our new home scarcely feels like home at all. And yet we are grateful. Our close friends and family are still safe, still healthy. For now.

Under the mandated lockdown, our new town soon transforms into a ghost town. With more restaurants and stores shuttering their doors, businesses clamber to stay afloat. Downtown is dotted with sad, boarded-up shopfronts. The city that once held so much promise now feels like a mirage, a Shangri-la. We can look, but alas we cannot enter any of the places we looked forward to visiting when we decided to move here. We cannot go to the movies. We cannot go to concerts or galleries or, to my 12-year-old's great disappointment, the mall. Anything that seems remotely fun or interesting has been cancelled for the foreseeable future. Since there is little else to do, we go for meandering walks and aimless drives around town. With thousands of people all over the world dying every day, our boredom pales in significance.

Come summer, the restrictions feel less oppressive. We go for hikes and visit outdoor markets and festivals. We sample takeout from various restaurants and eat al fresco. An indoor escape room pivots their business model by moving the experience outdoors. Part whodunnit, part scavenger hunt, an escape room sounds exactly like the sort of thing my Carson might be into. Typically a group activity for friends or colleagues, these "rooms" aren't exactly the mainstay of mother-and-son duos. But with so few options open to us, I decide to give it a shot.

I have no idea what to expect when Carson and I rock up at the escape room headquarters one hot summer afternoon. After greeting us, the hostess tells us there's a plot to murder the owner of a local pizza chain. She needs our help, she says, to crack the case. She hands over a bag filled with props and a pen and paper for notetaking, and insists that I text her after solving each clue. If we guess right, we progress to the next clue. If not, we have to keep on guessing until we get it right. There are a dozen clues in total. Once we find out who plotted to kill "Giuseppe," the fictitious pizza chain owner, we are to report back to HQ.

I am partial to a good mystery. When I was Carson's age, my family used to organize "murder mystery nights." Department stores sold kits that came complete with invitations (mailed out in advance by the host) and detailed character notes for each player. On the night of the "murder," everyone had to arrive at the host's place in full costume. One year, my heavily pregnant aunt showed up with pigtails and pompoms for her part as a cheerleader. Her brother, my uncle, came dressed in scrubs to play the role of a medic. To this day, I have no idea where he got the scrubs—there were no costume stores in my town back then. What was made clear to us kids was that this was an adult game. There was booze involved, obviously, and so much riotous laughter. I burned with envy. When I turned 14, my invitation landed in the mail. I couldn't believe it. Finally. For weeks I prepared for my big break. I was to play Lauren, a nerdy scientist. With a mouthful of metal braces, I was halfway toward the stereotype already. To complete the look, I popped the lenses out of a pair of black-rimmed reading glasses and wore one of my mom's white nursing smocks as a lab coat. With my long brown hair slicked and centre-parted, I was ready.

No one suspected Lauren, and why would they? Everyone was hiding something that night, and my character was no exception. My performance left a lot to be desired. But I never had so much fun as the night I pretended to be someone else—and a killer at that. Everyone knows the killer is always the best part.

⌐

You step out in the blistering July heat. The city is confusing. Not a grid but a labyrinth of old limestone. You would consult Google maps if you were on your own, but there's no need. Your 12-year-old already has all the streets committed to memory, and now leads you to the location of the first clue. Within seconds, he is working through the logistics, and you struggle to keep up. Clearly you are the Watson to his Sherlock, and you are more than content to follow his lead. It is a fun role reversal. You bumble along rather uselessly, notebook in hand, ready to take direction from your son. Carson is in his element. With virtually no input from you, he unscrambles anagrams and spots patterns hidden in the signage of local businesses. Each time you text the answer to the hostess, she gives you the green light to continue, and you move on to the next clue. You have just over an hour to complete all 12 clues and make your way back to headquarters. You are making good time.

By the fifth clue, though, you hit a wall. Carson is stumped. As the minutes elapse, you start to worry about the time you are losing on this one puzzle. You don't say anything to him, though. The last thing you want is to pressure him or add to his anxiety while he is in the zone. You, however, are not in the zone. You are nowhere near the zone. For starters, you forgot to pack a hat, and the sun broils your scalp. If you keep squinting like this, you're bound to end up with a headache. As it stands, you already feel a bit faint. If you hadn't been in such a hurry, you might not have left the water bottle in the car. Stupid. Who forgets water and hats on a humid day? The strap of the bag cuts into your shoulder. Why, in this heat, would the hostess load you down with so many cumbersome props?

You point out a bench and tell your boy you need to sit for a minute. Hordes of tourists and students mill around as you root through the bag for something that might help Carson solve this latest clue. A shirtless man with a long scruffy beard walks by pushing a grocery cart that does not contain groceries. He stares at you with your bag of tricks as though you are the curiosity.

After what feels like an eternity, you crack the fifth clue and manage to move on—or rather, Carson cracks it. You simply text the answer to the hostess. The clues are getting progressively harder; each one takes twice as long to solve as the last. At this rate the likelihood of you finishing on time is slim. Sweat gathers at your temples and the nape of your neck. You feel yourself growing flustered. Escape rooms aren't supposed to be this hard, are they? Or are you just spectacularly bad at this? Your husband should be the here right now, not you. Aidan would be good at this sort of thing, you think, or at least not half as useless as you are. Your inability to solve these puzzles makes you feel incredibly stupid and inept. And that current feeling of stupidity and ineptitude sets off a domino effect of all the other times in your life in which you have felt stupid and inept. Times when you couldn't seem to grasp something basic and obvious that everyone else could grasp. You remember the name they had for you, so long ago . . . Tard.

The escape room was a terrible idea. You can see that now; you won't solve the mystery in time. Your boy will be devastated, and he'll be right to blame you.

As your thoughts continue to free fall, you say nothing to Carson. You are determined to save face, even if that means faking it for his sake. But the fact remains, you are a terrible actor giving a terrible performance.

By now, your son's enthusiasm is starting to wane. When you break the bad news that you need to head back to headquarters, he doesn't protest. Unlike you, he seems resigned to take the defeat in his stride. To your astonishment, he doesn't cry or whine or scream. This is new. He has exploded over lesser disappointments. He's tired, and the heat is probably getting to him, too. You only wish you shared his equanimity.

As you retrace your steps to the escape room HQ, you try to regain some composure and perspective. *It's just a game*, you tell yourself, the way grown ups told you so many times when you were little. You always were such a sore loser. Not much has changed. Rage comes to a rolling boil inside you. You cannot hope to cool these thoughts. *Jesus, grow up. Get a grip.*

Once indoors you hand over the bag of props. You smile and thank the hostess while clenching your jaw and fists. You tell her you had fun, even though you didn't manage to solve the puzzle on time. Your words sound hollow, even to you. You truly are the worst actor.

In the car, Carson is unusually quiet. You pass him the water. He gulps down half the bottle. You crank up the air conditioning as high as it will go and drive home in silence. When you get there, you head straight for your bedroom. Aidan calls after you from his office, asking how the afternoon went. But you carry on into the master bedroom without answering. By the time he finds you, you are curled on the floor of the walk-in closet, rocking and sobbing uncontrollably.

Clearly taken aback, Aidan pauses in the doorway. He's never seen you like this before. You've never seen you like this before, for that matter. He has seen you cry many times throughout your long marriage. He has seen you distressed and upset before, but not like this. Never like this.

Crouching next to you, he rests a delicate hand on your shoulder. But you wrench yourself away. You hate yourself for rejecting him, but you can't help it. Unable to speak, you moan and bury your head between your knees. You pant and whimper like a wounded animal.

You have been together for over 20 years now. Aidan has seen you at your worst. Or what you thought was your worst. He has held back your hair while you puked your guts out during so many migraine attacks. The night before your wedding, you threw up seven times. That was a record, even for you. Eight years later, he watched you birth a baby boy in a pool of shit and mucous and blood. Watched you split yourself open.

But this, this is new territory—this rocking and crying so hard that your body convulses. And though he looks alarmed, Aidan gives you space and leaves you in the closet. You wish so much that he didn't have to see you like this. But rather him than your boy. You never want Carson to see you like this.

You don't want him to see you coming apart at the seams. That's how it feels. Like your row of careful stitches is finally unravelling. You don't know how you will begin to mend the damage, or if it's even mendable.

⌒

When the dust settles, my outburst seems absurd. And that absurdity makes me feel embarrassed and ashamed. Failing to escape an escape room is no big deal. Objectively I know this. But objectivity plays no part in in it. Both meltdowns and shutdowns are expressions of autistic overwhelm, although they manifest in different ways. Where a meltdown is an external reaction, a shutdown is more internalized. Meltdowns are often highly visible and even physical (crying, screaming, kicking, spitting, etc.). Shutdowns can look like withdrawal or non-responsiveness.[19] Carson tends to have meltdowns while I usually experience shutdowns. He explodes, while I implode.

Although shutdowns and meltdowns aren't exactly pleasurable, they are perfectly normal autistic behaviours. They are an innate stress response—not wilful acts of disobedience or manipulation. Everybody has different triggers. What sets off one person may not set off another. Sources of autistic overwhelm tend to be be cumulative and imperceptible to onlookers. Parents and teachers are often mystified, claiming a child's meltdown "came out of nowhere," but that's seldom the case. It has just been building up and gathering momentum internally.

For many of us, sensory overload is a major culprit. The culmination of the bag of props, the July heat beating down . . . Being thirsty or tired. Confusing social situations, unexpected events or changes in routine, too many demands, and too much stimulation are all recipes for disaster. Like many autists, I need more rest and recovery time than the average person to avoid burnout and autistic overwhelm. The "spoon theory," a popular analogy for people with chronic illness, also rings true for people on the spectrum. The idea is that everyone starts the day with a certain number of "spoons," which get used throughout the day on various activities.[80] Once the spoons are gone, they are gone. There are no more in the drawer to replace them. Since autistic people tend to have fewer spoons readily available in a given day, or use more spoons than neurotypicals for things like communicating and socializing, we need to be mindful about how we use these spoons throughout the day to avoid running out.

Nowadays, I am learning to be judicious with how I use my allocated number of "spoons." I cannot accomplish as much as the next person, so I must pace myself if I am to avoid running out of spoons (and risk experiencing a meltdown, shutdown, or burnout).

One of my biggest triggers is perfectionism. The need to succeed at all costs—even at something as trivial as an escape room—is debilitating. As an only child, I was perceived as spoiled and picky. Everything had to be *just so*. If I didn't have everything my own way, I fell apart. What looked like a compulsive need for control was nothing more than crippling anxiety.

When I was young, I had no awareness of these patterns or triggers and therefore no means to mitigate them. No one knew about autism in girls. My mother certainly didn't. Anxiety doesn't distinguish between an event you are looking forward to and one you are dreading. The start of every school year. Every birthday, every Christmas. The build-up started off slow: snow angels at dusk, the promise of Santa sneaking in after midnight. I loved Christmas—I probably loved it too much for my own good. And it was never just about the toys, although somehow my single mom always managed to put plenty under the tree. Our family was close then. We genuinely looked forward to being together. For such a small group, we were gregarious. Some years we cruised around the neighbourhood looking at the festive lights. Another year we huddled together on a wagon ride in subzero temperatures, belting out carols and getting half the words wrong. It was all part of our charm. Year after year, my nan pulled off a Dickensian miracle: a large bird with all the trimmings. I'm still not sure how she put together a feast on a shoestring budget. I remember those Christmases with affection, even those that ended in disaster. Like the year the television caught fire, thanks to an unattended candle sitting on a beaded doily on top of Nan's TV. (Those being the days of unattended candles, plastic doilies, and floor-model televisions.) Fortunately, no one got hurt, but the beaded doily couldn't be saved.

The only predictable thing about Christmas was my sickness. As soon as we arrived at Nan's, it would start. The throbbing on one side of my skull that made me dizzy, then nauseous. By the time everyone gathered around the table to eat, I was in bed in a darkened guest room. In no time at all, the throbbing gave way to a stabbing pain that fractured my vision. Greasy smell of turkey wafted into the room. Loud voices punctuated with bursts of laughter. Every sound a serrated edge in my brain. The faraway sound of my family having fun without me.

I lay writhing in bed, it seemed that I had landed from outer space. If you sliced open my veins, instead of red, the blood would run green, like the Visitors in the 1980s miniseries *V*. Back then,

I assumed this sense of disconnectedness, of *otherness*, came from not knowing my father. A part of me was missing, would always be missing. Maybe I was more like him and his side of the family than my mom's. I would never know, having never met any of them. For 44 years, I carried around this alien feeling until I finally learned its name: autism. Who knows, maybe my father is an alien, too. Maybe autism runs in his blood as surely as it runs in mine.

At some point the door would crack open. A shaft of light burning my retinas. My mom would appear, a shadowy Florence Nightingale figure at my side. Without a word, she would place a cool cloth on my forehead and a wastebasket by the bed in case I threw up (I often did). Then the door would shut behind her, and I was left alone in the dark all over again.

Sometimes, once the worst of the migraine has subsided—and I am left with a dull headache—I join the party. Having missed out on the turkey and the cranberries and the pumpkin pie, I join my cousin in front of the Christmas tree and wait to open our identical presents. Jess's hair is done up and she's wearing a new dress. In every photo from that time, there are dark, purplish circles under my eyes, and I'm wearing pyjamas instead of the pretty outfit I arrived in.

⌣

Perfectionism is not an autistic trait. However, many of us exhibit perfectionist tendencies.[81] Our attention to detail, combined with black-and-white thinking and cognitive inflexibility, can make us intolerant of mistakes and imperfections. Anxiety, always, is a factor.

When he was younger, Carson often fixated on the parts of a toy or game. If a piece had even the slightest manufacturing defect, he became distraught, insisting we throw the whole thing in the garbage. I can't count the number of times I rescued and hid various plastic or wooden components to avoid sending them to landfill.

Since he found it hard to use scissors, he would ask us to cut letters out of felt or construction paper for him. If any of the letters weren't perfect, he panicked, demanding we redo them.

Suffice to say, the apple doesn't fall far. It kills me to hear my son declare that he's stupid when he cannot master something that others can. Such times I remind him of all the things that come easily to him that stymie others. I remind him that he is the smartest person I know. This is not the ego-stroking of a parent besotted with her child. It's the absolute truth. And yet it doesn't help him any more than it helped me.

After almost every test and exam I sat in high school, I came home bawling and hyperventilating, convinced that I had "bombed" and would now certainly fail the class. (My definition of *bombed* being anything less than an A.) My mom or grandmother reassured me and picked up the pieces. Until the next time. The funny thing is, I never failed or even came close. And the pressure never came from my parents or teachers; it was all me. Knowing I was different, and that I struggled in ways that others did not, only made me push harder. I pushed and pushed, until inevitably all the pushing made me ill.

In elementary school I had real trouble learning to tell time. After a while all the other kids could read the big clock face in the classroom. I could not tell one hand from another or what intervals they signified. I was so ashamed, for a long time I lived in fear that I would be found out and ridiculed. Fractions were another source of anguish. No matter how hard I tried, I could not make sense of numerators and denominators. By high school, math was the most exquisite torture. If I couldn't solve an equation, I quickly grew flummoxed. With each failed attempt, my heart hammered. And my thoughts spiralled. Dumb, I was so fucking dumb and would never understand numbers. In a fury, I tore pages from my notebook and hurled my textbook at the wall. My anger was hot and exhilarating. But it didn't help me solve anything. Dyscalculia is a learning disability that affects a person's ability to understand math and number-based information.[82] If dyscalculia existed then, no one around me knew its name.

Every year, I made the honour roll, finishing near the top of my class. Come graduation, I won several bursaries and a scholarship to the university of my choice. By all appearances, I was a model student; no one knew that I was perpetually on the verge of dropping out of post-secondary. Every weekend, I begged my parents to pick me up. Every few days, I called up my nan in hysterics. "I can't do it," I'd tell her over and over. My grandmother would spend hours on the phone talking me off the ledge, only to do it all over again a week later. She might have recorded her pep talk to save herself the time. *Why is everything so much harder for me*, I wondered. I had no inkling that I was disabled, of course. I had no idea how to ask for the help I needed, assuming it was even available in the '90s.

One evening after a writing workshop, my professor pulled me aside and regarded me with an expression somewhere between pitying and patronizing. The worst. He was in his 40s, I guess, with a smattering of acne scars and an arrogance that took up the entire room. I wasn't doing great in his class. This was not news to either of us. Once the big fish in a small pond, I had suddenly found myself floundering in an ocean of sharks and whales. *What am I even doing here*, I wondered. I blamed my high school English teachers and Alien Woman for giving me false hope, letting me believe I had the chops to be in this program.

Surely if I just worked harder, I could improve. I may never be a writer, but at this rate I would settle for decent above mediocre. I asked him what I had to become a better writer.

The prof sat with his elbows planted on the desk. He leaned forward. So, I leaned forward too, certain that he was about to drop some great bomb of wisdom.

"Read Alice Munro," the professor said with his trademark smirk.

I sat back in my chair. *That's it?* I wondered. Don't get me wrong, Munro was one of the greats. A master of her craft. Still, as far as advice went, my prof's recommendation seemed a bit facile. Like saying to a budding filmmaker, "Go watch some Kubrick."

I left his office in a daze, utterly convinced of my own inadequacy. I had worked so hard to get here. Shitty retail jobs every summer from the time I was 14. Why did it never occur to me to question the man's credentials? What had he ever published, anyway, besides a feature once, in *Rolling Stone* magazine? He was no Alice fucking Munro.

Perfectionism is not the problem *per se*. The pursuit has resulted in some of the most creative and innovative works the world has seen. As with anything, it's a question of degree. If left unchecked, the quest for perfection can turn maladaptive, leading to physical symptoms such as panic attacks and ulcers and migraines, as well as mental ailments like malaise and antipathy and inertia. Someone (the smug-faced professor?) once likened writing workshops to being stripped naked in a roomful of strangers and pummelled with a baseball bat. No wonder I have stormed out of such rooms, unable to breathe much less write a single sentence.

These days, I am a staunch believer in art for art's sake. I understand that all art is subjective, and that all art has inherent value not determined by its price tag. I am nothing if not a grifter. I know that any draft (even this one) is never truly complete, only abandoned.

Now that I'm the proud owner of a cell phone with a built-in calculator, I tend not to rip pages from books or hurl them across the room anymore. Still, old habits die hard. The embers of self-loathing are still there, waiting to be stoked. No awards or accolades are enough to silence the voice inside my head—a voice that sounds suspiciously like the smug-faced professor. *You are not good enough. You will never be good enough.* Maybe so. Since that's the case, I might as well get on with it and quit being so precious.

When he sees me getting agitated one day, my 12-year-old pipes up and says, "Remember, Mom, the only thing in the world that's perfect is the word *perfect*."

I am floored. It's something I must have said to Carson years ago, and here it comes boomeranging back. Out of the mouth of babes.

The only thing that's perfect is the word perfect. I consider scribbling it on a yellow Post-it note and sticking it all over the house. A mantra for the ages. A mantra for mama. If I repeat it often enough, one day I might even come to believe it.

Loving the alien

"Mom, I need to tell you something."

One minute, my 13-year-old son is sitting at the dining table drawing. The next, he is staring expectantly at me. One minute, it's an ordinary Sunday afternoon. The next, it is not.

I stop whatever my hands are independently doing in the kitchen—emptying the dishwasher, cleaning the coffee filter—and look over at him.

"Promise you won't be upset?" he says.

I bite my lip. *How can any parent make such a blind promise?* I nod anyway.

Then Carson says, "I'm non-binary."

For a long time, I do not speak. Not because I disapprove exactly, but because this term, non-binary, has me somewhat perplexed. It calls to mind computers, strings of code. It belongs to Silicon Valley, not to a young teen in Canada. But then, the fact that I find myself in a world that is fast becoming unrecognizable and bewildering, must mean that I am officially old and past it. It has always been this way, and thus it will always be. If I am not careful, the gulf between my generation (X) and my child's (Z) will swallow me whole.

To buy time while I consider my response, I skirt around the table and glance over Carson's shoulder. It must be discreet, or else he will rush to cover it up. Where he used to race to show me his drawings, everything he works on now is cloaked in secrecy. Self-consciousness is the order of the day. *Ah*, I think, *puberty*. His script is elegant and formal-looking, hankering back to a bygone era when the artistry of such penmanship held value. Now the only time you see this kind of calligraphy is on wedding invitations. It's staggering how far my son has come from the days of chicken scratches on the page, the days when he could barely hold a pencil, let alone craft such beautiful scripts. Years of obsessively printing out the alphabet in various fonts have paid off.

"Are you sure you're not upset?" he asks.

It takes me a minute to remember what he's talking about. I shake my head. "No, I'm not upset," I offer. "A bit confused, maybe, but not upset."

Appeased, Carson goes back to his fancy letters.

The more I think about his declaration, the less surprised I am by it. The clues were there, after all, sprinkled across the years. There are always clues. Like the time we went to the bookstore. And Carson, who would have been around six at the time, asked me to read him a board book. The fact that he asked stands out in my mind because he was able to read fluently by then. He didn't need my help.

Still, I scooched over on the bench in the children's section, relishing the closeness of his little body squeezed in beside me. When I glanced down at the book he thrust into my hands, I could hardly believe it.

They say everything comes full circle. But seeing this throw-back from my own childhood floored me. *Strawberry Shortcake*. At Carson's age, Jess and I had been obsessed. I owned the books, a bedspread, several dolls. Each doll had brightly coloured hair that smelled of a particular fruit. Lemon Meringue, Orange Blossom, Huckleberry Pie, Plum Pudding . . . The blue one (Blueberry Muffin) was my favourite. I would bury my nose in her hair and inhale the synthetic berry smell. Bliss.

I cleared my throat, and as I began to read about Cherry Jam, a new character in Berry Bitty City, Carson snuggled into me. Instead of lapping up this moment of intimacy with my boy, I found myself distracted. Of all books, why did he pick one about Strawberry Shortcake, with its pink and glittery cover? Why not one about Thomas the Tank Engine or Spiderman instead? It was 2014—what did I care which kind of books and toys my child gravitated toward?

Aside from Strawberry Shortcake, when I was his age my own interests rarely adhered to gender norms. I watched *Dungeons & Dragons* and *The A-Team*. I watched *He-Man and the Masters of the Universe* just as often as *She-Ra and the Princesses of Power*. One minute I played with Transformers and G.I. Joe action figures, Cabbage Patch and Barbie dolls the next. I wore pants one day, and a dress another. My gender was never in question, never *questioned*.

Well, other than the time we stopped off at a tourist office one summer on our way to a campsite. My hair was cut very short. I'm not sure whether this was my mom's choice or my own doing. The woman at the desk was telling my mom about some nearby attraction (maybe a waterslide), adding that "your son will like it." I looked at my mom. She didn't bother to correct the woman, just smiled and took the pamphlet from her knowing we would never see her again. I was devastated. There was no question that I was a girl, even if I didn't look like one.

Carson was only six. What did it matter? In an ideal world, he should be free to like what he likes. Yet I knew the world we occupied was far from ideal. I wanted him to be true to himself, but if I was honest, what I wanted above all was to keep him safe.

Growing up, I was afraid of so many things. The theme songs from *The Twilight Zone* and *Doctor Who*. Spiders. Sharks. And of course, bears. The dark. Being left alone. The cold storage room in the house we moved into with Mitch. A tiny room in the basement with no light switch, just a string to a bare lightbulb. I dreaded when Mitch or my mom asked me to bring a can from the cellar. Reaching blindly into that cold dark space filled me with terror.

Now that I am older, different things scare me. I would still not be a fan of that cold storage room. Yet now that I am a parent, the things that really frighten me most are not found in basements or in closets. What scares me most are other people. Other children, teachers, parents, politicians . . .

Autistic people face an increased risk of being bullied and victimized.[83] Those who are non-binary or gender non-conforming are further marginalized—experiencing poorer physical and mental health, less access to health care, and a greater likelihood of sexual assault, sexual harassment, and verbal harassment compared with the general population. Even greater than non-autistic non-binary people.[84]

When Carson didn't ask me to buy the Strawberry Shortcake book that day, I breathed a sigh of relief. Sensing a bullet dodged. Immediately I felt guilty. It wasn't fair. I wanted him to have every freedom to be fully, utterly himself. At the same time, I was terrified of what might happen if he was. As an autistic person, he was already vulnerable. And if he expressed his gender in a way that fell outside of norms, he would be at an even greater risk of harm. As his parent, how would I protect him?

I need not have worried in those early years. He never showed an interest in playing with dolls or wearing dresses. He forgot all about Strawberry Shortcake and Cherry Jam. He moved on. So, for a while, I did too.

⌒

From that day forward, Carson's non-binary status becomes official. He insists that you stop referring to him as *him* and use *they* and *them* pronouns instead. In the weeks that follow, your teen polices your language at every turn, jumping to correct you and Aidan every time you slip up (which is often).

"He needs to brush his teeth."

"*They!*"

"I'm just waiting for him to get ready so we can leave."

"*Them!*"

The pronoun game quickly turns exasperating. You want to show your support, yet the constant corrections get on your nerves. You try, you really do. However, one day you call your *son*. The next, you can't. Making syntactical switches are hard when you've been on autopilot for 13 years. At the same time, you know you must get with the times, otherwise you risk being left behind.

"What makes you think you aren't a boy?" you ask Carson on the drive home from school one day. The question is not an accusation but one borne out of genuine curiosity.

Your best conversations always happen in the car. Perhaps that's the case with all teenagers, especially those who happen to be autistic. While you are driving, neither one of you has to make eye contact. That's the beauty of it. You are both free to look ahead or out the window and focus on what the other person is saying. For many people on the spectrum, eye contact can be uncomfortable, even painful.[85] Dogs have the right idea. If you stare at a dog directly, they feel threatened and may even bite you. In your case, eye contact is only an issue with people you don't know well. In other words: most people. Looking someone in the eye feels too intense, too intimate, and in many cases, it makes listening almost impossible. Plus, you never know how much eye contact is the right amount of eye contact. If you pass someone on the street, say, you might try to catch their eye. You smile and try to arrange your features a certain way to look friendly and kind. Instead, you end up smiling too hard or staring too long and wind up looking menacing and slightly deranged.

Suddenly contemplative, your kid stares out at the passing scenery, processing your words. Both of you love this route from school. The detour adds time to your journey. You don't mind, though, because you drive through open fields. There is a farm with a pond, and sometimes if you are lucky, you spot a few goats.

"I don't want to be a boy," Carson says at last, "because boys are bad, and girls are good."

"Well," you say, taken aback. This is not quite the answer you were expecting. "That's a pretty big stereotype. Not all men are bad and not all women are good, you know."

"Yeah," Carson says, "but more men are bad compared to women. Men fight and start wars. There's Putin and Trump and—"

"—there's also Margaret Thatcher," you interject, signalling onto your street. "There are good and bad people everywhere, Car. It has nothing to do with someone's gender. I think you'll find that what corrupts people, more often than not, is power."

Your teen considers this for a moment, then says, "Okay, but men are still worse."

To which you can only sigh.

Not long after this conversation in the car, Carson tells me they've decided to grow out their hair because "short hair makes me look like a boy." In between penis and fart jokes, they continue to insist, "I am not a boy." I take great pains to remind Carson that girls can have short hair and boys can have long hair. That hair itself is not a gendered issue. *Remember the '60s? Remember The Beatles?* My arguments fall on deaf ears.

All this talk of gender gets me thinking. Where do I land on this continuum? It's something I've never really considered in my 40-odd years on the planet. Androgyny has long been my sweet spot, my comfort zone. Though I've never been butch, I'm not exactly feminine, either. I am a woman—without the usual trappings of womanhood. And what are those trappings, if not more stereotypes? The fact that I'm deathly allergic to fashion. Nothing remotely delicate, lacy, frilly, or floral exists in my wardrobe. Nothing pink crosses my threshold. My bras and underwear are utilitarian affairs. Throughout my adult life, I have consciously boycotted dresses, heels, and jewellery—a decision partly informed by my sensory preferences but also because those items feel foreign to me. They don't feel like *me*.

Carson doesn't wear frilly things, either. However, they have taken to wearing the same hot-pink sweater to school several days a week. We can't wash it often enough. So far there is no fallout over the pink sweater at school, but I remain apprehensive.

Every day I make a concerted effort to use the new pronouns to show that I'm on board, even if doing so makes my head hurt and my ears bleed. Using the plural to denote the singular defies every grammatical convention I've been taught. Though it may never feel instinctive to me, I am aware that far from being static, the English language is constantly evolving. Every year, new words fall in and out of vogue. Vernacular changes, and pedants like me must grudgingly take stock. I figure if it's good enough for the *Oxford Dictionary*, it's good enough for me.

If Aidan and I struggle to get Carson's pronouns right, then my parents prove even more hapless. This brave new gender world confounds them both. My mom gets the semantics all jumbled. "What is *They* doing?" or "How is *Person* today?" I roll my eyes. If she wasn't my mother, I'd swear she was doing it to rile Carson. My stepdad is having none of it. Whenever my teen corrects him, Mitch simply throws up his hands in despair and resignation. My parents cannot wrap their heads around the possibility that there are other ways of being. It's as much a stretch as believing in alien life forms.

Unlike my Baby Boomer parents, I recognize that gender fluidity is not a new construct. Gender expression (much like autism itself) has long been a spectrum. Research indicates that autists are more likely to be gender diverse.[86] In fact, the more autistic traits a person exhibits, the more likely they are to experience gender dysphoria and gender non-conformity.[87] Why is this? Science has yet to provide us with a clear explanation for why we are the way we are. The answer, at least partly, surely lies in our neurology. As children, autists are slower to formulate a consistent gender identity.[88] Since we are less aware of social norms, it stands to reason that we are less influenced and shaped by them. Where gender norms are concerned, we march to the beat of our own drummer.

We autists are ahead of the curve, it seems. And speaking of ahead of the curve, maybe David Bowie was right. Maybe the binaries that matter aren't male or female, *his* or *hers*—not neurotypical and neurodivergent, even—but human and nonhuman. Maybe in the future there will be no labels or nomenclature of any kind. Maybe it will be enough for us to simply exist as one more species in the animal kingdom—no more and no less important than the next.

But as a species, we are not there yet. Not even close.

In the meantime, I must remain vigilant for my child's safety and well-being, even as one risks negating the other. A year from now, having chosen to spend their weekly allowance on makeup instead of candy, Carson will go to high school wearing thick, coral-coloured eyeshadow, and I won't have the heart to tell them their chosen shade is garish and deeply unflattering.

The teen years are a time rife with experimentation, as I know all too well. My own bids at self-expression (goth-black lipstick, combat boots) were hardly pretty. It's a process. No one needs to be judged or ridiculed while they try to figure out who they are.

I tell myself, Just because you don't understand something doesn't make it wrong. Despite my reminders to stay open-minded, I worry about how others will react to Carson's new look and how that reaction will affect my child. I'm a mom first and foremost. Still, I keep my worries to myself. For now it is enough to provide a tutorial on how to apply eyeshadow so as not to wind up looking like Tim Curry in *The Rocky Horror Picture Show*.

Over the coming months, the pronoun shift becomes progressively easier. Saying "my child," in lieu of "my son," may never be second nature. At least I'm trying. I want Carson to know that acceptance goes beyond lip service. It's my way of saying, *I see you and I love you no matter who you are, what you wear, or what you call yourself. I love you even when I don't understand you. I love you no matter what.* This, I tell them, is the textbook definition of unconditional love.

Carson looks thoughtful for a moment, then says, "All parents should love their kids this way."

"You're right," I say, nodding. "They absolutely should." Who is this wise young person? This changeling . . .

It's how we should love ourselves, too, I think as I undress in my room later that night. Climbing into bed (with my socks on, always), I try to untangle the day's events and make sense of my earlier conversation with Carson. One of several in as many weeks.

Loving my child and loving my husband, these are the easy things. Learning to love myself—that's not so simple. You'd think that I would have figured it out by now. That I am worthy of what I dole out so freely to others. But you'd be wrong. Showing myself the same love and compassion still does not come naturally. I'm working on it, though. I am nothing if not a work-in-progress. Why does accepting myself after all this time feel like such a radical act?

At 44, it feels as though I am just getting to know my true self— not one of the many iterations I used to present to the world. Since my autism diagnosis, I have been gradually peeling back the gossamer layers, to get at some essential core.

Now and then a memory reveals itself. Before Mitch came on the scene, my mom and I sometimes went to mass in a different part of town. That church seemed vast, maybe more so on account of my smallness. And I remember being awed by the exquisite beauty of the stained glass. The deep blue of the Virgin's robe, the cherry red of Jesus's open wounds. I remember vaulted ceilings, how the music rose and swelled in the space high above our heads. Like heaven itself. There was no organ, no majestic choir, just two vocalists harmonizing along to an acoustic guitar. The air rushed through my lungs, and I imagined it was the Holy Spirit itself inhabiting me. I was only a girl but as I sang the words, "The Lord is my shepherd, I shall not want," I felt so much, tears sprang to my eyes.

One Sunday while I sang along, an older woman in a kerchief sitting a few pews ahead spun around. She shot me a withering look. It was a look meant to silence me, to put me in my place. At that moment, I suddenly became aware of my voice. Was I too loud, too brash? Was I singing off-key? Probably. (I don't possess what Leonard Cohen called the "gift of a golden voice.")

Suddenly I was Eve in the Garden, self-conscious and deeply ashamed. That Sunday I learned there was something different about me, something *other* that people didn't like. I had to learn to make myself small, to rein myself in.

I never sang out loud in church again.

All these years later I wonder why it never occurred to me to second-guess the older woman. What kind of person belittles a young girl like that? Why is it always the autistic person who must contort themselves and distort who they are just to take up space in this world? And, furthermore, why is the world still grossly intolerant of other ways of being? What are we so afraid of?

Now I wonder where she went, that girl who sang her heart out at church, the one who dressed in kooky clothes and danced with wild abandon around the duplex apartment. I need to find her and tell her it's okay. She can come out now. She no longer has to hide or worry about what people will say. I want her to know that I will stand up for her. I will have her back no matter what happens. I owe it to her.

Acknowledgements

To my editor, Jen Sookfong Lee, for plucking me out of the slush, drying me off, and making me shine. Thank you for taking a chance on me and believing in this project. You are the best book doula a girl could ask for. Let's do it again sometime?

To the entire team at ECW. Thank you for making the sailing incredibly smooth for this anxious traveller. You guys rock!

To Ann Douglas and Misty Pratt for graciously propping me up. Writers need other writers. Thanks for making space at the table and for passing the potatoes!

To the friends and family who have stuck by me. Thank you for making this lone wolf realize she needs a pack. I'm glad you're mine.

To my parents for your steadfast love and for humouring my crazy notion to be a writer.

To my Irish Londoner. Stepping on your foot was the happiest accident of my life. Thanks for being my #1 crush and my #1 fan.

None of this would be possible without your unwavering faith and ardent cheerleading.

To my baby Magoo. Thanks for making me a mother and a better human. Every day that I get to watch you grow is a tremendous privilege. I'm so lucky to grow alongside you.

Author's notes

Parts of this memoir have appeared in different forms in the following publications:

- "I'm a Woman Who Was Diagnosed with Autism at 44," *HuffPost Personal*, August 25, 2021.
- "More Than Picky Eating: Understanding ARFID," *Healthline*, May 10, 2022.
- "One Toe in the Pink Pool," *The Globe and Mail*, March 31, 2015.
- "The Beatles Helped Bring Me Closer to My Autistic Son," *The Globe and Mail*, January 2, 2019.
- "The Day My Autistic Son Wandered from School," *The Washington Post*, July 1, 2019.
- "Why Being Gifted Isn't Always a Gift," *Today's Parent*, September 14, 2020.

Autism research is (thankfully) a continually evolving field. The birthing of a book, on the other hand, is a long, protracted process—much longer in fact than the birthing of a human baby! At the time of writing, I sought the most current and relevant sources to provide context to my experiences. Please note that as new data emerges, information throughout the book may naturally become dated.

Recommended further reading

Ashburn, Meghan, and Jules Edwards. *I Will Die on This Hill: Autistic Adults, Autism Parents, and the Children Who Deserve a Better World*. London: Jessica Kingsley Publishers, 2023.

Asta, Catherine. *Rediscovered: A Compassionate and Courageous Guide for Late Discovered Autistic Women (and Their Allies)*. London: Jessica Kingsley Publishers, 2025.

Bastow, Clem. *Late Bloomer: How an Autism Diagnosis Changed My Life*. Melbourne: Hardie Grant Books, 2021.

Brady, Fern. *Strong Female Character*. New York: Harmony, an imprint of Penguin Random House, 2023.

Douglas, Ann. *Parenting Through the Storm: How to Handle the Highs, the Lows and Everything in Between*. New York: HarperCollins, 2015.

Garcia, Eric. *We're Not Broken: Changing the Autism Conversation*. New York: Harvest, an imprint of HarperCollins Publishers, 2022.

Garvey, Niamh. *Looking After Your Autistic Self: A Personalised Self-Care Approach to Managing Your Sensory and Emotional Well-Being*. London: Jessica Kingsley Publishers, 2023.

Greene, Ross W. *The Explosive Child: A New Approach for Understanding and Parenting Easily Frustrated, Chronically Inflexible Children*. 6th ed. New York: HarperCollins Publishers, 2021.

Hendrickx, Sarah, and Jess Hendrickx. *Women and Girls on the Autism Spectrum: Understanding Life Experiences from Early Childhood to Old Age*. 2nd ed. London: Jessica Kingsley Publishers, 2024.

James, Laura. *Odd Girl Out: An Autistic Woman in a Neurotypical World*. London: Bluebird, an imprint of Pan Macmillan, 2018.

Jurkevythz, Renata, Maura Campbell, and Lisa Morgan. *Spectrum Women: Autism and Parenting*. London: Jessica Kingsley Publishers, 2020.

Katy, Emily. *Girl Unmasked: How Uncovering My Autism Saved My Life*. London: Monoray, an imprint of Octopus Publishing Group, 2024.

Kurchak, Sarah. *I Overcame My Autism and All I Got Was This Lousy Anxiety Disorder: A Memoir*. Vancouver: Douglas and McIntyre, 2020.

Layle, Paige. *But Everyone Feels This Way: How an Autism Diagnosis Saved My Life*. New York: Balance, an imprint of Grand Central Publishing, 2024.

May, Katherine. *The Electricity of Every Living Thing: A Woman's Walk in the Wild to Find Her Way Home*. New York: Melville House, 2021.

Nerenberg, Jenara. *Divergent Mind: Thriving in a World That Wasn't Designed for You*. San Francisco: HarperOne, 2021.

Price, Devon. *Unmasking Autism: The Power of Embracing Our Hidden Neurodiversity*. New York: Harmony, an imprint of Penguin Random House, 2022.

Prizant, Barry M., and Tom Fields-Meyer. *Uniquely Human: A Different Way of Seeing Autism*. Rev. ed. New York: Simon & Schuster, 2022.

Reber, Deborah. *Differently Wired: A Parent's Guide to Raising an Atypical Child with Confidence and Hope*. New York: Workman Publishing Company, 2020.

Silberman, Steve. *NeuroTribes: The Legacy of Autism and the Future of Neurodiversity*. New York: Avery, an imprint of Penguin Random House, 2015.

Toeps, Bianca. *But You Don't Look Autistic at All*. Translated by Fay MacCorquodale-Smith. Holland: Toeps Media, 2020.

Törnvall, Clara. *The Autists: Women on the Spectrum*. Translated by Alice E. Olsson. Melbourne: Scribe Publications, 2023.

Notes

LIKE SON, LIKE MOTHER: A PROLOGUE

1. James Harris, "Leo Kanner and Autism: A 75-Year Perspective," *International Review of Psychiatry* 30, no. 1 (2018): 3–17, doi.org /10.1080/09540261.2018.1455646.
2. Erin Digitale, "Study Finds Differences Between Brains of Girls, Boys with Autism," Stanford Medicine, February 17, 2022, med.stanford.edu/news/all-news/2022/02/autism-brain-sex -differences.html.
3. Beth Arky, "Why Many Autistic Girls Are Overlooked," Child Mind Institute, last updated October 31, 2024, childmind.org /article/autistic-girls-overlooked-undiagnosed-autism/.
4. Jonathan S. Beck, Rebecca A. Lundwall, Terisa Gabrielsen, Jonathan C. Cox, and Mikle South, "Looking Good But Feeling Bad: 'Camouflaging' Behaviors and Mental Health in

Women with Autistic Traits," *Autism* 24, no. 4 (May 2020): 809–21, doi.org/10.1177/1362361320912147.

5. Claire Sissons, "What to Know about Autism in Girls," *Medical News Today*, last updated November 26, 2024, medicalnewstoday .com/articles/325574.

6. Sissons, "What to Know about Autism in Girls."

7. Digitale, "Study Finds Differences."

8. Joanna Moorhead, "'A Lot Fell into Place': The Adults Who Discovered They Were Autistic—After Their Child Was Diagnosed," *The Guardian*, December 16, 2021, theguardian.com /society/2021/dec/16/adults-discovered-autistic-child -diagnosed-autism.

9. Associated Press, "Autism Now More Common in Black, Latino Children Than White in the U.S.," *NBC News*, March 24, 2023, nbcnews.com/news/latino/autism-now-common-black -latino-children-white-us-rcna76518.

DARK SIDE OF THE MOM

10. "Colic," Mayo Clinic, April 5, 2022, mayoclinic.org/diseases -conditions/colic/symptoms-causes/syc-20371074.

11. Özlem Bağ, Sevay Alşen Güney, Nagihan Cevher Binici, Tuba Tuncel, Aslıhan Şahin, Emel Berksoy, and Çiğdem Ecevit, "Infant Colic or Early Symptom of Autism Spectrum Disorder?" *Pediatrics International* 60, no. 6 (June 2018): 517–22, doi.org /10.1111/ped.13565.

12. Hülya Türkmen, Bihter Akın, Yasemin Erkal Aksoy, and Ayfer Erdoğan, "Maternal Attachment and Mental Health Status in Mothers Who Have Babies with Infantile Colic," *Midwifery* 110 (July 2022), doi.org/10.1016/j.midw.2022.103339.

13. A. L. Pohl, S. K. Crockford, M. Blakemore, C. Allison, and S. Baron-Cohen, "A Comparative Study of Autistic and Non-autistic Women's Experience of Motherhood," *Molecular Autism* 11, 3 (2020) doi.org/10.1186/s13229-019-0304-2.

THE GRINER

14. Deborah Muzikar, "Damage Over Generations: Quotes by Major Influencers in #Autism," *The Art of Autism*, April 27, 2015, the-art-of-autism.com/damage-over-generations-quotes-by-major-influencers-in-autism/.

15. Ian Sample, "The Truth about ADHD and Autism: How Many People Have It, What Causes It, and Why Are Diagnoses Soaring?" *The Guardian*, June 1, 2024, theguardian.com/society/article/2024/jun/01/the-truth-about-adhd-and-autism-how-many-people-have-it-what-causes-it-and-why-are-diagnoses-soaring.

16. T. S. Sathyanarayana Rao and Chittaranjan Andrade, "The MMR Vaccine and Autism: Sensation, Refutation, Retraction, and Fraud," *Indian Journal of Psychiatry* 53, no. 2 (April–June 2011): 95–96, doi.org/10.4103%2F0019-5545.82529.

17. Laura Eggertson, "*Lancet* Retracts 12-Year-Old Article Linking Autism to MMR Vaccines," *Canadian Medical Association Journal* 182, no. 4 (2010): E199–E200, doi.org/10.1503/cmaj.109-3179

18. Mitzi M. Waltz, "Mothers and Autism: The Evolution of a Discourse of Blame," *AMA Journal of Ethics* 17, no. 4 (April 2015): 353–58, doi.org/10.1001/journalofethics.2015.17.4.mhst1-1504.

19. Joyce E. Mauk, "Chelation Treatment for Children with Autism," *Science in Autism Treatment* 6, no. 1 (2009): 7, 14,

asatonline.org/research-treatment/resources/topical-articles
/chelation-treatment-for-children-with-autism/.

20. Brandy Zadrozny, "Parents Are Poisoning Their Children with
Bleach to 'Cure' Autism. These Moms Are Trying to Stop It,"
NBC News, May 21, 2019, nbcnews.com/tech/internet/moms-go
-undercover-fight-fake-autism-cures-private-facebook-groups
-n1007871.

21. Sample, "The Truth about ADHD and Autism."

22. Katharine Sanderson, "High-Profile Autism Genetics Project
Paused amid Backlash," *Nature*, September 27, 2021, nature.com
/articles/d41586-021-02602-7.

THE PROBLEM WITH EMPATHY

23. Anna S. Haghighi, "What to Know about Autism and Empathy?"
Medical News Today, March 30, 2023, medicalnewstoday.com
/articles/do-autistic-people-have-empathy#current-research.

24. Yukihiko Shirayama, Kazuki Matsumoto, Sayo Hamatani,
Katsumasa Muneoka, Akihiro Okada, and Koichi Sato,
"Associations Among Autistic Traits, Cognitive and Affective
Empathy, and Personality Traits in Adults with Autism Spectrum
Disorder and No Intellectual Disability," *Scientific Reports* 12,
3125 (February 24, 2022), doi.org/10.1038/s41598-022-07101-x.

25. Milton, Damian E.M., "On the Ontological Status of Autism:
The 'Double Empathy Problem,'" *Disability & Society* 27, no. 6
(2012): 883–87. doi.org/10.1080/09687599.2012.710008.

26. Troy Q. Boucher, Julia N. Lukacs, Nichole E. Scheerer, and
Grace Iarocci, "Negative First Impression Judgements of Autistic
Children by Non-autistic Adults," *Frontiers in Psychiatry* 14
(2023), doi.org/10.3389/fpsyt.2023.1241584.

27. Ido Shalev, Varun Warrier, David M. Greenberg, Paula Smith, Carrie Allison, Simon Baron-Cohen, Alal Eran, and Florina Uzefovsky, "Reexamining Empathy in Autism: Empathic Disequilibrium as a Novel Predictor of Autism Diagnosis and Autistic Traits," *Autism Research* 15, no. 10 (2022): 1917–28, doi.org/10.1002/aur.2794.

DADDY ELVIS

28. Mirta Stantić, Eri Ichijo, Caroline Catmur, and Geoffrey Bird, "Face Memory and Face Perception in Autism," *Autism* 26, no. 1 (2021): 276–80, doi.org/10.1177/13623613211027685.
29. S. L. Hartley, E. T. Barker, M. M. Seltzer, F. Floyd, J. Greenberg, G. Orsmond, and D. Bolt, "The Relative Risk and Timing of Divorce in Families of Children with an Autism Spectrum Disorder," *Journal of Family Psychology* 24, no. 4 (2010): 449–57, doi.org/10.1037/a0019847.
30. Hartley et al., "The Relative Risk and Timing of Divorce in Families of Children with an Autism Spectrum Disorder."

NO ALARMS AND NO SURPRISES

31. Alexia Ostrolenk, Baudouin Forgeot d'Arc, Patricia Jelenic, Fabienne Samson, and Laurent Mottron, "Hyperlexia: Systematic Review, Neurocognitive Modelling, and Outcome," *Neuroscience & Biobehavioral Reviews* 79 (August 2017): 134–49, doi.org/10.1016/j.neubiorev.2017.04.029.
32. Agnieszka Butwicka, Niklas Långström, Henrik Larsson, Sebastian Lundström, Eva Serlachius, Catarina Almqvist,

Louise Frisén, and Paul Lichtenstein, "Increased Risk for Substance Use-Related Problems in Autism Spectrum Disorders: A Population-Based Cohort Study," *Journal of Autism and Developmental Disorders* 47 (January 2017): 80–89, doi.org/10.1007/s10803-016-2914-2.

33. Steven Kurutz, "Employees with Autism Find New Ways to Navigate the Workplace," *The New York Times*, July 9, 2024, nytimes.com/2024/07/09/style/employees-autism-navigate-workplace.html.

34. Emily Anthes, "Parents Miss Signs of Autism in Their Daughters," *The Transmitter*, October 5, 2016, spectrumnews.org/news/parents-miss-signs-autism-daughters/.

35. Azeen Ghorayshi, "More Girls Are Being Diagnosed with Autism," *The New York Times*, April 10, 2023, nytimes.com/2023/04/10/science/autism-rate-girls.html.

36. Ghorayshi, "More Girls Are Being Diagnosed with Autism."

37. Bennett M. Liu, Kelley Paskov, Jack Kent, Maya McNealis, Soren Sutaria, Olivia Dods, Christopher Harjadi, Nate Stockham, Andrey Ostrovsky, and Dennis P. Wall, "Racial and Ethnic Disparities in Geographic Access to Autism Resources Across the U.S.," *JAMA Network Open* 6, no. 1 (January 23, 2023): e2251182, doi.org/10.1001/jamanetworkopen.2022.51182.

FRIEND IS A FOUR-LETTER WORD

38. Ananya Mandal, "Autism History," *News Medical Life Sciences*, last updated July 7, 2023, news-medical.net/health/Autism-History.aspx.

39. Mandal, "Autism History."

40. Juliann Garey, "The Controversy Around ABA," Child Mind Institute, last updated August 15, 2024, childmind.org/article/controversy-around-applied-behavior-analysis/.

41. Mandal, "Autism History."

42. Gary Shkedy, Dalia Shkedy, and Aileen H. Sandoval-Norton, "Long-Term ABA Therapy Is Abusive: A Response to Gorycki, Ruppel, and Zane," *Advances in Neurodevelopmental Disorders* 5, (2021): 126–34, doi.org/10.1007/s41252-021-00201-1.

43. Lydia Denworth, "How People with Autism Forge Friendships," *Scientific American*, April 8, 2020, scientificamerican.com/article/how-people-with-autism-forge-friendships/.

44. Rebecca Hymas, Johanna C. Badcock, and Elizabeth Milne, "Loneliness in Autism and Its Association with Anxiety and Depression: A Systematic Review with Meta-Analyses," *Journal of Autism and Developmental Disorders* 11 (2022): 121–56, doi.org/10.1007/s40489-022-00330-w.

SWEET SENSORY CHILD O' MINE

45. Elysa J. Marco, Leighton B. N. Hinkley, Susanna S. Hill, and Srikantan S. Nagarajan, "Sensory Processing in Autism: A Review of Neurophysiologic Findings," *Pediatric Research* 69 (May 2011): 48–54, nature.com/articles/pr9201193.

46. Cindy Hatch-Rasmussen, "Sensory Integration in Autism Spectrum Disorders," Autism Research Institute, accessed April 5, 2025, autism.org/sensory-integration/.

47. "Stimming: What Is It and Does It Matter?" Children's Hospital of Philadelphia Research Institute, last updated May 29, 2020, research.chop.edu/car-autism-roadmap/stimming-what-is-it-and-does-it-matter.

48. "Dermatillomania (Skin Picking)," Cleveland Clinic, last reviewed on April 11, 2022, my.clevelandclinic.org/health /diseases/22706-dermatillomania-skin-picking.

THE DREIDEL GAME

49. Erin E. Dempsey, Chris Moore, Shannon A. Johnson, Sherry H. Stewart, and Isabel M. Smith, "Moral Foundations Theory Among Autistic and Neurotypical Children," *Frontiers in Psychology* 12 (2022): 782610, doi.org/10.3389/fpsyg.2021 .782610.

TWICE EXCEPTIONAL, ONCE SHY

50. Beth Arky, "Twice-Exceptional Kids: Both Gifted and Challenged," Child Mind Institute, last updated December 17, 2024, childmind.org/article/twice-exceptional-kids-both -gifted-and-challenged/.
51. Simon Baron-Cohen, "Leo Kanner, Hans Asperger, and the Discovery of Autism," *The Lancet* 386, no. 10001 (October 3, 2015): 1329–30, thelancet.com/journals/lancet/article/PIIS 0140-6736(15)00337-2.
52. Herwig Czech, "Hans Asperger, National Socialism, and 'Race Hygiene' in Nazi-Era Vienna," *Molecular Autism* 9 (April 19, 2018), doi.org/10.1186/s13229-018-0208-6.
53. Hanna Steffenburg, Suzanne Steffenburg, Christopher Gillberg, and Eva Billstedt, "Children with Autism Spectrum Disorders and Selective Mutism," *Neuropsychiatric Disease and Treatment* 14 (2018): 1163–69, doi.org/10.2147/NDT.S154966.

54. Emily Laber-Warren, "The Benefits of Special Interests in Autism," *The Transmitter*, May 12, 2021, doi.org/10.53053 /UVVZ8029.

55. Maureen Bennie, "What Is Monotropism?" Autism Awareness Centre Inc., September 14, 2023, autismawarenesscentre.com /what-is-monotropism/.

56. Laber-Warren, "The Benefits of Special Interests in Autism."

#1 CRUSH

57. Ari Howard, "What to Know When Starting a Relationship with an Autistic Person," *PsychCentral*, March 30, 2022, psychcentral.com/autism/autism-and-relationships.

58. Fabienne Cazalis, Elisabeth Reyes, Séverine Leduc, and David Gourion, "Evidence That Nine Autistic Women Out of Ten Have Been Victims of Sexual Violence," *Frontiers in Behavioral Neuroscience* 16 (April 25, 2022), doi.org/10.3389/fnbeh.2022 .852203.

59. Francine Russo, "The Costs of Camouflaging Autism," *The Transmitter*, February 21, 2018, doi.org/10.53053/ZNSG1811.

60. Valencia Higuera, "What Is Rejection Sensitive Dysphoria?," *Healthline*, November 19, 2021, healthline.com/health/mental -health/rejection-sensitive-dysphoria#diagnosis.

61. Lorraine MacAlister, "Autism and Catastrophising," National Autistic Society, April 29, 2024, autism.org.uk/advice-and -guidance/professional-practice/autism-catastrophising.

62. "About Autism and Wandering," National Autism Association, accessed April 5, 2025, nationalautismassociation.org/resources /wandering/.

63. "About Autism and Wandering," National Autism Association.

FUNNY GUY

64. Marci Wheeler, "What Those Not on the Autism Spectrum Should Know," Indiana Resource Center for Autism, 2020, iidc.indiana.edu/irca/articles/what-those-not-on-the-autism -spectrum-should-know.html.

65. Rachel Aroesti, "'Maybe Everybody Feels Socially Awkward': The Standups Turning Being Autistic into a Comedy Superpower," *The Guardian*, March 15, 2024, theguardian.com /stage /2024/mar/16/autism-comedy-superpower-fern-brady -pierre-novellie-joe-wells-charlie-george.

RX

66. Sarah E. Fizpatrick, Laura Srivorakiat, Logan K. Wink, Ernest V. Pedapati, and Craig A. Erickson, "Aggression in Autism Spectrum Disorder: Presentation and Treatment Options," *Neuropsychiatric Disease and Treatment* 12 (June 2016): 1525–38, doi.org/10.2147/NDT.S84585.

67. Fitzpatrick et al., "Aggression in Autism Spectrum Disorder."

68. "Autism and Anxiety," Autism Research Institute, accessed April 5, 2025, autism.org/autism-and-anxiety/.

69. Alicia Sparks Akers, "Are Autistic People More Likely to Experience Migraine?," *Medical News Today*, December 18, 2023, medicalnewstoday.com/articles/autism-and-migraines.

70. Matthew J. Maenner, Zachary Warren, Ashley R. Williams et al., "Prevalence and Characteristics of Autism Spectrum Disorder Among Children Aged 8 Years—Autism and Developmental Disabilities Monitoring Network, 11 Sites, United States, 2020." *Morbidity and Mortality Weekly Report, Surveillance Summaries* 72, no. 2 (2023): 1–14, doi.org/10.15585/mmwr.ss7202a1.

71. "Autism Spectrum Disorder: Highlights from the 2019 Canadian Health Survey on Children and Youth," Government of Canada, last updated June 21, 2022, canada.ca/en/public-health/services/publications/diseases-conditions/autism-spectrum-disorder-canadian-health-survey-children-youth-2019.html#a3.1.

72. Nancy Doyle, "Neurodiversity at Work: A Biopsychosocial Model and the Impact on Working Adults," *British Medical Bulletin* 135, no. 1 (2020): 108–25, doi.org/10.1093/bmb/ldaa021.

73. Ian Sample, "The Truth about ADHD and Autism: How Many People Have It, What Causes It, and Why Are Diagnoses Soaring?" *The Guardian*, June 1, 2024, theguardian.com/society/article/2024/jun/01/the-truth-about-adhd-and-autism-how-many-people-have-it-what-causes-it-and-why-are-diagnoses-soaring.

74. "Medication Treatment for Autism," Eunice Kennedy Shriver National Institute of Child Health and Human Development, last updated April 19, 2021, nichd.nih.gov/health/topics/autism/conditioninfo/treatments/medication-treatment.

75. Elizabeth Shea, "Eating Disorder or Disordered Eating? Eating Patterns in Autism," National Autistic Society, May 24, 2016, autism.org.uk/advice-and-guidance/professional-practice /avoidant-eating.

76. Tanner Koomar, Taylor R. Thomas, Natalie R. Pottschmidt, Michael Lutter, and Jacob J. Michaelson, "Estimating the Prevalence and Genetic Risk Mechanisms of ARFID in a Large Autism Cohort," *Frontiers in Psychiatry* 12 (June 8, 2021): 668297, doi.org/10.3389/fpsyt.2021.668297.

THE PERFECT CURSE

77. Ofir Y. Pinto and Raanan Raz, "Employment Outcomes After a Birth of a Child with a Developmental Disability: A National Nested Case–Control Study," *Journal of Autism and Disorders* 51 (2021): 697–703, doi.org/10.1007/s10803-020-04581-6.

78. Zuleyha Cidav, Steven C. Marcus, and David S. Mandell, "Implications of Childhood Autism for Parental Employment and Earnings," *Pediatrics* 129, no. 4 (April 2012): 617–23, doi .org/10.1542/peds.2011-2700.

79. Jasmine Phung, Melanie Penner, Clémentine Pirlot, and Christie Welch, "What I Wish You Knew: Insights on Burnout, Inertia, Meltdown, and Shutdown from Autistic Youth," *Frontiers in Psychology* 12 (2021), doi.org/10.3389/fpsyg.2021.741421.

80. Claire Jack, "What Is the 'Spoons Theory' of Autism?," *Psychology Today*, November 4, 2022, psychologytoday.com /ca/blog/women-autism-spectrum-disorder/202211/what-is -the-spoons-theory-autism.

81. James Coplan, "The 8-Ball from Hell of ASD: Perfectionism," *Psychology Today*, September 7, 2016, psychologytoday.com /ca/blog/making-sense-autistic-spectrum-disorders/201609 /the-8-ball-hell-asd-perfectionism.

82. "Dyscalculia," Cleveland Clinic, last updated August 2, 2022, my.clevelandclinic.org/health/diseases/23949-dyscalculia.

LOVING THE ALIEN

83. Jessica Schroeder, M. Catherine Cappadocia, James M. Bebko, Debra J. Pepler, and Jonathan A. Weiss, "Shedding Light on a Pervasive Problem: A Review of Research on Bullying Experiences Among Children with Autism Spectrum Disorders," *Journal of Autism and Developmental Disorders* 44 (2014): 1520–34, doi.org/10.1007/s10803-013-2011-8.

84. J. Navarro, N. Lachowsky, R. Hammond, D. Burchell, F. S. E. Arps, C. Davis, J. Brasseur, S. Islam, B. Fosbrook, K. Jacobsen, M. Walker, C. Lopez, A. Scheim, and G. Bauer, "Report—Health and Well-Being Among Non-binary People," *Trans PULSE Canada* 7 (July 6, 2021), transpulsecanada.ca/results/report-health-and-well-being -among-non-binary-people.

85. Nouchine Hadjikhani, Jakob Åsberg Johnels, Nicole R. Zürcher, Amandine Lassalle, Quentin Guillon, Loyse Hippolyte, Eva Billstedt, Noreen Ward, Eric Lemonnier, and Christopher Gillberg, "Look Me in the Eyes: Constraining Gaze in the Eye-Region Provokes Abnormally High Subcortical Activation in Autism," *Scientific Reports* 7, no. 3163 (2017) doi.org/10.1038 /s41598-017-03378-5.

86. Laura Dattaro, "Largest Study to Date Confirms Overlap Between Autism and Gender Diversity," *The Transmitter*, September 14, 2020, doi.org/10.53053/WNHC6713.

87. Aimilia Kallitsounaki, David M. Williams, and Sophie E. Lind, "Links Between Autistic Traits, Feelings of Gender Dysphoria, and Mentalising Ability: Replication and Extension of Previous Findings from the General Population," *Journal of Autism and Developmental Disorders* 51, no. 5 (2021): 1458–65, doi.org/10.1007/s10803-020-04626-w.

88. Kallitsounaki, Williams, and Lind, "Links Between Autistic Traits."

P.D. GREEN

JULIE M. GREEN is a writer whose work has been featured in *The Washington Post, HuffPost, The Globe and Mail, Today's Parent, Chatelaine*, and more. In 2024, she was longlisted for the CBC Nonfiction Prize. She has appeared on CTV, BBC Radio, SiriusXM, CBC Radio, and HuffPost Live. She writes *The Autistic Mom* on Substack.

After studying Creative Writing and English literature at Concordia University in Montreal, Julie moved to London. She stayed in the U.K. for 10 years, then relocated to Toronto following the birth of her son. Julie now lives in Kingston, Ontario, with her husband, teenager, and Olde English Bulldogge. In her spare time, she paints, runs a women's book club, and volunteers at an arts centre for adults with developmental disabilities.

For more information, visit juliemgreen.ca.

Ententertainment. Writing. Culture. ───────

ECW is a proudly independent, Canadian-owned book publisher. We know great writing can improve people's lives, and we're passionate about sharing original, exciting, and insightful writing across genres.

─────────────────── **Thanks for reading along!**

We want our books not just to sustain our imaginations, but to help construct a healthier, more just world, and so we've become a certified B Corporation, meaning we meet a high standard of social and environmental responsibility — and we're going to keep aiming higher. We believe books can drive change, but the way we make them can too.

Certified

Corporation

Being a B Corp means that the act of publishing this book should be a force for good — for the planet, for our communities, and for the people that worked to make this book. For example, everyone who worked on this book was paid at least a living wage. You can learn more at the Ontario Living Wage Network.

This book is also available as a Global Certified Accessible™ (GCA) ebook. ECW Press's ebooks are screen reader friendly and are built to meet the needs of those who are unable to read standard print due to blindness, low vision, dyslexia, or a physical disability.

The interior of this book is printed on Sustana EnviroBook™, which is made from 100% recycled fibres and processed chlorine-free.

FSC
www.fsc.org
MIX
Paper | Supporting
responsible forestry
FSC® C016245

ECW's office is situated on land that was the traditional territory of many nations, including the Wendat, the Anishinaabeg, Haudenosaunee, Chippewa, Métis, and current treaty holders the Mississaugas of the Credit. In the 1880s, the land was developed as part of a growing community around St. Matthew's Anglican and other churches. Starting in the 1950s, our neighbourhood was transformed by immigrants fleeing the Vietnam War and Chinese Canadians dispossessed by the building of Nathan Phillips Square and the subsequent rise in real estate value in other Chinatowns. We are grateful to those who cared for the land before us and are proud to be working amidst this mix of cultures.

ecwpress.com